THE SHAN
OF BURMA

The **Institute of Southeast Asian Studies (ISEAS)** was established as an autonomous organization in 1968. It is a regional centre dedicated to the study of socio-political, security and economic trends and developments in Southeast Asia and its wider geostrategic and economic environment. The Institute's research programmes are the Regional Economic Studies (RES, including ASEAN and APEC), Regional Strategic and Political Studies (RSPS), and Regional Social and Cultural Studies (RSCS).

ISEAS Publishing, an established academic press, has issued more than 2,000 books and journals. It is the largest scholarly publisher of research about Southeast Asia from within the region. ISEAS Publishing works with many other academic and trade publishers and distributors to disseminate important research and analyses from and about Southeast Asia to the rest of the world.

CHAO TZANG YAWNGHWE

THE SHAN OF BURMA

Memoirs of a Shan Exile

ISEAS

INSTITUTE OF SOUTHEAST ASIAN STUDIES
SINGAPORE

Published by ISEAS Publishing
Institute of Southeast Asian Studies
30 Heng Mui Keng Terrace
Pasir Panjang
Singapore 119614

E-mail: publish@iseas.edu.sg
Website: <http://bookshop.iseas.edu.sg>

The responsibility for facts and opinions in this publication rests exclusively with the author, and his interpretations do not necessarily reflect the views or the policy of the publishers or its supporters.

ISEAS Library Cataloguing-in-Publication Data

Yawnghwe, Chao Tzang.
   The Shan of Burma : memoirs of a Shan exile.
   (Local history ; 16)
   1.   Ahoms (Indic people)—Burma—History.
   2.   Ahoms (Indic people)—Burma—Politics and government.
   3.   Shan State (Burma)—History.
   I.   Title
   II.   Series: Local history and memoirs (Institute of Southeast Asian Studies) ; 16.
DS501 1595L no. 16   2010

ISBN 978-981-230-396-7 (soft cover)
ISBN 978-981-230-601-2 (E-book PDF)

Photo Credit:
Cover photographs (from left to right): Shan United Army recruits attending a class, Saw Yanda, and Yawnghwe Hall.

Photographs on Yawnghwe Palace (on the cover and page 4) and the Shan United Army (on the cover and page 28) were reproduced with the kind permission of Bertil Lintner.

Typeset by International Typesetters Pte Ltd
Printed in Singapore by Utopia Press Pte Ltd

Contents

Foreword

The second printing of Chao Tzang Yawnghwe's *The Shan of Burma: Memoirs of a Shan Exile* is a timely re-introduction to the world of political literature of the most poignant and ground-breaking study of all the ethnic conflicts that followed the independence of Burma (Myanmar[1]) in 1948. Since its first publication in 1987, the book has remained essential reading for anyone seeking to understand the patterns of state failure and humanitarian tragedy that have befallen the long-suffering peoples in this deeply troubled land. Chao Tzang's insightful writing is never an armchair analysis nor a militant polemic. It is the riveting description by a remarkable intellectual, who was eyewitness to many of the most controversial and epoch-shaping events in Burma's ethnic politics from the mid-20th century onwards.

Born into a leading political family, Chao Tzang's life was a personal odyssey during which he constantly engaged with the many challenges of his age. The different names by which he was also sometimes known — Eugene Thaike, Khun Loumpha, and Sao Hso Wai — reflect different passages in his career. However, neither the privilege of his background nor the many hardships he suffered deflected his life-long determination to see democracy and equality established for all the peoples of Burma. As a boy, he was in Panglong during the historic conference; as a tutor, he was at Rangoon University during General Ne Win's military coup that led to the deaths of one brother and, later, his father in prison; and into middle-age, he served as a key leader in the Shan resistance movement until a combination of ill-health and political encirclement forced his retirement from the field.

The Shan of Burma is a vibrant analysis of this first, turbulent period of his life. Chao Tzang structured his study around three main prisms: that of personal narrative, historical commentary, and vignette biographies of the leading actors, many of whom were previously unknown in the outside world. The book was prodigious in new insights and rare detail on many unrecorded aspects of Shan history, from the pre-colonial era through to the modern. The writing has a seamless flow that brought lucidity and explanation to what had, until then, been regarded by many international observers as only intractable problems in one of Asia's least studied lands.

After independence, Burma's national landscape had become characterized by militarized politics, ethnic division and countrywide impoverishment in which a rampant trade in illicit narcotics developed a powerful momentum of its own. Chao Tzang confronts these issues head on, and it is his always frank depiction of events in the conflict-zones that forms the cornerstone of his account. The day-to-day struggles of the Shan nationality movement are starkly illuminated as Chao Tzang describes how the Shan State Army became caught between the competing pressures of military government offensives, China's support to insurgent communists, the thriving opium trade, Kuomintang remnants, and rivalries with other ethnic and militia forces that, at times, become almost too numerous to detail.

Chao Tzang, however, never loses sight of his conviction that all the conflicts that caused such precipitate, socio-economic decline in Burma are, at root, political in nature and can only be addressed by political solutions. In particular, he argued that since independence there had been two unresolved struggles for state power taking place: one for control of power among the ethnic Burman-majority "at the centre", and the other for control between the centre and the "homelands" of the non-Burman peoples around the international frontiers. The result was that the whole country had become entrapped in what he describes as a "politics of violence" that had to be ended. Equally important, he forewarned the international community that only "good government" could resolve Burma's illicit opium trade; "military" approaches, he reasoned, would never do this.

I first met Chao Tzang in 1984 when he was finishing his manuscript. From the outset he made clear his belief that peace would be very quickly brought to Burma if only the country's military leaders would — as in other Southeast Asian countries — choose a political path. The book was written towards the end of the Cold War when communist actors were still influential in the field. But in the 21st century, all of Chao Tzang's hopes and convictions for political solutions through dialogue continue to have meaningful resonance.

Following completion of "The Shan of Burma", Chao Tzang joined other members of his family in exile in Canada. Here he completed his Ph.D. in Political Science at the University of British Columbia under the thesis title: "The Politics of Authoritarianism: The State and Political Soldiers in Burma, Indonesia, and Thailand". During these exile years, he also taught at the University of British Columbia and Simon Fraser University. He became a renowned analyst on both Burmese politics and narcotic issues, frequently attending international conferences and contributing to different publications.[2]

However Shan politics and the cause of ethnic peace in Burma remained his abiding passion, and from the mid-1990s he returned closer to the field. He became co-founder of the United Nationalities League for Democracy (Liberated Area), advisor to the National Reconciliation Programme and the Shan Democratic Union, and chair of the working committee of the Ethnic Nationalities Council, where he tirelessly promoted dialogue and political solutions to Burma's continuing conflicts.

In a democratic world, there can be no doubt that Chao Tzang Yawnghwe would have become an exemplary leader in his country. It is a tragedy therefore that his life was prematurely cut short by illness when he died in July 2004 at the age of sixty-five just at a time when a new generation of young people and international academics was coming to learn more of his experiences and work.

The re-publication of *The Shan of Burma* thus marks the most fitting epitaph to his life of both personal struggle and scholarship in the field. In the Preface Chao Tzang, who was then taking sanctuary in Thailand, is modestly aware that he was writing his memoir without access to primary sources. He was, he wrote, having to deal with "living history" that had not yet been "anointed" by the works of "established scholars". However from the first moment of publication, *The Shan of Burma* set a new benchmark in writing about ethnic politics and the long-standing challenges of socio-political reform in the country. The "living history" he so personally captured is as relevant to Burma scholars in the 21st century as it was at the very first printing. There can be no more vital legacy than this.

Martin Smith
Author of Burma: Insurgency and the Politics of Ethnicity
September 2006

Notes

1. In 1989, the official name of "Burma" was changed to "Myanmar" by the military State Law and Order Restoration Council that had assumed power

the previous year. The terms can be considered alternatives. In the English language, Burma is still widely used, including for historical writing. This reprint will retain Burma, as in the original edition.

2. See example, Chao Tzang Yawnghwe, "The Burman Military: Holding the County Together?", in *Independent Burma at Forty Years: Six Assessments*, edited by Josef Silverstein (Ithaca: Cornell Southeast Asia Program, 1989), pp. 81–101; Chao Tzang Yawnghwe, "Burma: The Depoliticization of the Political", in *Political Legitimacy in Southeast Asia: The Quest for Moral Authority*, edited by Muthiah Alagappa (Stanford: Stanford University Press, 1995), pp. 170–92; Chao Tzang Yawnghwe, "Shan State Politics: The Opium-Heroin Factor", in *Trouble in the Triangle: Opium and Conflict in Burma*, edited by M. Jelsma, T. Kramer and P. Vervest (Chiang Mai: Silkworm Books, 2005), pp. 23–32.

In Memorium

"Chao Tzang" or "Uncle Eugene" as he was affectionately known amongst Burmese democracy activists was a man of many contrasts. His neighbours in Canada would not have guessed that the mild-mannered absent-minded academic had lived through one of the most turbulent periods of Burmese history and that he was himself a key actor in the making of that history. True to his self-effacing and democratic aspirations, few of his friends actually even knew his real name, let alone his royal lineage. Eugene was a name given to him by nuns in primary school and Tzang — "Elephant" — was his nickname as a child. As a son of the ruling "Saopha" (Celestial Lord) of Yawnghwe, he was officially named Sao Hso Lern Hpa — "Prince Tiger of the Celestial Moon". In those days, the ruler of Yawnghwe ruled his territory as a traditional Shan monarch.

Chao Tzang was born on 26 April 1939 in Yawnghwe in the waning years of the British Empire. His earliest memories were of World War II. He witnessed the historic Panglong Conference where modern Burma was born. Later, his life was transformed from that of a royal prince to that of the son of the first democratic republican president of the Union of Burma. His political consciousness was awakened by the civil war that broke out soon after independence. While studying at Rangoon University, he was disturbed by the direction the country was taking under General Ne Win and soon established clandestine ties with the Karen and Shan resistance. He also began touring Shan State to see what was happening at the grassroots level. In 1962, he had two narrow brushes with death. First, in the early hours of 2 March, when the Burma Army surrounded our home in Rangoon and opened fire. Miraculously, only one brother was killed. Chao Tzang, who rolled off his bed on the ground floor, later found his mosquito net riddled with bullet holes. On 7 July, he was visiting his future wife on campus and was attracted by the noise of students protesting the military coup. As he watched, he saw the troops facing the students cocking their arms and opening fire. Students fell to the left and right of him. These incidents brought home to him the reality of military rule and he was once again transformed — this time into a revolutionary to rid his homeland of injustice. Chao Tzang joined the Shan resistance after our father died in prison, and for the next twelve years lived in the jungle as a guerrilla commander. But as the fortunes of war declined, his life was once more transformed and he became a stateless refugee in Thailand, living at the mercy and generosity of friends and strangers. When he, his wife, young son and young daughter were accepted by Canada for resettlement in 1985, he decided to continue his studies and finally earned his Ph.D. in political science when he was close to sixty — a time most other people retire. He wanted to learn, apply his knowledge to resolving the intractable problem that has plagued his homeland for the last half a century. To the end, he dedicated his life to finding a political solution, to educating, encouraging and mentoring young people, especially women to think for themselves and to fight for justice and equality.

Having lived as one of the highest in the land and also as one of the lowest, he did not stand on ceremony. He was very approachable and was able to put everyone at ease. He did not put on airs as a prince or pretend to be a macho military man. Instead of regaling his listeners with his military prowess and with his many brushes with death as a guerrilla commander, Chao Tzang would often entertain his guests with hilarious stories of his inexperienced and inept military leadership. Although Chao Tzang is to be admired and emulated, he could not have lived as he did without the equally strong commitment and support of his faithful and long-suffering wife of forty years — Nu Nu Myint of Kengtung. She sacrificed her career as a headmistress and joined him in the jungle when he had no future to offer her. She stuck by him through thick and thin and took care of the family in order that he could pursue his dream. In commemorating the life of Chao Tzang, we must pay tribute to Nu Nu's dedication and to her family.

Friends and family noticed a change in Chao Tzang in March 2004. He was very subdued and started to lose his balance and memory. After numerous consultations, he was finally diagnosed as having a tumor in his brain stem in late April. After a brief recovery from chemotherapy, he passed away quietly on 24 July 2004.

Harn Yawnghwe
Director
Euro-Burma Office
Brussels
September 2006

Preface

Shan State in Burma today has its capital at Taunggyi. Administratively, there is a Northern and Southern Shan State with their capitals at Lashio and Taunggyi respectively. At the time of the Tai Mao kingdom around the twelfth century, there were nine Shan principalities or states, seven of which are in present-day Burma. Although the British were in the Shan area by the late 1800s it was only in 1922 that they grouped the Shan principalities into the Federated Shan States.

Shan State has generally been out of bounds to foreign visitors since the military coup of 1962. The few places open include Taunggyi and the Inle Lake of Yawnghwe. Given the situation where accounts of Shan State politics are sensationalized with reports of opium wars, narcotics armies, drug trafficking, warlords and opium kings, and given the current paucity of knowledge regarding socio-economic, political, and historical realities, I felt despite feelings of inadequacy, that I should try to fill the information gap with respect to not only the Shan, but the politics of Burma as well. I am not a scholar.

My problem was compounded in that books dealing directly with the Shan and their homeland are few. Moreover, except for Chao Saimong Mangrai's *The Shan State and British Annexation* (1965), none deal with politics. Of course, all histories of Burma by such distinguished historians as Hall (1955), Harvey (1925), Christian (1945), Tinker (1967), Htin Aung (1967), Maung Maung Pye (1951), Trager (1966), Silverstein (1977), and Steinberg (1982) do contain references to the Shan and Shan States. However, in the parts dealing with post-1948 Burma, one is able to perceive, it seems, the reluctance of these scholars to dig too deeply into areas which would offend the powers that be in Rangoon. In reading some of these works on Burma, one can almost imagine these otherwise scholarly writers muttering curses against the non-Burmese, especially the Shan Chaofa (or *Sawbwa*, in Burmese) for surly opposition to Burmese leaders nobly engaged in the task of nation-building.

I feel that the greatest flaw in current works dealing with post-1948 Burma is the confusion over the term "nation-building" in general, and more specifically, its connotation within the internationally recognized political perimeter known as Burma, which, in reality is a composite of many homelands. That is, it is composed of the homeland of the Burmese, a broad plain lying on both sides of the Irrawaddy River that flows into the sea between the Gulf of Martaban and the Bay of Bengal; and surrounding this Burmese plain in an elevated horseshoe (comprising 60 per cent of the total land area of Burma) are the homelands of the Arakan, Chin, Kachin, Shan or Tai/Thai, Karenni, and Karen.

Although the Burman or Burmese are more numerous, the non-Burmese ethnic groups constitute collectively quite a large minority. Census taking in independent Burma has strong political overtones in addition to obvious flaws such as the lack of trained personnel, the state of war, lack of roads and communications infrastructure. It appears to be in the interest of Rangoon to deflate figures for Shan, Karen, Kachin, and to inflate the Burmese population. For example, the Tai or Shan population was 1.6 million in 1973 as compared to 1.3 million in 1931 (an increase of only 0.3 million within 42 years), whereas the Burmese population reportedly increased from 10 to 20 million in the same period. Moreover, both British (1931) and Burmese authorities (1973) included in Burmese figures substantial numbers of Shan, Mon, Karen, Chin, and others who dwell in Burma Proper. The Arakanese were counted as Burmese, much to their displeasure. Finally, as an example, the government of Kawthoolei (Karen nationalist movement) claims there are roughly 7 million Karen even though Burmese authorities fiercely dispute this figure.

Taking into account the geographic and demographic factors and even ignoring the complex political and historical circumstances shaping these ethnic entities, it must be recognized that the task of nation-building in Burma is not easy as it requires great wisdom and statesmanship which flashed — alas, too briefly — in the person of Aung San, Burma's George Washington. The subject of this monograph is, then, nation-building in Burma from the viewpoint of a Shan nationalist, and covers the relationship between the Shan and the various Burmese centres of power from the Pagan period (1044–1257) to the 1980s.

I write on those few momentous and dynamic years before independence (1945–48) without recourse to important primary sources — that is, participants who played important roles then, and also in Shan politics and administration up to 1962. This is so for the following reasons. At present I cannot return to the Shan State; also, the voices of these men have been silenced, some by death, but the majority by the fact of their being on the "wrong" side of the political struggle. As such, they not only suffered for their convictions, but have since the coup of 1962 been cast into the wilderness — becoming a "lost and silent generation" of Shan leaders.

Nonetheless, though I was involved in the Shan rebel movement (1963–76), and though I lack academic qualifications, as well as access to primary sources, I will try my best to be factual. Though footnotes to documents will be scanty, what I put down as facts can be checked by anyone who cares to speak to and question any knowledgeable native of Burma or the Shan State. I am fully aware that I am treading on uncertain ground because I am dealing mostly with living history, the realities of which have not become facts since they have not been thus anointed between covers of published books by established scholars.

In keeping therefore with such circumstances, I shall in the first part of my monograph relate my involvement in the Shan nationalist movement which, I hope, will give the readers a feel for the forces and events shaping the lift and the thoughts of one man, a native of the Shan hills — rather like serving a few glasses of Shan wine before the main meal.

One more word in conclusion to this introduction: I do not claim that in the Shan struggle to preserve their identity and rights as a nation which has since the late 1950s taken the form of open warfare — as it did before 1885 — that Right is always on the side of the Shan. At any rate, in politics, Right is seldom Might. In other words, those powerful and ruthless enough will have no difficulty in achieving what they want, in committing grave injustices, or riding roughshod over truth. Nowadays, no matter what, Might usually triumphs over Right. However, one must not forget that Might, like Fortune, is not only fickle, but in the end, only creates more problems. After all, the embracing of Might is but a rejection of Wisdom, and, stupidity gets no one anywhere.

Chao Tzang Yawnghwe
(Eugene Thaike)
Chiangmai
1984

Acknowledgements

For a person such as myself whose life has been eventful, having been born in the midst of political turmoil which still rages on in my homeland, the debt of gratitude I have accumulated from the people I have come across — fortunate for me and unfortunate for them — needless to say, is indeed overwhelming. Everyone I have met in Thailand and particularly in Chiangmai has been not only courteous and kind, but also generous and compassionate. I am, as such, humbly grateful to all and deeply regret that I am unable to list all their names.

I would, however, like to cite some of those who have provided assistance in the writing of this book: M.R. Dr Sukhumbhand Paribatra, and Mrs Piensuvan Nakpreecha, for their most valuable help; Dr K. of Chiangmai, a scholar and a man of all seasons, who has been not only a great teacher but an inspiring example as well; Mr Bertil Lintner, a serious student of politics and history, for kindly lending me books and materials on Burma and providing photographs; Mrs Frederika Scollard and a friend for editing and correcting my all too numerous errors in grammar and composition; Nu Nu Myint Yawnghwe, for making numerous trips to buy stationery supplies and to make photocopies, and generally keeping things in order; Khun Kya Nu, a long-time colleague and friend for checking out facts and dates; and the Director of the Institute of Southeast Asian Studies, Singapore, Professor K.S. Sandhu for his encouragement and support.

And last, but not the least, Mr Adrian Cowell and Mr Chris Menges, of ATV, London, for bringing to the attention of the outside world, at great risk to their well-being, the tragic plight of the poor peasants of the Shan State with its anarchy and war which has made life for them meaningless and devoid of hope.

PART ONE

AN AUTOBIOGRAPHICAL INTRODUCTION

1

A Native of the Shan Hills

The Early Years

I was born in 1939 in the Federated Shan States, then under the British flag, in a princely manor — the *Yawnghwe Haw* (Shan for Yawnghwe Palace). My birth took place in a temporary hut in the northern garden of the palace, built specifically for childbirth[1] as was customary among Shan ruling families. My earliest memories are of World War II, of delicious Japanese rice-cakes, bespectacled Japanese officers with long swords and shining boots, sounds of aeroplanes, being carried by adults in the dark of night to earthern bombshelters, and looks of fear and uncertainty on adult faces. Then, the balmy days in the Inle Lake, and always on the move, we children enjoyed running across green and fragrant padi fields, hiding in cool bamboo groves, and swimming in the lake. Japanese soldiers often appeared, but so did, I recall vividly, two men with blue eyes and red hair clad in green (in contrast to the dusty yellow of Japanese uniforms). They were, we were told, men belonging to the *Maha-mate* army, that is, the Allied forces. We enjoyed the strange texture and taste of cheese and chocolates, and pored over magazines filled with photographs and coloured cartoons (mostly caricatures of Hitler, Mussolini, and Tojo) brought by these strangers.

When the war ended, we children travelled with my mother and relatives from Yawnghwee to Hsenwi, her hometown (a distance of 200 miles by car).[2] On the way, we saw for the first time men who were blacker than the *kula* (Indians), whose teeth shone in their dark faces like half moons in the starless night. Men of importance (we were told), of different races came and went, many staying for days at Yawnghwe Haw.[3] We, like the adults around us, were greatly amused at seeing Burmese men in sarongs and pink silken caps perched daintily on their

3

Yawnghwe Haw, where I was born. It was built by Sir Sir Chao Mawng, the Chaofa of Yawnghwe (1864–85) and my grand-uncle (1897–1927). It is the only Shan Palace not destroyed in World War II. Photo courtesy of Bertil Lintner.

heads since men in the Shan State always wore Shan trousers — similar
to Chinese ones. We were also taken to a town called Panglong, where
two very important and historic conferences were held resulting in the
Panglong Agreement of 1947 which shaped and changed the course of
our history. But as children we noticed only the stalls selling cooked food
and toys; the nightly entertainments (*zat-pwe* or Burmese opera, movies,
dances by hilltribe performers, Shan men tattooed all black doing fierce
sword dances); the sporting events (pillow fights, sack races, climbing
the greased pole, football matches); and gambling booths offering games
to suit every pocket and taste.

Around the age of six, I was sent with my elder brother to a Roman
Catholic convent in Kalaw (Loi Ann in Shan), but we contracted typhoid
and came home in an ambulance. We recovered and were dispatched to
the far north to Hsenwi, again as boarders at a convent. At one time my
father, Chao Shwe Thaike, while President of the Union of Burma, came
on tour to Hsenwi, where he also attended the wedding of his eldest
son.[4] We stood in line with other school children, waved little flags as
the motorcade passed, and later joined the family at Hsenwi Haw.

Due to a congenital heart defect, I was not allowed to fly,[5] and was
left at Hsenwi when my older brother flew with the rest of the family
from Maymyo (where we joined the family during the summer vacation)
to Rangoon. While at Hsenwi, I was caught in a battle lasting two days
between Kachin mutineers of Captain Naw Seng[6] and Kachin battalions
loyal to the government.[7] It was a confusing period filled with rumours
and movements of armed men. My uncle, Chao Hom Pha, the Prince
of Hsenwi, was at one time abducted by Naw Seng, which caused great
excitement among his subjects.[8]

There was fighting everywhere, and it seemed to me at the time that
every male adult was a soldier of some sort.[9] I was then living with
different relatives, passing from one family to the next, like an orphaned
child, and moving from town to town. Finally, perhaps in 1950, I rejoined
my family in Rangoon, no longer a nomadic orphan, but as one of the
sons of the Union President.

Although my father's term as President ended in 1952, his services
were retained by U Nu's AFPFL (Anti-Fascist Peoples' Freedom League)
government,[10] as Speaker of the House of Nationalities (the Upper Chamber of Burma's unicameral Parliament), up to 1960. My family moved
into our own house which had formerly belonged to an Indian tycoon,[11]
on Kokine Road, Rangoon. My days were like those of any growing

schoolboy — school, homework, play, "boy scouting", friends (from among children of ministers, top military officials, senior civil servants, prominent politicians, wealthy merchants, aristocratic landowners, and so forth from the Methodist English High School,[12] considered exclusive, and the best in Burma).

I matriculated at eighteen, and enrolled at Rangoon University in 1957. In this institution with its political tradition, which had nurtured nationalist leaders such as Aung San, U Nu, Ba Swe, Kyaw Nyein, I was introduced to politics. Here, I met people who vehemently opposed the government and who could talk about nothing but the armed overthrow of capitalism — seditious but exciting for one who was keen on history, and had visited Mao's China when the family was invited to do so by Premier Zhou Enlai (Chou En-lai). The private family tour of the People's Republic of China (April and May 1957), the meeting with legendary revolutionaries[13] who figured so prominently in Edgar Snow's *Red Star Over China*, as well as seeming happiness and buoyancy of the people under communism,[14] not surprisingly gave me much food for thought. It impressed on me that oppression and exploitation of the humble and poor were very wrong and inhumane.

It was at Rangoon University that I first met other young Shan, and got to know personally Kachin, Karen, Mon, Arakanese, Chin, and other students. The more vocal and outgoing ones were as political as their Burmese counterparts though less anti-government, but all distrusted Burmese intentions which they perceived to be Burmese domination and subjugation of other ethnic groups. Noticeable was that all these young non-Burmese regarded communism as the ultimate evil, and thus shunned or avoided the Rangoon University Students Union leaders and activists who professed Marxism, and allegedly had contacts with secret communist cells in Rangoon.

Having gained friends from my homeland, I began, every summer, touring as much of the Shan State as I could — travelling on motorcycles, local buses, bullock carts, and on foot; and putting up in monasteries or homes of friends, relatives, and casual acquaintances. On these exploratory trips, I often heard tales of atrocities involving Burmese soldiers: villages razed, wholesale looting, disappearance of people, beating and torture under questioning about secret arms caches, molestation and rapes, shooting of livestock and poultry, and wanton killings.

My involvement in the politics of national awakening was further deepened when my mother, the Mahadevi of Yawnghwe was elected MP

(Member of Parliament) of the Lower House (Deputies) for Hsenwi in 1956.[15] Thereafter home became a political headquarters of sorts. All day and for half the night people ranging from Shan *chaofa* (princes), to MPs and other political leaders (Burmese, Shan, and other ethnic groups), Shan monks, and student leaders drifted in and out.

It was my father, the Yawnghwe prince who had encouraged my mother to enter politics. He was very much disturbed by the apparent Burmese disregard for the Shan State government and Shan autonomy.[16] Burmese soldiers acted in a manner that made the natives see them as predatory foreign occupation force (which seems to be still the case today). But since my father was also the Speaker of the Upper House, he could not directly interfere. He therefore devoted his energy to having Buddhist texts translated from Burmanized Pali to Shan — a move which "Shan-ized" Buddhism. It catalyzed a mini-cultural revolution and resulted in the revival of Shan literature which in turn increased national awareness and activities.

I myself was swept along by the rising tide of nationalism, initially as a shy and nervous participant. But after the first military takeover (1958) when several Shan student activists[17] from the university went underground to join the Noom Suk Harn, the first Shan resistance organization at the border, and the remaining student leaders dropped out in fear, I worked at keeping the spirit of nationalism high on campus.[18] I was not only successful in this task, but was by 1961 able to unite all on-campus non-Burmese student associations — Kachin, Karen, Arakan, Pa-O, Karenni, Chin, and Shan — under the wing of the Nationalities Students United Front which was as powerful as the Rangoon University Students Union.

While thus engaged on campus, I established clandestine contacts with both the Shan and Karen movements, often slipping into the jungle to meet their leaders.[19] It was a dangerous venture and, in retrospect, of dubious value. However, being young and fired with zeal and patriotism, I did not lose much sleep over the risk I was taking.

After the head of the Burma Army, General Ne Win, was invited in 1958 by the then Prime Minister U Nu to take over power, the military really got down to, in its own unique style, restoring stability and law in Shan State. Units were sent into the countryside to clear the whole region of rebels, foreign intruders, and those planning rebellion and secession.[20] This vigorous exercise[21] to restore stability resulted instead in an armed uprising in which Shan rebels captured the town of Tangyan in 1959,[22]

Chao Kyaw Toon, hero of the battle of Tangyan in 1959. This picture was taken at Camp Pang Tong (1960).

retreating only after about a week of fierce fighting and intense strafing by the Burma Air Force. Though the Burma Army won the battle, the rebellion smouldered on in the form of small armed bands scattered all over the Shan Country.[23]

This development put those directly responsible — the Head of Shan State, the Shan civil administration, the *chaofa*, MPs, politicians, and Shan political parties in an awkward position. Since anything concerned with the military and defence was beyond their jurisdiction, they became mere on-lookers. What was most worrying was that the numerous military sweeps were alienating the bulk of the rural population.

If peace and stability in Shan State were to be restored and rebellion nipped before it developed into anything threatening, it was imperative that some control be imposed on the Burmese military which meant that the Shan government should be given more power. Responsible Shan leaders reasoned that if more power was vested in the Shan government under a genuinely federal arrangement,[24] nationalist extremists would lose whatever support they hitherto enjoyed. Besides, the correction of imbalances in the hastily[25] drawn 1948 constitution would, Shan leaders reasoned, remove all serious friction within the Union and thus strengthen unity.[26]

These thoughts and ideas took on a more concrete form after the general election of 1960 in which all parties and personalities seen as pro-military throughout the Union were defeated. This took the form of a proposal by the Shan State government to U Nu whose party had won a landslide victory at the polls (on an anti-dictatorship platform), for reform of the Union constitution. It in time became a movement as the Karenni government, as well as the Kachin, Mon, Arakanese, Chin, and Karen leaders and parties expressed support.

Needless to say, the constitutional movement captured the imagination of all classes in Shan State. I attended several meetings organized by the Shan government at Taunggyi to explain the movement's aims, and in 1961, I even persuaded delegates of the Shan literary and cultural seminar to march around the town in support of the proposal for federation.[27] Like everyone else then, I believed that with the rejection by voters throughout the Union of anti-democratic tendencies, whatever conflict there was between the Burmese centre and the non-Burmese would in time be resolved through peaceful and democratic give-and-take.

However, this was not to be. I was rudely awakened at about 4 a.m. on the morning of 2 March 1962, by sounds of gunfire, faintly at first

but growing louder as I grew more awake. The gunfire was directly outside the home, and bullets smashed through window panes and frames,
thudded against or ricocheted off walls. A military unit had crept up
to our home in the dark, and surrounding it on two sides, had opened
fire.[28] My younger brother, Chao Mee who was only seventeen years
old was killed "while resisting the armed forces in its performance of
duty", according to the authorities concerned.[29]

Amidst the smell of cordite, the Yawnghwe prince, Chao Shwe
Thaike, who was former Union President, twice Speaker of the Upper House, and MP (Upper House) for Yawnghwe, was taken away at
bayonet point and put in an army van that morning before the light of
dawn.[30] That was the last time I saw my father. One day in November
1962, I received a phone call from a Major Thein Shwe who said he
was a classmate of my elder sister, Chao Sanda.[31] He wished to meet
me. The Major took me to meet Colonel Lwin, the head of the dreaded
MIS (Military Intelligence Service) who informed me that "the President"
had expired in jail.

The meeting took place at Dagon House, a special meeting place
for top army brass and for the reception of foreign military guests. I
was offered cigarettes (Benson & Hedges) and scotch and soda. While
I sat there numbed by the news of my father's death, wondering if he
had been tortured and finally injected with some poison, the Major and
his boss solemnly discussed, of all things, the fighting between the
Chinese People Liberation Army (PLA) and the Indian Army at their
mutual border.

The cremation of the Chaofa *Luang* (Shan for "senior") of Yawnghwe
was held in Yawnghwe tow, drawing large crowds from far and near —
the Padaung with their long-necked women, Pa-O men and women in
traditional black, the Intha (Inle Lake dwellers) in brown homespun,
the townspeople in sombre clothes, and relatives in the white of royal
mourning. A couple of Burma Army men[32] resplendent in green and
red bands on caps and tabs on collars, coloured ribbons on chests, and
gold insignias on shoulders were there for a while, and left without the
usual pomp.

That year, 1962, I had another brush with shots fired in anger, again
in Rangoon. Following the coup in March, feelings against the military
on campus were high as the takeover was seen as an usurpation of
power by neo-Nazi elements. Aware of this the new regime introduced

new campus rules and regulations which resulted in a series of student protests. On 6 July, there was one such protest, and the next day the police were sent in. Shots were fired wounding several students,[33] but the police were chased out. The students then proceeded to close all campus gates, hoisted red banners of the Students Union all over the campus, made fiery speeches against the military, and declared the university a "fortress of democracy".

On the evening of 7 July, the regime unleashed its soldiers, armed with newly issued West German G-3 assault rifles, against the student body. I worked as tutor in the Department of English, and that evening I found myself near the campus main gate (on my way home from the judo gym). I had stopped to talk to several students from my tutorial class. Many students were waving red banners and hurling insults at the military when a volley rang out. I jumped into a nearby ditch. When the firing stopped, those not hit, myself included, ran. Another volley was unleashed. We hit the dirt. The firing ceased. We then started running again, and another volley was fired. And so it went.

The military declared that soldiers had had to break up an unruly student mob, and maintained that minimum violence had been used. Only sixteen shots were fired resulting, most unfortunately, in sixteen deaths.[34] The university was declared closed, and the Students Union Building — popularly regarded as a home away from home of the young Aung San, Burma's Architect of Freedom, during his university days — was flattened by demolition charges, the sound of which was heard throughout the capital. It is still widely believed that dead and wounded students were dumped into this building before it was demolished.

The violence of 1962 heralded the supremacy of force, and the death of democracy and reason. I felt there was no other choice left but to answer the call to battle — for the Shan, as well as for democracy. This I did in April 1963, several months after the cremation of my father.

Answering the Call

Before I proceed to give an account of my personal experiences in the Shan nationalist movement, I wish to first give a very brief sketch of the Shan.

The people known to the outside world as the Shan, do not refer to themselves as such. The name they use for themselves is "Tai", and like their brothers, the Thai or Siamese, they believe that their original home was in south China covering the provinces of Sichuan (Szechuan), Yunnan, Guizhou (Kweichou), Guangxi (Kwangsi) and Guangdong (Kwangtung) — a belief which is dismissed by almost all Chinese scholars, and Western ones too, as being without factual foundation. However, neither the Shan nor Thai should be blamed because if this story of origin is a fabrication, it was the invention of Western scholars. Before the coming of Westerners, the Shan or Tai and their brothers, the Lao, northern Thai or Tai-Ping and the Tai-Ahom, all believed that they were descended from Khun Lu and Khun Lai who came down from heaven on ladders of, according to different chronicles, gold, silver, or iron. In all chronicles there is a story of a servant of Khun Lu and Khun Lai, named Pang-ku, or Lang-ku, who tricked his masters into letting him eat the head of the chicken sent from heaven, and as a result, he became the king of Muang Kae (China). A very tall tale, scoffed Western scholars when they heard the story, and the natives, very much impressed by Western wonders and wisdom, could not help but agree. Somehow, they did not seem to have wondered why similarly fanciful tales of Adam and Eve, Noah and his Ark, among others, were not summarily dismissed by the West as was the story of Khun Lu and Khun Lai. Perhaps it was because they were so overawed.

Since a comprehensive research on the early history of the Tai-speaking people (Shan, Thai or Siam, Lao, Tai-Ping or Khon Muang, Tai Chuang, Tai Chong, Thai Dam, White Thai, Tai Nua, Tai Mao, Tai Lue, among others) has yet to be undertaken, all that can be said about the Tai or Thai is that by the late twelfth century, they had evolved somehow into a people with enough skills and prowess to establish kingdoms. At about this time, coinciding with increasing pressure of the Mongol rulers of China on the kingdom of Nanchao, the Tai had established various kingdoms near the southern rim of Nanchao.[35] These were the Tai Ahom kingdom of Assam, the Shan kingdom of Ava, the Tai Mao kingdom, the Lao kingdom of Lan-Chang, and in present day Thailand, the kingdoms of Payao, Chiang Rai (later moved to Chiangmai), and Sukhothai and the Shan kingdom at Martaban.[36]

The Tai people known as the "Shan" — the subject of this paper — are those who constituted and established the Tai Mao and Ava kingdoms which had close connections and continuing relationships with Burmese kingdoms. Within the context of the history of Burma, it will be seen that there were then two Shan centres of power — Ava, and the Tai Mao kingdom.

I shall deal with the details of the long and turbulent relationship between the Shan and the Burmese in the chapters to come. Here it will suffice to say that after the fall of the Shan kingdom of Ava to the great Burmese conqueror, Burinnong, in 1555, and the destruction of the Mao kingdom by the Chinese in 1604, the Shan, though without a central focus and splintered into principalities, clung stubbornly to their identity and independence. They resisted all Burmese moves to subjugate them. At times they submitted to strong or wise monarchs, but they rebelled whenever they could.

The Shan enjoyed some peace during the British period[37] since there was no Burmese centre of power. However, following World War II there again appeared a Burmese centre of power which brought to the forefront the old question of the relationship between the Shan and the Burmese.

Though the British had blunted Shan nationalist sentiments by allowing them to slumber in a pastoral idyll cut off from the whole world, World War II with its marching armies of various nationalities, fire and death from the skies, and stirring call to arms by both the Allied and Japanese protagnoists — awoke the Shan nation, rousing them to the perils of trust and dependency on external powers. And since the desire to be free, to be the master of one's fate was the order of the day — from the Gulf of Tonkin to the Suez Canal and even beyond — the Shan were naturally no less affected than the Burmese by this flame.

Thus with the lowering of the Union Jack, the stage was set for a continuation of the struggle between two national imperatives — the Burmese centre, for greater control of "regained" possessions,[38] especially the Shan tributary; and the Shan, for greater control of their destiny. Thus, I was born a Shan and lived in the period of Shan awakening. I saw, heard and experienced the drama of two forces pulling in opposite directions. I was drawn like thousands of my compatriots into a Shan-Burmese struggle similar to, or a continuation of, the kind which had existed during the days of my grandfather, and further beyond.

It was towards the end of April 1963, that I found myself in a jungle camp of the 4th Battalion, SSIA (Shan State Independence Army)[39] — really a couple of lean-tos roofed with leaves and multi-coloured plastic sheets.

After a rudimentary basic military training by instructors (one an ex-police sergeant, and another formerly of the 1st Shan Rifles, Burma

Army), I was appointed political officer of the SSIA Northern Command. After a series of adventures and misadventures, I was given an escort of two squads by the SSIA northern commander.[40] In response to my wish to travel further south to meet with other SSIA senior officers, namely, Sai Myint Aung (Hso-khan),[41] acting chief of staff, and Khun Kya Nu,[42] the most dynamic and active of all SSIA leaders.

Around July 1963, the new Burmese regime invited all armed opposition groups to hold peace talks with the Revolutionary Council. This resulted in my first important assignment as head of a joint SSIA-SNUF (Shan National United Front)[43] team to co-ordinate preliminary talks with Burmese authorities. We had no expectations and viewed the call for peace talks as Rangoon's public relations stunt.

In this role, I — complete with shoulder length hair and a sort of beard — was once more back in Rangoon. Due to my status as the son of the former Union President, and a "Rangoon boy", the Rangoon press was naturally very intrigued and gave much prominence to the youthful Shan delegation[44] which somewhat elevated the status of the Shan rebels in the public's eyes — from Shan bandits to nationalist rebels. It was a major propaganda victory for the SSIA, in particular, and the Shan cause in general.

At this point, I think it would be of general interest to readers to give an account of my experience during the peace talks. In July 1963, Colonel Tint Swe (at present Minister of Industry I) in charge of a tactical command at Loilem, Shan State, contacted the joint SSA-SNUF team for peace talks in response to our acceptance of the Revolutionary Council's offer. A rendenzvous was fixed at a village on the Panglong-Laikha road. On hand to welcome us was a tall and elegant gentleman who spoke excellent English, Lt.-Col. Kyaw Khine of the 12th Burma Regiment (Buregt), who had at one time been to the United States for further training. He was courteous, and like all officers we met, seemed genuinely desirous for peace though unsure how and if the war would end. Like us, Burmese officers were uninformed about the direction of the Revolutionary Council. But being career soldiers, they were committed to serving loyally.

While in Loilem, we heard over the radio that an SSIA representative had landed in Rangoon from a foreign country. Though bewildered by this new development I, nevertheless, requested Colonel Tint Swe for this "representative", Sai Pan, to be included in our team when meeting with the Revolutionary Council in Rangoon. It was most worrying because we had no idea what Sai Pan had in mind. Our mission was exploratory, and would thus avoid taking any definite stand at this early stage.

After several days in Loilem, we were taken to Taunggyi, the capital of Shan State, and then to the airport at Heho (Hai-wua). After the flight to Rangoon, we were met at Mingladon Airport by several MIS officers and taken to a house within the grounds of the Rangoon Turf Club (then closed following a ban on horse-racing). The SSIA "representative" from abroad, Sai Pan, was already there, and we had a heated discussion out of ear-shot of MIS officers, presumably, on the deserted race track.

It became apparent that the SSIA exiles abroad responded because they were convinced that the Burmese army was on the verge of collapse and would agree to share power with rebels, and with regard to Shan State, federalism. Hence Sai Pan's view was that we should lay all our cards on the table without further waste of time. We replied that on the contrary, bringing up federalism would amount to showing a red rag to an enraged bull. The call for peace was, I argued, but a ploy by the coup-makers to neutralize anti-military feelings in the country, and more importantly, to win the sympathy of the international community. As such, our aim should be to keep the talk and ceasefire going on for as long as possible and thus gain maximum favourable exposure. We argued back and forth inconclusively until Sai Pan was threatened with exclusion from the team which would have made him merely a representative of a few exiles abroad.

The meeting with the Revolutionary Council took place in a luxurious mansion formerly owned by a Chinese tycoon, Y.H. Kwong, a friend of the Yawnghwe family who was expelled earlier from Burma by General Ne Win. At the talks, only two members of the Revolutionary Council spoke — that is, General Ne Win and Dr Hla Han (a doctor of medicine and Burma Independence Army [BIA] veteran who was then quite influential). Ne Win's opening passage was to the effect that he was determined to mercilessly uproot all disloyal elements, but was giving misguided elements a chance to co-operate with the government. In closing, the General asked what sort of proposals we had in mind. Thereupon, Sai Pan whipped out a paper and laid it on the table. It was a demand for federalism.

Dr Hla Han picked the paper up, studied it, and passed it on to Ne Win who, after reading it, passed it on to others. A stony hush descended, smiles disappeared replaced by scowls, and twelve more pairs of eyes stared at us coldly. Although I was in a state of shock at such an unexpected stab in the back, nonetheless I managed to blurt out that we, officers in the field, had not been consulted and had no opinion on this matter. However, since the Revolutionary Council had seen the proposal, we would like to have time to study it, and would again contact the government.

Dr Hla Han replied heatedly, which made him stammer more than usual, that federalism and secession could not be allowed; that all races of Burma had to stand united behind the Revolutionary Council in its march towards socialism. No divisions would be tolerated, he warned. I replied that due to difficult communications, we would like an extension of the ceasefire in place, and assured that we were eager to establish peace. General Ne Win replied that we should discuss this with the Northeast and Eastern Military Command, and after a round of handshaking, the meeting ended on a slightly less cold note.

It was a close call. A young officer on the team later told me that he had expected all of us to be bundled out, lined up on the beautiful lawn outside, and shot. More seriously, an abrupt ending to the talks would have deprived us of public exposure in the Rangoon news media which was one of our reasons for responding. However, because we did not insist on federalism, we continued as emissaries, giving a press interview (more successfully), and taken on tours of factories and other sights of the capital. We even managed to extend the ceasefire till the end of 1963. The Eastern Command continued to co-operate with us, even flying one SSIA leader, Khun Kya Nu, from Loilem to Loilang on the Thai border.

The talks,[45] however, came to nothing as none of the rebel organizations were interested in joining the Burmese way to the Socialist Party — which was Rangoon's alternative to continuing with the war. The Burmese military made it clear that there would be no return to plurality in politics for a long time to come.

One very significant by-product of the peace talks of 1963, in the Shan State, was that it inspired thousands of young people (mostly from middle and high schools) to join whichever rebel band was nearest. The people as a whole and especially the rebels, being ill-informed and politically unsophisticated, became wildly optimistic and believed that victory was just round the corner.

With a flood of recruits coming in, the SSIA's main task was to get as many arms as possible, there being but one rifle to every five soldiers.

Saw Yanda (holding the microphone), founder of the Noom Suk Harn, the first Shan resistance organization (1959).

My next assignment was to purchase arms from Laos and Thailand. This was a difficult task as Chinese syndicates and merchant-warloads[46] who were in control of the border trade disapproved of strong nationalistic Shan armies.

At this juncture, my mother, the Mahadevi of Yawnghwe, arrived in Thailand with two daughters and a son, and a young Shan graduate of Rangoon University as escort.[47] It was reported that as soon as the military heard that she had left Rangoon, a hunter-killer team was dispatched to bring her back dead or alive, and checkpoints were alerted.

It is believed that the Burmese team even crossed the border into the town of Maesod (Thailand), and on Burmese soil had mistakenly arrested a woman who was travelling with two daughters.[48]

The Mahadevi, a political leader in her own right, at once set out to unify the feuding factions — the Noom Suk Harn (established in 1958),[49] the SSIA (1960), the SNUF (1961), and the Tailand National Army or TNA (1963).[50]

However, since it was thought that victory was just around the corner, she was regarded by, in particular, Saw Yanda ("Chao" Noi)[51] of the Noom Suk Harn, and U Gondra (self-styled Chao, or Prince Nga Kham)[52] of TNA as a "Johnny-come-lately" about to steal the soon-to-be forthcoming glory and power. The Yawnghwe Mahadevi therefore failed to achieve unity, and had to settle for merging the SSIA and the SNUF in a new organization, the SSA (Shan State Army) in early 1964.

In early 1964 Khun Sa,[53] who served as chief of the Loimaw *Ka-kwe-ye* (KKY or Local Defence Force) — one of the many anti-insurgency auxiliaries encouraged and supported by the Burma Army — turned against the Burmese. The causes for this were Rangoon's blanket nationalization measures[54] and he demonetizing of Kyat 100 and 50 notes. He set up the United Anti-Socialist Army and called upon all Shan armies to unite. He held a series of talks with Saw Yanda, U Gondra, and Bo Deving (a dissident SSIA battalion commander from Muang Yai area who broke away in 1962).

However, before much was accomplished, the three Shan leaders turned against Khun Sa, and his border camp was raided by Thai authorities. Khun Sa, angered by this betrayal, was soon back with the Burma Army as chief of Loimaw KKY.

While these events were unfolding at the Thai border, I was with the SSA 1st Brigade whose jurisdiction covered Namsan, Muang Mit, and Hsenwi.[55] My main task was to reorganize the 4th, 5th and 6th Battalions, and to set up the infrastructure for civil administration and the upkeep of law and order. I was charged with liaison with the Kachin Independence Army (KIA)[56] operating in parts of Hsenwi and Muang Mit, and the responsibility for bringing in small Shan groups in areas east of Hsenwi town which were rich in opium and under the loose control of units belonging to the former KMT (Kuomintang — Chinese Nationalist) 5th and 3rd Armies based at Mae-salong and Tum Ngop respectively in Thailand.

Just as our reorganization was complete, the Burma Army launched a six-month sweep. We counter-attacked, raiding the mining town of Namtu Bawdwin,[57] ambushing convoys and trains between Lashio and Hsipaw, sniping at Burmese foot columns, all of which put more than 200 enemies out of action.

At this juncture, an unexpected and favourable event occurred. There was trouble for the Burmese in Kokang, a narrow strip of land between the Salween River and the Chinese border in the northwest of Shan State, arising from the detention of Olive Yang.[58] Her elder brother, Jimmy Yang, a former MP (prior to the 1962 coup) for Kokang, and Rangoon-based businessman, made his way back and raised the banner of revolt.[59]

The Kokang KKY had been recognized as an auxiliary force by the Burma Army since the early 1950s, and under Burmese protection, had engaged in opium and gold trade across the Thai border. It also had extensive connections with the ex-KMT armies (3rd and 5th) on the Thai border, and hence was a formidable and well-funded force.

The main concern of the SSA was to win over this force, or at least to keep it from falling under the control of the ex-KMT armies. The fact that its new commander Jimmy Yang was well educated and politically-inclined seemed to be in the SSA's favour.

Therefore the SSA 1st Brigade commander, Sai Hla Aung (Colonel Hso-lane) and I journeyed to Kokang via Namkham, but our column (500 men) ran into a Burmese operation against Bo Mawng[60] and Bo Kang Yoi,[61] due to earlier attacks by the two against Burmese outposts. We inflicted moderate losses on the enemy in three major clashes, but lost five men with ten missing. Nevertheless, we crossed the Salween into Kokang and met with Jimmy Yang. We were shown well-constructed strong points and were impressed by the smart performance of his Kokang troops on parade. We were asked to bring more SSA commanders so that future strategies could be devised.

I recall that it was in early 1965 that I again went with a high-level SSA team[62] to Kokang. While the talks had barely begun, the Kokang KKY collapsed as Lo Hsin Han,[63] its senior most commander, defected. There was widespread panic and people, both armed and unarmed, fled for ferry points on the Salween. We were, it seemed, the only ones left in Kokang.[64] We followed the fleeing horde in the hope of resuming talks with Jimmy Yang on the western side of the river. However, there was a large Chinese force (from the ex-KMT 3rd army) waiting to escort him to safety in Thailand, and off he and his force went with them.[65]

In the meantime, I received information by wireless that matters at the Shan State War Council (SSWC),[66] the highest organ of the SSA, headed by the Mahadevi of Yawnghwe, was not going well due to bickering and intrigues among members. I was asked to return to settle matters as soon as possible.

Late in 1965, by coincidence I met the head of the KIA, General Zau Seng. He asked me to escort him to the border. Having accomplished most of my assignment for the SSA 1st Brigade, and receiving instructions from the SSWC chairperson, the Yawnghwe Mahadevi, to escort the Kachin president, I accompanied the Kachin column to the Thai border.

While I was on my way — which took five months due to the need to evade Burmese blocking forces who were out in strength — the situation took a turn for the worse. There were not only extensive enemy sweeps, but Khun Sa and his Loimaw KKY were on the offensive. He smashed Bo Deving's force and scattered units of the Noom Suk Harn (which was loosely allied to Bo Deving) in the Laikha and Muang Nong area.[67] The Loimaw KKY also clashed with SSA units because Khun Sa regarded Bo Mawng, the hero of Tangyan (and nominal commander, then, of the SSA 2nd Brigade) as an ally of Bo Deving. However, since neither the SSA nor Khun Sa desired direct confrontation, open warfare was avoided.[68]

While Khun Sa's Loimaw KKY was on the rampage, a coup within the Noom Suk Harn unseated its chairperson, Saw Yanda and control fell into the hands of younger officers who were formerly of Rangoon University.[69]

Around this period (the mid-1960s), there were changes in the TNA operating in Kengtung (covering more than 12,000 sq miles). Its president, U Gondra was assassinated, and after a year of internal strife, a dark horse, Khun Myint,[70] commander of Muang Yang Brigade, emerged as undisputed leader. Although uneducated, he saw beyond local interests, and appeared sincere about uniting all Shan armies under the SSA. He renamed the TNA, the SSA/East.

From mid-1966 to 1968, I was in charge, jointly with Khun Kya Nu, of the SSA's army general headquarters (GHQ).[71] I was therefore in a position to work for Shan unity under a favourable environment due to changes within the Noom Suk Harn (renamed SNIA for Shan National Independence Army), and in Kengtung.

Taken at a summit meeting of rebel commanders (c. 1965). Left to right: Naw Louisa Benson, widow of Brigadier Lin Tin, 5th Kawthoolei Brigade (Karen), at the time acting brigade commander; General Zau Seng, supreme commander of KIA (Kachin) from its founding in 1961 to his death in 1975; General Li Wen Huan, paramount chief of ex-KMT 3rd Army.

As unanimously agreed by the three Shan armies, a working committee for unity, named the Shan Unity Preparatory Committee (SUPC) was formed.[72] It got down to work, formulating a plan to merge all armies under one political and military command. The main and immediate Shan concern was the CPB (Communist Party of Burma, initially called the Burmese Communist Party) which was from 1967, with help from Chinese cadres, building up its military muscle along the Kachin and Shan borders with China. We saw clearly that the Chinese-CPB strategy was none other than to use the Shan State as a killing ground, and to use local recruits as cannon fodder. Only by uniting could we hope to prevent our homeland from being ravaged by two warring Burmese centres of power, similar to a scenario nightmarishly unfolding in Indochina. Also, we reasoned, Shan unity would create a situation conducive to a negotiated and peaceful settlement of the Shan-Burmese conflict with Rangoon since the conflict did not involve irreconcilable ideological or power contradictions.

Just as preparations for unity were coming along smoothly, the situation took a turn for the worse as events overtook carefully drafted plans.

First, the SNIA (Shan National Independence Army) collapsed when Saw Yanda deposed in late 1965, staged a counter coup capturing the strategically placed SNIA's GHQ camp on the Thai border.[73] Another blow was struck when the then SSA chief-of-staff, Moherng detained some senior SNIA officers after inviting them to a conference,[74] which was quickly followed by a declaration from Moherng that he had set up jointly with Saw Yanda a new organization to combat communism — the Shan United Revolutionary Army (SURA).[75] With "anti-communism" serving as a common ground, Moherng, the erstwhile SSA chief-of-staff, allied himself with the ext-KMT 3rd Army of General Li.

Though Moherng's action was highly disloyal, and shocked the entire SSA, I nevertheless saw that my responsibility as general secretary of the Shan Unity Preparatory Committee (SUPC) was to keep the momentum for unity in motion. I tried to meet personally with Moherng, but all my overtures were ignored. The option of military action against Moherng was briefly considered but rejected since Moherng had the backing of the ex-KMT 3rd Army. A fight would have been protracted, and there was the growing danger of the CPB.

Another novel and dangerous Burmese threat was emerging. Burmese authorities had unrolled in late 1967 a new strategy to undermine Shan armed resistance which came in the form of the *Ka-kwe-ye* (KKY)

Turbaned figure, Moherng then SSA chief-of-staff, and right of turbaned figure Sai Zam Muang (now believed dead), SSA 1st Brigade. Front row (extreme right): Sai Lek, present (1984) SSA chief-of-staff.

policy. According to this policy anyone wishing to do so would be permitted to raise auxiliary local defence forces which would be allowed to engaged in trade (mainly opium and contraband goods) to the Thai and Laotian borders, and any rebel group surrendering would be given KKY status.

With everyone apprehensive of the CPB inroads, backed by the communist Chinese[76] in Shan areas that shared a border with China, the Burmese KKY policy was an extremely attractive way of meeting the communist threat, and most lucrative too.[77] Already, the SSA 2nd Brigade (in Muang Loen and parts of Muang Yai), and the 6th Brigade (Muang Hsu and Muang Nong), had begun responding to this policy.

Meanwhile in Kengtung, Khun Myint and the SSA/East were facing increasing pressure from Chinese cadres and the CPB, and as such would not be of much help in the event of a war with Moherng and the Chinese merchant-warlord army. It therefore made more sense to first meet the more immediate threats, that is, the Burmese KKY policy and the CPB expansion into Shan State.

At a top-level meeting of SSA officers in May 1968, I was assigned, together with Sai Zam Muang, 1st Brigade chief-of-operations, and Sai Sa Toon, 4th Brigade chief-of-operations, the task of consolidating the SSA's position in Hsenwi, Namsan, Hsipaw, Muang Yai, Khesi, Muang Loen, Muang Hsu, and Muang Nong, covering some 24,000 sq miles.[78] The SSA liaison office and army general headquarters was put under the charge of Khun Kya Nu, Sai Hla Aung, and Sai Mawng (Lao-leng). Its task was to keep alive the spirit of unity, and more important, establish close links with other resistance movements such as the Karen National Union (KNU), Karenni, Pa-O and others, and keep an eye on political developments in the outside world as well.

Against the Dark Tide

By late 1968, I was once again in the frontline, moving around with a command staff and escort of fifty men in the Hsipaw, Muang Yai, Khesi, and Muang Hsu areas. I remained in the field until early 1972 as commander of the SSA 1st Military Region. I was not involved in any fighting but played hide-and-seek with enemy columns and search units for at least six months of every year.

My first task was to raise morale which took the form of frequent military parades, situation briefings and discussions with officers and

Reviewing an SSA march-past on Shan national day, Muang Kho, 7 February 1969. Front row (from left to right): Lt.-Col. Bo Kang Yoom, director civil administration department 1st Military Region; myself, commander of 1st Military Region; Lt.-Col. Ngaa-muang, director, military department, 1st Military Region.

NCOs (non-commissioned officers), political mass meetings at market villages, formation of propaganda units, inspection tours of units and villages — all of which restored overall confidence, making the SSA less susceptible to Burmese offers of shares in the lucrative border trade being carried out by ex-rebels and KKY units.

My most important task was, however, to weld the two SSA Brigades, the 1st and the 4th, which hitherto had scarcely co-operated with each other, into one cohesive whole. It meant reshuffling men and officers; forming new battalions;[79] introducing uniform rules and regulations in command and control (adapted from U.S. army manuals); and leadership courses for NCOs and officers. In addition, I had to re-structure the civil administration, by setting up new administrative bodies; laying down rules governing local administration at various levels, taxation, education and schools, law and order, health and sanitation, administration of justice and the appointment and training of administrative personnel. In these very formidable tasks, I was assisted by experienced SSA officers.[80]

However, Burmese offers to share in the lucrative opium and contraband trade proved too tempting for two battalion commanders who defected with about 200 men in the midst of the SSA 1st Military Region's operation to recover Namsan and parts of Hsenwi from the KIA. It demoralized the troops who were already not having an easy time. My mistake was to undertake a major military venture while the troops were new to each other and also to their NCOs and officers, and vice versa.

The months following were chaotic with officers and NCOs losing control of the men deserting in twos and threes, or whole squads asking to go home. At this grave moment in early 1969, had the Burma Army struck, the SSA 1st Military Region would have been destroyed. However, the enemy was apparently unaware of the extent of its demoralization. Burmese inaction was also probably due to on-going secret talks between me and a cousin of mine, Lt.-Col. Chao Saw Ohn of the Burma Army.[81] The main subject discussed was the increase in strength of the CPB, and the threat this posed to the country as a whole.[82]

Fortunate too was the fact that Khun Sa,[83] the most influential and powerful KKY leader, at this crucial stage, secretly contacted the SSA, expressing interest in joining the resistance, and even helped us capture one renegade battalion commander.

Due to these fortuitous events, and assisted by loyal officers[84] I was able to rebuild the army and its morale. Further, mandate given by the people (through votes cast at a series of public meetings throughout the SSA 1st Military Region) to continue with the resistance, and their subsequent active support was crucial.[85]

Just as we had restored the SSA's spirit and discipline, the Burma Army launched a major sweep using the newly formed 77th Division fresh from its victory against the CPB in the Burmese delta and the Pegu Yoma range. There was, however, not much fighting as we responded with evasion and hit-and-run tactics. About 100 enemies were put out of action while we lost ten killed or wounded. The sweep lasted about three months.

The following year (1970) was for Rangoon a very busy one as the CPB debouched in strength from redoubts on the China border began operations in the Wa State, Kokang, north and west of Hsenwi, and Muang Mit. From the right, another threat materialized in the form of former Prime Minister U Nu (deposed by Ne Win in the 1962 coup, and imprisoned) who had left Burma for medical treatment, and upon arrival in London declared war against Ne Win's regime. He declared that he was the legitimate Prime Minister and called on all in Burma to rally around him.

U Nu's call to arms raised great hopes and excitement in Burma, and we too, were quite encouraged. Our spirit was further boosted when Khun Sa made overtures for joint operations and said he was ready to fight the Burmese. However, while secret talks were underway, MIS arrested Khun Sa,[86] but a Colonel Chang[87] managed to bring Khun Sa's army into the jungle. After extensive talks, the Loimaw KKY agreed to eventual unification of the two armies, and adopted a new name — the Shan United Army (SUA). Though less disciplined and smaller in number, the SUA (Loimaw) was better armed and better off financially because of its close relationship with a commercial interest[88] (part of the commercial and financial network of ethnic Chinese dominating Southeast Asia).

At the end of 1970, the joint SSA-SUA (Loimaw) force went on the offensive which included a grenade attack on the Burmese top brass attending an Independence Day parade (4 January 1971) at Lashio,[89] ambushes of military trains between Hsipaw and Lashio, destruction of bridges between Kyaukme and Lashio, attacks on enemy outposts including a battalion headquarters in Kyaukme, with the re-assertion of SSA control in Namsan and the southwest of Hsenwi. The enemy struck with a counter-offensive using the crack 88th and 99th Divisions. In the sixth

The Shan United Army (of Khun Sa): recruits learning the three R's, 1983. Photo courtesy of Bertil Lintner.

months of fighting covering the whole of the SSA 1st Military Region, our men put out of action over 600 enemy personnel.[90]

In Namsan, fighting was more complicated as the SSA-SUA forces under Lt.-Col. Sai Zam Muang had to deal with three opponents: the Burma Army, ex-KMT 3rd Army, and the KIA. Fighting was therefore three-cornered and extensive. For instance, one SSA unit under Captain Khun Hpung fought almost 30 actions with various enemies all in a month.

From March 1971 onwards things were relatively quieter as the Burma Army was engaged with the CPB under the Kachin, Naw Seng, in the Eastern Shan Sate (from Kokang, Vieng Ngun, Muang Loen, and to the northeast of Kengtung) and in the north (Hsenwi and Muang Mit).

During this period I was occupied with touring and inspecting various units and making adjustments to rules and structures where needed, and was busy with drafting plans for setting up a political party. It had become necessary to take this step because we believed that the resistance movement should be controlled by, and responsive to the will of the people, more so since the people did participate fully in the war. The formation of a party would bring the resistance and the army under their control which would consequently eliminate undesirable tendencies within the army such as warlordism, and deviation from nationalist aspirations.

When the draft party constitution was ready, I convened an all-SSA general conference in mid-1971. This coincided with another enemy push and we therefore had to hold a mobile conference, moving about with a security force of 600 men. There was no major engagement but SSA units in Namsan managed to put out of action close to 200 enemy personnel. In August 1971, a political party — the Shan State Progress Party (SSPP) — was born.

In the period in which I commanded the SSA 1st Military Region, the most troubling problem was that concerning the CPB. It had been making overtures[91] since 1969 for joint efforts against Rangoon under the banner of a united front.[92] Enjoying the full support of Chinese leaders such as Marshal Lin Biao (Lin Piao) and Jiang Qing (Chiang Ching), it had abundant funds, arms and ammunition, uniforms, shoes, medicine, and access to hospitals in Yunnan province. In addition it had a radio station which broadcast weekly in the Shan language. Being thus equipped the CPB was able to engage in spectacular battles inflicting heavy losses on the Burma Army (600 to over 1,000 killed in some major engagements).[93]

The tide of communism seemed to be rising higher and higher in Southeast Asia. From 1966, Thailand was faced with a major communist uprising, and in the Indochinese states, the United States, the world's mightiest power was floundering, and its resolve clearly weakening. For the politically naive who were themselves in a war situation — which best describes all those within the SSA, with few exceptions — the argument that victory of communism in general, and the CPB in particular, was all but inevitable, was naturally most convincing.

This being the case, the SSA leadership's insistence on independence and refusal of the CPB's offer of arms "without strings", was not well received, especially by those commanding units. The CPB also waged whispering campaigns labelling SSA leaders as militarists and reactionary bureaucrats. I was branded a feudalist reactionary since I was of the ruling House of Yawnghwe.[94] However, CPB representatives cultivated senior SSA officers, flattering each in turn as being the only "truly revolutionary leader of the Shan people".

The CPB's credible battle performances, its stores of military supplies, the limited international knowledge of SSA people, and infantile desire for plentiful weapons — all conspired to push the SSA into the open arms of the CPB.

To prevent this, I and other SSA leaders, and Khun Kya Nu as party president and army chief-of-staff, developed a two-pronged strategy whereby (1) a base was to be set up in the south adjoining the Thai border which would serve as a fall-back point and distance the SSA/SSPP from the CPB, and (2) the formation of a united front comprising non-communist nationalist movements (the Karen, Kachin, Pa-O, Karenni, Mon among others) to keep the CPB at bay and which would hopefully develop into a "third force" in Burmese politics.

Accordingly, I came down to the Thai border with a task force of 800 men in early 1972. I was to work for a united front, and explore avenues for co-operation or alliance with U Nu's Parliamentary Democracy Party (PDP).[95]

Khun Kya Nu, whose task was the establishment of an SSA base in the south, accordingly set out with the task force (which had escorted me down to the border). However, while in Muang Pan, the ex-KMT 3rd Army and SURA (set up by former SSA chief-of-staff, Moherng, in 1968) struck. The SSA/SSPP units though out-numbered and out-gunned, managed to put about 200 attackers out of action, but were forced to disengage when Burmese troops appeared.[96] In the confused melee,

Khun Kya Nu was cut off from the main column which made its way back to the north. Fortunately, he managed to contact Thaton Hla Pe,[97] a political veteran and president of the Pa-O group operating west of Muang Pan. By the end of 1972, with the Pa-O president's help, Khun Kya Nu, with less than 40 men under him, was able to establish a southern base covering Mawkmai, south Muang Nai, and part of Muang Pan (about 2,000 sq miles). The base headquarters was at Muang Mai, about three hours' walk from the Thai border.

In the meantime, I met the former Burmese Prime Minister U Nu and other PDP leaders, and in the ensuing talks made it clear that the SSA/SSPP could not ally itself with the PDP without at least a plentiful supply of ammunition because of our promixity to both the CPB and the Burma Army.[98] The PDP leaders were quite displeased with our "quibbling" but at any rate, the talks became irrelevant as the PDP had run out of funds, and its leadership was splintered.

With regard to the setting up of a united front, the attempt was more successful especially since the Karenni president, Saw Mawrel, and the vice-president Bo Kha, were enthusiastic. After a series of conferences with various non-Burmese national organizations, the Nationalities Liberation United Front (NLUF) composed of the SSA/SSPP, KNU (Karen), KniNPP (Karenni National Progress Party), the Padaung, Mon, and Arakan, was formed.[99]

Though the objectives set up by the SSA/SSPP in 1971 had been tentatively achieved, the situation in the north, our main operation base, was not promising. The absence of Khun Kya Nu and myself allowed the CPB to freely sow disunity. Soon, a gulf developed between those wishing a military alliance with the CPB and those opposing it — the former being stronger since Lt.-Col. Sai Zam Muang, SSPP chief-of-operations, badly wanted arms, and was convinced (in 1972 and 1973), that communism was everywhere undefeatable (which was understandable since the Americans were on the verge of defeat in South Vietnam). However, inspite of growing dissension and ferment within the SSA, Khun Kya Nu and I were able to keep things under control through daily wireless communications with the leaders concerned.

In mid-1973, a glimmer of hope appeared in the form of overtures by Lo Hsin Han, the Kokang KKY leader. This stemmed from the dismantling of KKY units by Rangoon because the KKY programme had become a political liability due to the international furore against opium and heroin from Burma's Golden triangle.[100] Lo Hsin Han, being part of the trade and profit-orientated cross-border brotherhood, unsurprisingly, was all for a strong base on the Thai border. He also expressed support for Shan unity and the idea of a "third force" in the politics of Burma.

Though SSA leaders were quite sceptical, we recognized that Lo Hsin Han could contribute to the building of Shan unity, and that he was valuable to us in focusing international attention on the plight of the Shan people. We had hoped to do this by offering our service in the eradication of opium growing on Shan soil. He was particularly important in this respect since his elevation in 1972 by Western media as the "Opium King of the Golden Triangle".

However, no sooner had Lo Hsin Han arrived at the SSA southern headquarters, Muang Mai, than he was enticed on board a Thai helicopter and eventually extradited to Burma amidst much crowing by American and multinational bureaucrats and policemen who hailed it as the end of the narcotics trade. (Lo was flown from Bangkok to Rangoon in late 1973.)

While the effect of Lo's capture on the narcotics trade can only be described as absolutely minimal, it radically weakened the non-communist leadership of the SSA/SSPP. The involvement of Thai, American, and other Western governments and agencies in this sordid bureacratic game turned the SSA rank and file against the non-communist world. It goes without saying that it yielded the CPB a bumper harvest in political credit, and subsequently pushed the SSPP army chief-of-operations to accept gifts of arms from the communist.[101]

Well aware that the SSA/SSPP was about to fall into the CPB's embrace, party president, Khun Kya Nu, made for the north at the end of 1973. Soon after his arrival, the Burma Army launched a sweep, but the SSA armed with new weapons from the CPB was victorious. Within a span of two months, almost 900 enemy personnel were put out of action.[102] Thus, the CPB's prestige rose to newer heights.

Meanwhile, in the southern base the leaderless Kokang KKY split into two following a series of assassinations among the remaining leaders. One faction tried to wrest control of the southern base from the SSA, and there was a mini-war lasting seven months. The Kokang KKY finally withdrew in mid-1975.[103]

The crucial question regarding the relationship with the CPB was resolved in a most unsatisfactory manner, but the best to be hoped for under the circumstances. The northern SSA under Sai Myint Aung, party vice-president, and Sai Zam Muang as chief-of-operations, would work closely with the CPB[104] in order to obtain more arms, while the president would return south and maintain the base there.

Our position was precarious since most of our troops were homesick northerners, and worse, our mini-war with the Kokang KKY had diverted trade to safer routes depriving us of much needed revenue.[105] Both SURA (under the erstwhile SSA chief-of-staff, Moherng) and the ex-KMT 3rd Army, naturally saw the southern SSA as a threat to their control of trade and trade routes. The CPB as well as the northern SSA conspired to disaffect the men and officers under us. These intrigues, bribery and other enticements finally achieved results culminating in the ousting of the party president, Khun Kya Nu, in early 1976. As secretary-general, I was asked to take medical leave, but since I was already on leave following heart surgery, I got the message, and resigned.

Thus ends the tale of this native of the Shan hills insofar as my involvement in events which gave shape and complexion to the history and politics of my people and homeland is concerned. I am now in exile, a man without a country, and in the manner of such men, I live with undying if fluctuating optimism.

Though my efforts in the Shan resistance (1963 to 1976) have not been blessed with any particular success, and might even be considered wasted — Moses emerging from the wilderness without God's commandments, as it were — I can honestly say that I am not bitter. Unsound as it may seem to an objective reader, I feel that what transpired was inevitable. I felt compelled to fight because I had, as the Shan say, "Eaten the rice of the people, and drunk the water of the land." And, having committed myself, I tried my best, discharged whatever task fell upon my shoulders as well as it was possible under the given circumstances. Far from being embittered, I am, on the contrary, thankful for the experience. It has enabled me not only to be unafraid of adversity and hardship but also to understand fully and deeply the Buddhist credo: "You come into the world with nothing, and so shall you leave...."

Notes

1. I am unaware of the origin or reason for this practice.
2. There was much going and coming by Shan of all classes at that time since World War II had separated families. There were many tearful reunions and marathon gossip sessions.

3. See Chapter 5.
4. See Chapter 5.
5. I had what in medical terms is known as PDA. The alarm about flying proved to be false. I made my first flight in 1951, and flew often thereafter.
6. See Chapter 5.
7. The government battalions was also commanded by a Kachin officer, Brigadier Lazum Tang.
8. The story is that Captain Naw Seng attempted to persuade the Hsenwi Chaofa to turn against the Burmese, but without success.
9. Most able bodied men were either in the Burma Army (that is, 1st Shan Rifles), the UMP (paramilitary police), Shan State police, the *chaofa*'s police, or were levies raised by the princes for combating rebels (that is, Naw Seng's Kachin, Leftist People's Volunteer Organization [PVO], White Flag Communists, Pa-O rebels, and KMT intruders) on Shan soil.
10. A coalition of Burmese groups formed in 1945 on the eve of Japan's defeat to fight against the Japanese. Under Aung San, it successfully negotiated for independence. It monopolized power till 1958 when it split into two factions and many cliques.
11. The Prince of Wales was said to have dined here once in the 1930s. It was the headquarters of the Japanese Kempetai during the war, and until purchased by my family in 1953, was occupied by a unit of the Rangoon Armed Police.
12. For example, the children of U Nu, U Kyaw Nyein, General Ne Win, Union President U Win Maung (1956–60) attended this school.
13. Mao Zedong, Zhou Enlai, Zhu De (Chu Teh), Liu Shaoqi (Liu Shao-chih), Marshals He Long (Ho Lung), Peng Dehuai (Peng Ta-huai), Lin Biao, Chen Yi, among others. And also, in a prison, several Japanese generals (war criminals) and Henry Pu Yi, at one time proclaimed Emperor of China by the Japanese.
14. This was during the period of "Let a Hundred Flowers Bloom, and a Hundred Thoughts Contend".
15. Her tenure was cut short by the 1958 military takeover on the "invitation" of U Nu, the Prime Minister. In the 1960 election, the Mahadevi was defeated by her elder brother, Chao Mun Pha, the *kyem-muang* or heir-apparent to Hsenwi State as the Prince had no children until the early 1950s.
16. With the back of the communists in Burma broken, and the Karen losing cohesion and steam due to the death of Saw Ba U Gyi, their supreme leader, the Burma Army was able to send more units into Shan State in the early 1950s, and by the mid-1950s it had established itself as an extra-legal (and unconstitutional) super-authority in Shan State.

17. They included Sai Toon Aye, Chao Kyaw Toon (Hso-won), Sai Hla Aung, Sai Myint Aung, Sai Pan (Boontai), Sai Kyaw Sein (Hso-tyen), Sai Gaw Kham, Sai Yawt, Khun Thawda, Khun Kya Nu (Sengsuk). For details, see Chapter 5.

18. This was through the Shan State Students Association and the Shan Literary Society, and the publication of *Tai Noom* magazine (in English, Burmese and Shan languages), which was very popular. The students organized annual Shan cultural seminars at various towns.

19. Among the Shan, I met with Khun Kya Nu, Sai Myint Aung, Sai Pan, Sai Kyaw Sein, and Sai Gaw Kham, the last named being with the Noom Suk Harn, while the rest were SSIA leaders. Among the Karen, I had regular contact with the movement's president, Saw Hunter (who after the 1963 peace talks emerged from the jungle, and was for a time Burmese ambassador to Israel); Brigadier Lin Tin (emerged in 1963, but was killed a few years later by the Burmese army in a planned shoot-out); Brigadier Truman who also emerged in 1963, but his whereabouts later were not known. (Bo Mya, the present Karen president was during those days not prominent).

20. As provided in Chapter X of the 1948 constitution. This right is to be exercisable by the Shan and Karenni after ten years.

21. This took the form of mass arrests of leaders at village level, questioning under torture about arms caches and plans for rebellion, accompanied by looting, rapes, among others.

22. Rebels, mostly Wa and La ("Shan-ized" Wa) under Bo Mawng (an officer in the paramilitary UMP), captured Tangyan town and in Muang Loen state, the towns of Muang Seng and Muang Gao. A Rangoon University student, Chao Kyaw Toon, also figured prominently.

23. Each band has not more than thirty men, loosely organized, and led by assorted types ranging from former village level leaders such a Bo Gang Yoom, Hso-gyam, Pawlam Ho Mang; adventurous souls such as Bo Ngaa-muang, Bo Wa, Bo Deving, Bo Gunzate; former Shan bandits such as Gun-hok, Bo Paan, Hso-lae; Chinese bandits such as Pao Yung, to name but a few.

24. The arrangement of 1948 was weakly quasi-federal since the constituent components were not, strictly speaking, constituent states, but semi-autonomous appendages of a mother-country, Burma. This is similar to British colonial arrangements with regard to British possessions prior to the 1920s.

25. The Union Constitution was drawn up in 1947. According to my mother (the Mahadevi of Yawnghwe), and other Shan leaders, they were made to understand that changes, if desired, would be made after independence. The important point was to gain independence as soon as possible.

26. It is strange that so many Western scholars should view the constitutional reform as a diabolic plot by Shan princes to protect their feudal privileges and dismember the Union. That the Burmese military should take this stand is comprehensible but odd for outsiders, especially so when it is obvious to all who visit Burma that the climate there is not conducive to free discussion of politics and political events.

27. This numbered a few hundred including some monks, and high school students.

28. Strangely enough not a shot was fired at the residences of the Prime Minister and cabinet ministers which were heavily guarded by paramilitary police.

29. It is still not known why and how he was killed. As for "resisting the armed force", one might as well say that the mouse was killed by the cat for resisting.

30. I accompanied my father to the waiting army van at bayonet point. While in prison, he was not allowed to see any of us. In fact, none of those detained by the coupmakers was allowed to see their families until released four or five years later.

31. Also known as Mrs Sanda Simms, at present with her husband in Oman.

32. They were accompanied by Namkham U Toon Aye, appointed Head of Shan State by the coupmakers.

33. Among the wounded in the clash with the police was a Shan student from Taunggyi.

34. Real casualty figures are not known. When the university reopened in December 1962, several hundreds were missing. It could be that some of the missing just dropped out, while some may have gone "underground" to join the communist or Karen rebels, and the rest must be presumed to have been killed that 7 July evening.

35. This phenomenon, establishment of Tai kingdoms around the southern rim of Nanchao before, during, and after, the fall of this kingdom — within a span of about a hundred years — must surely have a significant bearing on the argument that Nanchao is not Tai.

36. Actually, Shan chronicles mention the Pong kingdom (established 80 A.D.), and state that Muang Mao was already in existence since 568 A.D. Also, the Payao and Chiangrai kingdoms, according to chronicles, were established well before the end of the twelfth century.

37. From the late 1880s to 1942, the annexation of Burma to the outbreak of fighting in Burma between the invading Japanese units and British defenders. Actually, the Japanese spearhead crossed into Burma from Siam (Thailand) at Victoria Point, then up to Mergui and Tavoy at end of 1942. John Leroy Christian's *Burma and the Japanese Invader* (1945), gives a good account of the war in Burma.

38. Burmese politicians and nationalists believed strongly that the British colonialists dismembered the already united Burma, and encouraged separatism and divisions.

39. Established in 1961 by former university students who broke away from the Noom Suk Harn, the first Shan resistance organization. The students felt that the cause of the Shan would go nowhere with Saw Yanda as leader due to the latter's lack of qualifications and dictatorial pretensions. In 1964, the SSIA accepted the leadership of the Mahadevi of Yawnghwe.

40. Sai Hla Aung who was SSA 1st Brigade commander (1964–67); SSA vice chief-of-staff (1971–79); acting president of SSA and SSPP (Shan State Progress Party) up to 1983 when he surrendered to Burmese authorities.

41. After the formation of SSA in 1964 he was a member of the SSWC; after formation of SSPP he became first vice-president (1971–76); acting president from 1976, and was killed in action 1978.

42. After the SSA was set up, he was commander of 3rd Brigade; commanding officer of army general headquarters (1967–71); chief-of-staff and president of SSPP (1971–76); and since 1976, in exile and self-employed.

43. Jointly founded in 1962 by SSIA Khun Kya Nu, and Noom Suk Harn commander, Moherng, of Laikha and Muang Kung area, who from 1950–58 was with the White Flag communist unit operating in Shan State. In 1964 the SNUF merged with SSIA to form the SSA under the Mahadevi of Yawnghwe.

44. Composed of myself; Sai Kyaw Sein who in 1966 surrendered, returned in 1970, and in 1975 defected to the Burmese communists; and Hsai Won, surrendered in 1968, returned in 1982. The team was joined in Rangoon by Sai Pan who had been living in Thailand.

45. The final peace team was composed of three Shan groups — the SSIA, Noom Suk Harn, and TNA of Kengtung area, and led by Khun Thawda of the SSIA. The talks were held at Taunggyi and quickly terminated by Rangoon because the rebels received more favourable publicity than the military.

46. Part of the inter-Asia community of trading and finance houses dominating all financial activities of, for example, Burma, Thailand, Vietnam, Laos, Cambodia. This particular segment dominated the Shan opium trade as early as the 1950s, and controlled opium and arms markets outside. After the 1970s, their control extended to gems. From the early 1960s to the present, they also control the black-market economy of Burma.

47. See Chapter 5.

48. These stories were related to me by the Mahadevi and many Thai officers and friends.

49. See Chapter 5.

50. Originally formed as SSIA Kengtung Brigade by Chao Kyaw Toon, the hero of Tangyan battle, and Sai Hla Myint who gained fame for daring deeds in Kengtung as "Bo Farang". When both were killed in action, the brigade was commanded by Chao Way, a member of the Kengtung ruling house. He was also killed, and U Gondra who succeeded in late 1962, broke away from the SSIA, establishing the TNA.
51. See Chapter 5.
52. See Chapter 5.
53. See Bangkok newspapers as well as the *Far Eastern Economic Review*, *Newsweek*, *Time*, and other publications reporting on Burma beginning from 1978 up to the present.
54. After the coup of 1962, the Revolutionary Council passed a number of laws which nationalized all retail businesses and trade, banks, factories, and mills, budding industries, cottage industries, among others. For details see *Area Handbook for Burma* (Washington D.C.: American University, 1971).
55. Other forces operating in the area were the Kachin (KIA), ex-KMT Chinese bands involved in opium, and small Shan bands (for example, Bo Paan, Bo Su, Bo Hso-lam, Bo Zingda) all of which were gradually corporated into the SSA 1st Brigade.
56. See Chapter 5.
57. Worked by Chinese since olden times, and improved, it is said by Herbert Hoover (U.S. President 1928–32) in the 1900s. After the British bought the mine in 1918, it was worked by a British firm, the Burma Corporation. It was then regarded as the most productive silver and lead mine within the British empire. (For details see paper by U Aye Kyaw for Seminar at Payab College, Chiangmai, Thailand, 1983).
58. She was in the early 1950s involved with a KMT attempt to retake mainland China via Shan State. Later, she managed to persuade Burma Army to retain its Kokang KKY as an auxiliary border force, but concentrated more on gold and opium trade under the protection of various Burmese commanders at Lashio, Northern Shan State.
59. The ruling house was "Shan-ized", but about two-thirds of the natives were Haw Chinese, or Hill Chinese, and spoke a Yunnanese dialect; the remaining third were Shan and Palaung. Before World War II, Kokang was a *myoza* (township) under Hsenwi. The Chaofa himself had an English name, Eddie, as do all his siblings — Jimmy, Olive, Francis, Jane, Kenneth, Judy — the legacy of a convent education.
60. See Chapter 5.
61. See Chapter 5.
62. The team comprised Sai Pan, then SSA vice chief-of-staff; Sai Hla Aung, commander 1st Brigade; Khun Kya Nu, commander 3rd Brigade; Sai

Mawng, chief-of-operations, 4th Brigade; and myself, the 1st Brigade adjutant.

63. See Chapter 5.

64. We had during the flight of the Kokang KKY, as our escort three platoons — one each from the 1st, 3rd and 4th Brigades.

65. Upon arrival at the border, Jimmy Yang set up his command post near the GHQ of the ex-KMT 3rd Army. Nevertheless, he was made a member of the SSWC, and the Kokang KKY was renamed SSA 5th Brigade, but for various reasons, he was closer to the ex-KMT (and the KIA). However, in 1967 the SSA 5th Brigade (Kokang) commanded by Francis Yang surrendered at Lashio.

66. The SSWC was composed of the Yawnghwe Mahadevi (chairperson), Moherng (vice chairperson and chief-of-staff), and as members were Sai Myint Aung, Sai Pan (vice chief-of-staff), Khun Thawda, and in 1966, Jimmy Yang (or Chao Ladd).

67. Khun Sa's offensive against Bo Deving and the Noom Suk Harn stemmed from the raid by Thai authorities on his camp at the border in 1964, as related earlier in this chapter.

68. See Chapter 5.

69. These were Sai Gaw Kham (Rangoon University); Sai Kyaw Win (Rangoon University), Sai Tin Pe (Rangoon University). See Chapter 5.

70. See Chapter 5.

71. The SSWC was by mid-1966 so badly splintered that it became ineffective and incapacitated. Together with Khun Kya Nu, I had to set up from scratch a new command centre for the SSA — the army GHQ — which reported directly to the SSWC chairperson till 1969 when the Mahadevi had to leave, for various and personal reasons, for Canada. It was envisioned that with the merger of the three Shan armies, a Shan State Command Council (SSCC) with the Mahadevi as honorary chairperson, and Moherng as chief executive, would be set up.

72. I served as SUPC's general-secretary. Others were Khun Kya Nu, Sai Zam Muang, Sai Sa Tun, Khun Myint, Khun Zom, Khunsing and Sai Gaw Kham (see Chapter 5).

73. Due to gross over-confidence, the camp (at Piangluang) was unguarded, and was captured without a single shot being fired by about two dozen men under Saw Yanda. The camp was then quickly taken over by a joint Chinese (3rd Army) — Shan (Moherng's) force — a co-ordinated operation. Piangluang in 1984 was still the GHQ of Moherng's SURA.

74. Moherng was apparently unhappy with the merger of his SNUF with the SSIA in 1964, and displeased with the appointment of Khun Kya Nu as 3rd Brigade (former SNUF) commander. And like all Shan of that period who lacked formal education, he did not trust intellectuals, particularly student leaders of the SSIA.

75. In 1983, Moherng who had throughout refused to talk of Shan unity, made an appeal to all patriotic elements to unite so as to restore Shan independence and fight the CPB. Moherng was been able to set up a Tai Revolutionary Council composed of the SURA and the southern wing of the SSA (led by Zam Mai). The other remaining army, Khun Sa's SUA had expressed interest.

76. Beijing's support for the CPB has been on party-to-party basis, and rises and falls in accord with what China's power imperatives, internally and externally, are. Support was highest from the rise of Marshal Lin Biao to the fall of Jiang Qing. It is thus difficult to arrive at any definite conclusion, or make hard and fast rules.

77. It is lucrative because the price of opium is three to four times higher at the Thai border, so are contraband goods from the border, more so since the unofficial rate of exchange between baht and kyat is about more or less equal.

78. In 1968, approximately 9,000 sq miles were under other armed bodies, chiefly, the CPB, and to lesser extent, the Burmese-sponsored KKY forces.

79. These were, special forces 101, 104, and 16th, 17th, 21st, 24th, and 25th Battalions, each 200-strong. Total SSA strength (1970s) was about 3,000 men.

80. In addition to Sai Zam Muang and Sai Sar Toon, others were Bo Ngaa-muang, Bo Kang-yoom, Nyunt (Khun Siri), Sai Toon Hlaing, Sai Kyaw Zam (Khun Gaw Hpa), and Sai Nyan Win (see Chapter 5).

81. See Chapter 5.

82. The talks were discontinued as the Burmese could offer nothing but KKY status.

83. He was considered according to Western governments "king of the international drug trade", after Lo Hsin Han, an earlier "opium and drug king" was removed from the scene in 1973.

84. See Chapter 5.

85. In reality, the SSA was only a front for the people (the ordinary villagers), for they not only armed, fed, clothed, sheltered us, but gave us timely and correct intelligence, and took care of our sick and wounded. Had the people in 1969 not voted to continue resistance, we would have disbanded the SSA there and then.

86. He was released in the mid-1970s, and rejoined the SUA. While in Mandalay Prison, the SUA kidnapped two Russian technicians from the Russian Hospital in Taunggyi in 1973 and there were secret negotiations involving the then Thai Prime Minister, General Kriangsak Chommanand. The release of the Russians probably expedited Khun Sa's release.

87. See Chapter 5.

88. A mutually dependent relationship, but with merchants holding the purse. It reveals a striking dilemma within an armed movement as regard "support". If support elements are commercial or alien, the movement will have to compromise its political goals and national interest. But if its "support" is the people, the rural folks, who form the poorest section of the population, the movement though assured of survival and vitality, will not be able to speedily attain its goals.

89. One enemy colonel was killed. Many spectators were also killed and wounded not because of the grenade but as a result of soldiers firing into the crowd.

90. In one action alone in Loikho, the enemy lost more than 100 men, killed and wounded. The battle was bought under the personal command of Lt.-Col. Sai Zam Muang, with able assistance of Major Leng Zeun, SUA (Chinese national whom I gave a Shan name).

91. The earliest communist representative was Sai Aung Win.

92. CPB's representatives were unable to explain what form such a front would take. It main interest obviously was to obtain cannon fodder.

93. For example, the battle of Kunlong, which lasted two months; the raid on Lashio; the battles for Muang Ko, Muang Yang, Vieng Ngun, Muang Yong, Tong-Ta, in the early 1970s, Burma Army units such as the 101, 102, 105 LIR (Light Infantry Regiment), and the 1st Shan, 1st Kayah, 4th Chin, and 17th Buregt, 12th Buregt were some of those which lost all combat components in battles and had to be re-formed.

94. Communist mischief and petty intrigues within the SSA resulted in a motion adopted by military commanders in conference that I should be court-martialled and executed for, among other things, holding secret talks with the enemy, not being patriotic enough, and high-handed. However, this motion was squashed at a meeting of the party central committee. I became aware of this incident only in 1974 or early 1975.

95. When U Nu formed the PDP in 1970, it was obvious that he had received some money which was not very substantial from foreign sources. However, PDP leaders were over optimistic and did not plan for a protracted struggle, and by early 1974, the movement had completely run out of both steam and funds.

96. It is not clear whether it was a coincidence that Burmese units appeared. However, up till 1980, there was some co-operation between the SURA and the Burmese to block the passage of CPB units into Muang Kung, Laikha, Muang Nai, and Muang Pan. Here again, we ran into the "support" factor, that is, non-native merchants and finance-houses had no interest in politics, trade and profit being their main concern.

97. See Chapter 5.

98. Both Rangoon and the CPB greatly feared U Nu since he enjoyed the support of not only the Burmese, but the Shan and other ethnic groups in general considered him a good man. An alliance with the PDP without getting any military aid in return would be disastrous for the SSPP/SSA since both Rangoon and the CPB would pounce on it at once.

99. After 1976, the front was enlarged to include other Shan State based small groups such as the Pa-O, Lahu, and Wa, and Palaung, though the last named was under KIA control. The KIA joined only in 1983, tentatively. Unfortunately, the front failed to develop into a meaningful organization, and became in content and nature very like the United Nations, and still is.

100. A name coined by the international media referring sometimes to the Shan State, and sometimes to an undefined place "where meets the borders of Burma, Laos and Thailand". As a consequence of the second definition, visiting American secretaries of important departments, congressmen, presidential aides, and ignorant tourists, are obliged to visit a patch of grass and sand where meets the three borders — the confluence of the Maesai with the Mekhong River.

101. Not too many actually. About 200 pieces, mostly various models of AK rifles, a few light machine guns, a couple of 60 mm motars, one or two 57 mm recoiless rifles or guns, a number of B40 rockets, very large quantities of ammunition, anti-personnel mines, explosives, and grenades. However, for SSA rank and file this quantity was generous considering that it had difficulty even in buying arms, much less given any.

102. In one action alone in Wan Pan area, more than fifty Burmese soldiers were killed within the first twenty minutes. In another, twenty-four enemies died where they stood, and the rest fled in panic. All enemy casualty figures given, if they err, do so on the conservative side. SSA's policy is strict on battle claims. Usually arms must be captured from the enemy's dead. There are also other methods of checking which are still confidential.

103. The Kokang KKY evacuated after being attacked at Ho Muang, near Muang Mai, by an SSA force, assisted by a company of KNU troops. The news of a large SSA column on its way down from the north also shook them up. Actually, the troops from the north was one which accompanied Khun Kya Nu, and the attacking units were escorting me from the border to the Salween where we had agreed to meet. The exchange of fire at Ho Muang was accidental. At any rate, we could have without difficulty expelled the Kokang force, but it would have taken some time.

104. The northern SSA did not stay with the CPB for long since the communists asked for undisputed political leadership which reduced the SSA to being just

an armed auxiliary of the CPB. Sai Zam Muang, the key man, repudiated the alliance, and came down south, arriving in mid-1978, and mysteriously disappeared. Acting party president Sai Myint Aung was killed in action earlier. Thus the SSA became a leaderless army, but managed to totter along until 1982 when acting chief-of-staff, Chao Hso-noom (son of the Muang Loen Prince), and acting chief-of-operations, Sai Lek, once more approached the CPB for military and other assistance, in the manner of a prodigal son returning. The key person this time, Chao Hso-noom died of illness in November 1983. A splinter group led by Zam Mai accepted Moherng's call for unity in the same year. The politics of the Shan being highly fluid, and governed more by imponderables than logic, nothing should be taken for granted.

105. The southern SSA base required at least 20,000 baht a month for food (rice, in the main) and medicine for base support troops, staff, and dependents, numbering about 400. Combat units, three battalions, required only ammunition and occasional uniforms.

PART TWO

SHAN-BURMESE RELATIONS

2

An Overview of Shan-Burmese Relations

Politics in Burma

Von Clausewitz's dictim, the "War is but the continuation of politics by some other means", seems a particularly apt description of the state of Burmese politics. This is particularly true with regard to the relations between the Shan and the Burmese. The only significant historical period without war was from 1885 (when both came under the British flag) to 1959 and peace was broken by the first shot fired at the town of Tangyan. Even then, there were wars in between — World War II, and the insurgencies following independence in 1948.

Except for a short period under the Union Jack, there was always a war on in Burma. First, between tribes flowing into virgin land, more fertile and warmer than the lands further to the north from whence they came.[1] Then city states appeared, and Mon fought Mon to build a Mon kingdom, likewise the Burmese and Shan. Next, the Burmese kingdom fought the Mon, and Mon the Shan, and Shan the Burmese. Also, Burmese fought Burmese, and Shan fough Shan.[2]

Foreign wars were also fought whenever a "unifier" appeared, and the Mon, Burmese, Shan, all followed the royal standard of Burinnong (1551–81), Alaungpaya (1752–60), Hsinphyushin (1763–76) to invade and lay waste Chiangmai, Ayuthia, Vieng Chan, Luang Prabang, Chiang Rung, and smaller kingdoms or principalities such as Zanta, Chefang, Muang Kawn. All these kingdoms were Tai or Thai (that is, Shan or Siam) kingdoms and principalities. The current state of affairs in Burma — from 1948 to the present — is thus but a return to an environment of battles and wanton destruction natural to Burma.

Basically, the protracted current armed conflict in Burma revolves around the question of power — the control of power at the centre and the control of the centre over other components states which in turn is related to the question of how much autonomy the states should have over their respective destinies.

The protagnoists in the first type of conflict are the ethnic Burmese and the struggle has ideological overtones as it concerns the non-communist leftists and the communists. The civil war began with the attempts by Thakin Than Tun and Thakin Soe, leaders of the White and Red Flag[3] factions respectively, to seize power, and the AFPFL led by U Nu tried to keep the communists out.

The present post-1962 "anti-communist" incumbents in Burma, unlike their counterparts in Thailand, Malaysia, Indonesia, South Korea, are not by any means advocates of free enterprise nor do they even pay lip-service to democracy as is understood in the West. In fact, they have set up political and economic super-structures modelled after nations and states professing communist ideals, complete with a monolithic political party, People's Courts, People's Council, People's Co-operatives, and such others. Even the national ideology — the Burmese Way to Socialism — is in essence marxist, though given a metaphysical touch with Buddhist thoughts thrown in here and there.

It would therefore be quite misleading to view the struggle between the present incumbents, the Burmese military, and the CPB as simply ideological, or an anti-communist crusade. Rather, it is more of an in-house struggle between two groups of the same school fighting for the whole cake — monopolistic control of national life.

The second type of struggle for control in Burma involves the question of autonomy or the degree of autonomy to be given to other ethnic groups. This struggle which has taken the form of open warfare between Rangoon and the Shan, Karen, Karenni, Mon, and so forth, has unfortunately been branded by the West in general as nothing more than a tribal uprising. This is due perhaps to the inability of the West to grasp the fact that the concept of a bureaucratic nation-state is relatively new. In Asia, the traditional form of governance is one based on the loyalty of a person to the nearest overlord, and so on up the ladder, and finally, to the person of the king. Hence, it is not easy, even among one people who share a common language and culture to bring about a national loyalty focused on an alien and impersonal bureaucratic arrangement. The difficulties are further compounded when a nation-state is composed of different ethno-linguistic groups.

MAP 2.1
Burma (States and Divisions)

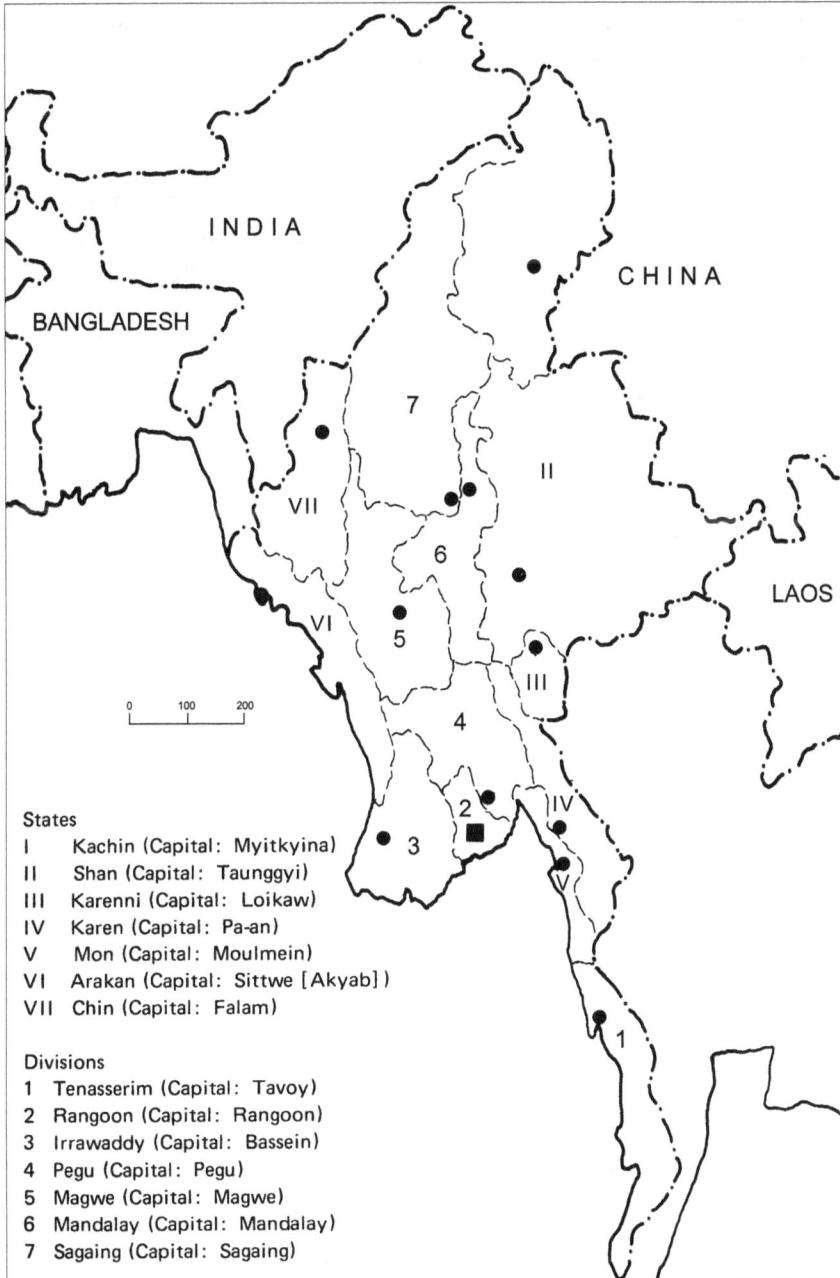

States

I   Kachin (Capital: Myitkyina)
II   Shan (Capital: Taunggyi)
III Karenni (Capital: Loikaw)
IV   Karen (Capital: Pa-an)
V   Mon (Capital: Moulmein)
VI   Arakan (Capital: Sittwe [Akyab])
VII Chin (Capital: Falam)

Divisions

1 Tenasserim (Capital: Tavoy)
2 Rangoon (Capital: Rangoon)
3 Irrawaddy (Capital: Bassein)
4 Pegu (Capital: Pegu)
5 Magwe (Capital: Magwe)
6 Mandalay (Capital: Mandalay)
7 Sagaing (Capital: Sagaing)

Source: Government of Burma (1980) publication (obtained from Tai Revolutionary Army personnel).

The complexities are further heightened by the facts of history and politics. That is, the Shan and Mon in particular had, like the Burmese, evolved into kingdoms well before the coming of the West to this region. In fact, the Mon civilization was much more developed than either the Burmese or Shan, and both borrowed heavily from the Mon in some form or other.

Such being the realities of history, the stand taken by most Western scholars and historians that the Burmese power centre equals an "egalitarian, modern state", while Shan nationalism is "reactionary feudal tribalism" is untenable. Such an attitude is certainly not scholarly since it ignores the historical and qualitative factors governing the status and development of the various ethnic groups in Burma, especially the major ones.

It must also be remembered that before the impact of the West, there was no such concept as national unity in Burma or elsewhere in Asia. There was the king and his court in the golden capital, and there were vassal lords and princes who may, or may not have been of the same ethnic group as the king. When a king was strong or dynamic, vassal lords and princes enjoyed less freedom, and more often than not, such a king would invade neighbouring kingdoms. The aim of engaging in foreign wars was not for country or nation, but for reasons of personal glory. The Burmese, like the Cambodian, the Siamese, the Shan, the Indian, even the Chinese, were not, prior to the nineteenth century, conscious of nationalism or nationhood in the sense it is understood today.

Burmese consciousness of nationalism was engendered only after a period of British rule. Burma opened up to the world under Britian and it brought to Burmese minds, knowledge and consciousness of the outside, of sweeping changes, and historical events — the Russo-Japanese War, the birth of modern China, World Wars I and II, the Irish uprising, the agitation for freedom by Gandhi and Nehru in India. Intellectual stimuli as in the introduction by the British to Burma of the trappings of a modern bureaucratic state, and the gradual introduction of self-government in Burma[4] from the 1920s onwards — were the seeds of Burmese nationalism.

As the Burmese emerged under Britain into the modern world, Burmese élites began to define the meaning of Burma, and in the process interpreted her history in a strongly nationalistic manner. They envisioned the Burmese as a nation whose kings had by feats of valour created a Burmese kingdom, bringing under the sway of the golden peacock throne, the various subordinate peoples (the Arakanese, Shan, Karen, Chin, and so forth). This unity was shattered by Britain, the kingdom dismembered, and separatism encouraged in keeping with the "divide and rule" strategem of foreign imperialists. However such a perception does not quite fit the facts.

In the 1930s, when Burma was to be separated from India and constituted as a self-governing entity,[5] British policy-makers had in mind the amalgamation of the Frontier Areas (homelands of the non-Burmese), and in particular the Shan State. The official view was that it was "inevitable that sooner or later some form of union must take place, and ... the policy now to be adopted with regard to the Shan States should be framed with reference to this contingency..." (September 1931).[6]

British administrators made the Burmese language a second language in Burma Proper which killed the Mon language. The British never encouraged any languages except Burmese as can be seen from the fact that all schools in Shan States and other Frontier Areas taught Burmese and English in classes.

Britain certainly did not have any plan to create a Balkan-type situation, and seemed to be working towards creating a nation-state out of Burma Proper and the Frontier Areas.[7] This was to take its place in the British scheme of things as a self-governing dominion, but this plan was overtaken by momentous events — World War II and the Japanese invasion.

Indeed when Burma emerged in 1948 as an independent nation-state from the ashes of World War II and with the sun setting on the British empire, Burmese nationalists and leaders saw themselves as heirs not only to the Burmese kings (that is, the Burmese imperial legacy) but also the British colonial administrators. The Frontier Areas were in their eyes either restored lost possessions or colonies of sorts.

Whilst the peoples of the Frontier Areas had been kept in isolation from the rest of the world by the British, they were rudely awakened by the Japanese war. Their villages were bombed, and Japanese, Chinese, Indian, British, American, and even African soldiers marched freely across their fields and valleys, and they were harangued to rise, to stand and fight for their motherland, and to expel alien rulers or invaders as the case may be. These pleas struck a different chord in the "minority" leaders (most of whom had had military training of some kind, or combat experiences under foreign flags) who felt that within the context of what befell them so suddenly, they could no longer afford to have their destinies under the control of others, no matter how benevolent or powerful. Certainly, they had no intention of becoming anyone's subjects, or inferiors.

Nationalism then, was at fever pitch among both the Burmese and the non-Burmese ethnic groups after World War II. The 1948 Union constitution which tied the Burmese and other ethnic groups in political matrimony was a hasty compromise between Burmese nationalism (with overtones of Burmese imperial motives and British colonial attitudes) and the awakening national awareness of the non-Burmese groups.[8]

Today, this basic contradiction remains unsolved, though the problem is probably one more of method than of interest. It is Burma's misfortune that Burmese policy-makers have not, and are still reluctant to re-think the framework of the relationship between the major and minor components of what could become a real nation. Given a correct perception and grasp of political and historical realities and politics by Burmese leaders, there seems little reason why national unity cannot be achieved without resort to war and bloodshed. That this is possible had once been proved by no other than Aung San. It would serve present Burmese leaders as well as future ones to examine why leaders of the Frontier Areas agreed to sign the Panglong Agreement with him.[9] Was it because they knew him well, or was it because they feared him, or were they dazzled by his personality? The fact is that they were practically strangers to him, and he to them. More than anything, it was because the leaders of the Frontiers Areas, lacking education and political sophistication were nonetheless very practical men, and Aung San, in his own way, was one of them.

Those who hold power in their hands also hold the answer, or at least half the solution to the very basic problem of national unity, or lack of unity, afflicting the country and ravaging national life since independence. The correct handling of the relationship between the Burmese power centre and constituent components is, in my opinion, the key not only to the problem of national unity, but also the question of national development, progress, peace, and — in the interest of Burma and all humanity — the problem of opium cultivation and heroin trade.

Shan State Politics and the Opium Question

The most widely held view, popularized by the Western media and encouraged by Rangoon, is that opium cultivation in the Shan State is widespread because the people are forced by Shan rebels and warlords to grow poppy. Opium thus obtained is then escorted by rebel armies to Thailand where it is refined into heroin which is shipped, presumably by a Shan network of couriers and agents, to cities all over the world. Money thus obtained is used to finance rebellion against Rangoon.

The above is a very simple and plausible story which infers that an easy and uncomplicated solution is at hand: this being no other than the elimination of Shan rebels, through the eradication of opium and heroin (benefiting humanity), and military victory for Rangoon (which would allegedly contribute to the peace and stability of the region).

However, the elimination of Shan rebels is easier said than done and can be achieved only with a massive influx of military and other assistance from external donors, which in turn, implies the "blind" participation of donor countries in Burma's civil war in Rangoon's favour. The word "blind" is chosen because Rangoon though obviously needing and desiring military and other assistance, just as obviously, does not like outsiders to see for themselves what the problems and conditions in Burma are. International participation in Burma with the view to eradicating opium and heroin should be modelled on such programmes as exist in Thailand. They involve not only the government but the growers themselves and give development assistance to uplift the opium growing region. This is the key. No solution will be found in a headlong rush into a war in blind support of one or the other participant in a conflict which is now more than twenty years old.[10]

At any rate, despite attempts by policy-makers in Rangoon (and elsewhere) to tie the eradication of opium and heroin to the obliteration of the Shan and other rebels in Burma, the link is in reality incidental. In fact, the opium business in Shan State, and the international trade in heroin, are essentially non-political. That is, those in this business, and making money are a class of apolitical people whose sole interest in life is trade and profit. The majority are Chinese whose relatives, partners, friends, organizations, finance, loyalties, interests, and obligations straddle national frontiers. Their creed, "commerce is commerce", pays little heed to the legality or morality of the merchandise — and who can blame them for this attitude given the historical fact that two wars were fought by Western powers to impose opium and its trade on China?

There is little evidence as to how opium and heroin dealers are organized. However, it can be assumed that the organization is informal and close-knit. Drug financing appears to be no different from the financing of, say, trade in soya beans. It is very difficult to point out which Chinese trading-house or financial dealer is involved because of the system of informal or non-institutional borrowing and investment practices among the Chinese. It is clear though that Chinese syndicates, though informal and decentralized, are extremely powerful since their members are involved in many businesses within and outside the law.

With regard to the much publicized involvement of Shan rebel armies in the narcotics trade, their role is limited to taxing growers and the buying agents, and at times escorting caravans to the border for an agreed fee. Even the "narcotics kingpin" Lo Hsin Han who commanded the Kokang KKY (1965–73), did not own all the opium that was traded, or the refineries or have access to international markets, much less control over heroin beyond the Shan border.

Why is opium extensively cultivated in Shan State? Is it, as alleged by Rangoon, because the Shan and tribal peasants are forced by Shan rebels and the CPB to do so? It is not easy to force peasants to grow anything since there are many ways to get around such compulsion. For forced cultivation of opium to succeed, it must be run plantation-style with peasants forced into barracks under guard among other things which implies that rebel armies must hold secure areas, and this has never been the case.

The next question logically is, do they grow opium for profit? The fact is, as anyone who is acquainted with the mechanism of rural economies knows, cultivators rarely make substantial profit from what is grown, be it onions, sugarcane, or opium. Besides, a peasant family with an optimum work-force of four, given favourable weather and soil conditions, will at most produce about 12 kg a year. The field price of one kg of opium is as follows: 300 kyat in the mid-1960s; 600 kyat in the early 1970s; and 1,000 kyat in the early 1980s (kyat and baht are about equal, unofficially). It is indeed rare for a family to be able to produce the maximum amount. However, let us say that a certain peasant family did produce 12 kg of opium in 1980. Its annual income would be 12,000 kyat (or 12,000 baht). But a sarong costing 30 baht in Thailand in the same year, costs 90 kyat (or 90 baht) in Shan State; and a cheap cake of soap at 3 baht would cost that rural Shan family 9 kyat. In terms of purchasing power, the family's maximum income would therefore be only 4,000 baht (less than US$250) per year.[11] The vast majority earned far less for the year 1980. Most opium cultivators

MAP 2.2
Opium Cultivation in Shan State after 1963

Before 1963

After 1963

Source: Compiled from "Situtation Reports and Intelligence" data, Shan State Army GHQ Office, 1963.

moreover like most peasants of Southeast Asia, are indebted to buying agents or local moneylenders before planting and have to hock the yield, or borrow usually at 30 to 50 per cent interest per season. It is thus amply clear that Shan and other tribal peasants are not growing opium for profit.

The answer must thus be sought in another area. In 1958, the figures given by the Shan State government in response to questions by MPs on opium production was 12,000 viss (1 viss is about 1.5 kg), or roughly 18 tons.[12] However, let us assume that the figure was grossly underestimated due to the inefficiency of the officials involved. Even allowing room for a very wide margin of error, the annual production could not have been more than 60 to 80 tons in 1958. And after the 1962 coup and the blanket nationalization of all private businesses retail trade, factories, agricultural trade and marketing and demonetizing of 100 kyat and 50 kyat notes, the annual production figure in the early 1970s (according to Rangoon, Washington, and the United Nations) was 400 to 600 tons. This increase from 18 (or 60–80) tons in 1958, to 400–600 tons annually in the early 1970s, is really incredible. A revolutionary leap never seen before in agricultural history, and this achieved without UN assistance or a single cent of the American taxpayers' money. As one person who is considered an expert on Third World affairs, puts it: "Perhaps there is a lesson in the Shan opium production phenomenon for the UN's FAO, and related agencies".[13]

In 1963–64, when I passed through Muang Nai, Muang Pan, Laikha, and toured extensively Muang Yai, Hsipaw, and Hsenwi, though opium cultivation had increased, I rarely saw poppy plants in or around villages. However, in 1969, poppy plants were everywhere, in backyards, and around the hamlets.

While I agree that opium cultivation is widespread in the Shan State, I seriously doubt any figure given by officials. The main reason is that Rangoon does not control the rural areas. There is no love lost between Burmese authorities and the populace and therefore there has been little effort by Rangoon to survey opium production. Furthermore no outsiders have been into the Shan rural areas to assess the situation for themselves. Thus, the internationally accepted Shan opium production figure — 400 to 600 tons annually, seems quite unreliable. It is a sad fact that despite all the hue and cry, and the millions of dollars spent on suppressing Shan opium, practically nothing is known about this main opium growing area of Southeast Asia, the Shan State.

Shan nationalists and rebel spokesman have claimed time and again that opium and heroin trafficking is caused by a deep economic, social, and political malaise arising from Rangoon's harsh rule, economic foolhardiness, and arrogant defiance of socio-economic and political realities. More-over, the Shan have in all their proposals to end the opium problems, welcomed foreign observers and agencies,[14] which contrasts sharply with that of Rangoon's attitude. The Burmese attitude is one which seems to say: "The opium and heroin problem is our internal affair, and concerns no one. But if you are concerned, you must support us unconditionally. We will solve it in our own way".

I do not claim that the Shan rebels are in the right, or condemn Rangoon's stand on this very serious international problem which is the cause of so much misery the world over. I will leave it to the readers to form their own judgement.

To clarify, the worldwide furore and condemnation of the flow of opium and heroin from Burma in the early 1970s presented Rangoon with a serious threat since it focused international attention on the Shan State, the main opium growing area. It was therefore imperative to formulate a strategy which would turn the situation around in its favour. Rangoon admitted that a massive amount was flowing out of Burma's Shan State. However, this was because, the Burmese claimed, the centre had no control because of the Shan rebels. As such, the elimination of Shan rebels would be the first requirement in solving the opium question.[15]

In other words, Rangoon's answer to the problem is no other than the continuation of the decades-old war, but with military and financial assistance from governments interested in suppressing opium and heroin. In effect this means that the West must assist Rangoon in achieving a military victory in Shan State, and presumably elsewhere too. Such being the case, it would not be out of place therefore to examine the viability of Rangoon's military plan to eradicate opium.

On the purely military aspect in the Shan State, it is doubtful if Rangoon can field more than 70,000 combat troops due to rebellions elsewhere. As against this, there are 7,000 to 9,000 Shan nationalists; 1,000 rebel tribesmen (Wa, Palaung, among others); 2,000 KIA contingent in Shan State; and a 20,000 to 30,000 strong force under the CPB.[16] In numbers and arms, the Burma Army enjoys a great advantage, but rebels are natives, know the lie of the land, and to some extent, enjoy the support of the populace. Moreover, while the Burma Army is able to apply its strength fully for only a limited period, the rebels operate in full strength all year round. As for combat capabilities, the rebels are just as tough, and perhaps even more skilful in bush warfare.

Again, from a military angle, rebel armies are not the American Indians of John Wayne's movies. For instance, it is evident from the film, *Opium Warlords* (Adrian Cowell, ATV, London, 1975) that the Shan armies are well-armed, and organized, use modern communication systems, and have battle-tested officers possessing more than the rudimentary knowledge of modern military concepts and tactics.

In 1961, all Shan rebels totalled not more than 1,500 men[17] — excluding the ex-KMT Chinese armies.[18] Compare this to the 7,000 to 9,000 men at present. In addition to the increase in Shan military strength, the Burma Army is at the moment having to care for its casualties, and at one time in 1978, it suffered 20–30 casualties daily in the Shan State alone.[19]

It is therefore, doubtful, even with Western military assistance, that there will be any quick or decisive outcome. Though the chances of the rebels defeating the Burma Army are slim, there is also no possibility that they will give up meekly whatever the pressure. A possible scenario is that with increasing Western assistance to and proximity with Rangoon, the rebel rank and file as well as the peasants would lose confidence in their non- or anti-communist leaders. The only winner then would be the CPB since it would, through its ability to provide arms, be able to take over the various nationalist movements and armies.

It is obvious that the purely military approach being advocated and practised by Rangoon to deal with narcotics, and other more fundamental problems (national unity, for example) creates more problems than solutions. The realities of the conflict in Burma and the Shan State are very different from the fight between law-enforcers and Mafia godfathers within a politically stable society such as New York. In the case of Burma, one ethnic group is trying to impose its concept of nationhood on the other by force. These groups are in turn resisting what they see as attempts to subjugate them or destroy their ethnic identity.

Rangoon's attempts to gain control over the various homelands is therefore linked to the problem of narcotics only because of negative and short-sighted policies. A solution lies not in the escalation of violence and destruction, but in something simpler and more basic — this being no other than what is known as "good government", a relevant and rational point which international policy-makers, bureaucrats, and scholars gloss over when discussing the problem of drug trafficking in Burma.

Notes

1. These include the Pyu, Kayan, Thet, Mon, Burmese, Shan, to name some major ones. The Burmese claim to be descended from the Pyu, known as Piao to the Chinese and Shan. Scholars are still uncertain who the Kayan and Thet are. But Karen folklorists claim the Kayan are the Karen's forefathers (*Kayan* means "human beings" in the Padaung dialect), and Thet are natives of the Thai Thet country, that is, forefathers of the Thai or Tai.

2. Arakan was another Burmese kingdom, but it did not submit to the main Burmese power centre until conquered by Bodawpaya in 1784. There were two Shan centres of power, Ava and Muang Mao. The former submitted to Burinnong in 1555, and the latter was destroyed by a Chinese invasion in 1604.

3. Since receiving aid from the Chinese fraternal party in the late 1960s, the name was changed from the Burmese Communist Party (BCP) to Communist Party of Burma (CPB). It was most powerful in the early stages of the civil war having won over the majority of the AFPFL-controlled auxilary (the PVO), almost all of the 1st, 2nd and 3rd Burma Rifles, and enjoyed the support of students, labourers, oilfield workers, and militant peasants. Though reduced in strength by the 1950s, it still controlled the Pegu Yoma (just over 100 miles north of Rangoon), the Irrawaddy deltas, and had strongholds in Central Burma. But in the mid-1960s the party, following the Chinese example, staged a cultural revolution resulting in the liquidation of top-line leaders such as Goshal, Yebaw Htay and most military commanders, plus many hundreds of experienced political cadres. Consequently many more hundreds in anger and in fear for their lives surrendered and divulged party secrets, thus enabling Rangoon to break the communists resulting in the decimation of top leaders such as the chairman, Thakin Than Tun, and also Bo Zeya, Thakin Zin, Thakin Chit, Thakin Tin Tun, and Bo Pu. Were it not for Beijing, the Burmese communist movement would have ended there and then. But Chinese assistance prolonged the life of the CPB. It remains today as an alternative Burmese power centre, but only by virtue of Beijing's support and the prop of a non-Burmese (Wa, Kokang, Kachin, Akha, and Shan) armed force. Thakin Soe's Red Flag did not attain much importance, except during World War II when it spearheaded resistance against the Japanese, and attracted only the extremists. It ceased to exist after Thakin Soe surrendered in late 1970. To add to the confusion, the official name of the Red Flag is the Communist Party of Burma (CPB).

4. Self-government with its executive and legislative organs, judiciary, elections, and so forth, was introduced only to Burma Proper or later, Ministerial

Burma. The homelands of the Shan, Chin, Kachin, Arakan, and Karenni were excluded from self-government, though the Shan and Karenni enjoyed some form of self-rule through hereditary princes.

5. Burma Proper, or the Burmese homeland became a self-governing entity under Britain by the *Government of India Act 1935* (Schedules X to XV). See J.L. Christian (1945).

6. See Taylor (1983). Quoting from letters by H.L. Nichols, officiating Chief Secretary, Government of Burma.

7. For bureaucratic reasons these were known variously as Excluded Areas, Scheduled Areas and Frontier Areas, which were separately and varyingly administered by the British. The Frontier Areas were recognized by both the British (in possession of Lower Burma) and King Mindon (1853–78) as independent in a treaty signed in 1875.

8. The constituent assembly met on 10 June 1947, and the constitution was formally adopted on 24 September of the same year. For a good account of the negotiation with the British for independence, see Cady (1958).

9. Signed on 12 February 1947 between Aung San as head of the interim government of Burma and leaders of the Frontier Areas whereby the amalgamation of the Frontier Areas with Ministerial Burma was agreed upon and the form of amalgamation defined.

10. Actual fighting with Shan rebels began in 1959; Karen in 1949; Mon and Pa-O following closely; Kachin in 1961; Arakanese in 1947; and Karenni, about the same year as the Karen.

11. Though the figures given may not be accurate in totality since no professional survey has ever been made, whatever the actual price or cost, the comparative indicators, for example, price difference of opium and consumer goods, are correct, in terms of percentage and effects. (Compare Shan price to international price, that is, 1 kg at US$0.5 million. *Bangkok Post*, 16 June 1984.)

12. Union of Burma Printing Office, *Records of the Shan State Council 1957–58 Session* [in Burmese].

13. In a discussion with Dr David A. Feingold, Director, Centre of Opium Research, Institute for the Study of Human Issues, Philadelphia, U.S.A., in Chiangmai, May 1984.

14. See Lintner (1984).

15. See statements by Burmese authorities, reports to the United Nations by Rangoon, government press releases concerning the Burmese narcotics problem, especially from 1976 to the present.

16. Figures obtained from SSA field reports, interviews with leaders and officers of the armies mentioned, which were then cross-checked with traders and others. Incredibly enough, top leaders in rebel organizations are not prone

to exaggerating their strength though junior officers are. Talks with people of the locality are quite revealing because villagers are not over-awed by rebels whom they support.

17. These include more than 400 in the Noom Suk Harn; SSIA, below 400; Kengtung around 400; scattered bands with more than 300 men.

18. According to Rangoon's report (*Kuomintang Aggression against Burma*, 1953), there were over 10,000 men under the KMT in Shan State. According to Thai officials (Seminar at Chiangmai University, Political Science Department, 1982) there were then over 20,000 KMTs in Thailand, as far as is known.

19. I heard about it from several sources particularly people with close relatives (who were officers holding the rank of major and above) in the Burma Army.

3

The Development of Shan-Burmese Relations

Shan or Tai Nationalism and the Burmese Centre

The relationship between the Shan or Tai and the Burmese power centre has always been long and turbulent, stretching back more than 900 years. Yet to the present day, the origins of the Shan are shrouded in mystery and surrounded by controversy. For instance, the ancient city of Tagaung which the Burmese claim to have established as their first capital is disputed by Shan and Tai chronicles which claim that by 568 A.D. the Tai, descendants of Khun Lun and Khun Lai, had founded a kingdom in Upper Burma with their capital at Muang Maorong in the same environ as the Burmese kingdom of Tagaung.[1] The Burmese claim that their kingdom was founded during the life-time of the Lord Buddha, whilst the Shan claim that Tagaung is a Shan or Tai word, *Ta-Gong*, meaning "Drum Ferry" town.

Another controversy surrounding the early Shan (Tai/Thai) is the Nanchao question, and whether the "Ai-Lao" mentioned in early Chinese annals were Tai/Thai. Shan nationalists, and some historians subscribe very strongly to the theory that the Thai (Tai/Shan, or Siam), as the "Ai-Lao", even before the Han, had established themselves between Tibet and the Chang Jian (Yangtze) River, a few thousand years ago. Later, they set up the Nanchao empire (650–1236) which together with China and Tibet, was a major power in the region for a time. According to this theory, some time before and immediately after Nanchao fell to Kublai Khan, the Shan or Tai (Thai/Siam) migrated south and westwards, founding Tai/Thai kingdoms in Assam (well established by 1229);[2] in Upper Burma and present-day Shan State, the Tai Mao kingdom (well before 1215 to

1604);[3] the kingdom of Ava in Central and Upper Burma (1287–1555);[4] in Lower Burma, Wareru, the Shan son-in-law of Sukhothai's King Ramkhamheng (1275–1317) established the kingdom of Martaban;[5] in present-day Laos, the Lan-Chang kingdom; in Vietnam, the kingdom of Sipsong Chu-Tai; and the kingdoms of Payao, Chiangsaen, Chiangmai, and Sukhothai in present-day Thailand, all founded well before 1238, except Chiangmai (in 1296).

Though the belief that the Ai-Lao and Nanchao kingdoms were Tai is ridiculed by quite a few scholars, especially Chinese of both Taiwan and mainland China, as a pan-Thai pipe dream, the fact remains that they did found kingdoms stretching from northeast India to the upper Tonkin in the tail period of the Nanchao empire, and more importantly, all these Tai or Thai kingdoms touched upon were not very far from Nanchao's southern rim.

My opinion is that this has much bearing on the question of whether Nanchao was Tai (Thai) or not. If Nanchao was Lolo, would these kingdoms not be Lolo instead of Tai/Thai? Perhaps, some people would find it more acceptable if it were suggested that the Tai/Thai (Shan/Siam) magically appeared from nowhere, complete with kings and kingdoms. If Nanchao was Lolo, why was it the Tai, not the Lolo, who founded new kingdoms when Nanchao declined?

The Thai or Siamese are referred to by the Karen and Burmese of Lower Burma as "Shan". In fact, in old Burmese stone inscriptions and sometimes even now, the word "Shan" is spelled as "Syam",[6] but as in all Burmese words ending with "m" it is, pronounced with the "n" sound. The word for road, for example, is spelled *lam* but pronounced *lan*. When the British arrived, they adopted the Burmese pronounciation of the word "Siam", thus giving the impression that the Shan (Tai) and Siam (Thai) are two different groups.

The Wa, Kachin, Palaung, and others, refer to the Tai as "Sam" or "Syam". This is strange because the Shan never refer to themselves as anything but Tai. No one really knows the meaning of the word "Siam" a name given by others to the Tai/Thai people, although theories abound.[7]

Shan kingdoms of old were relative to their time, well organized. Drawing upon old terms and usages, we can deduce that there was a *Chao Haw Kham* (Lord of the Golden Palace), or a king.[8] Above the king, there was *Chao Haw Seng* (Lord of the Palace of Gems), or *Chao Wong*, the Emperor (King of Nanchao, perhaps, or the ruler of China).

Below the *Chao Haw Kham* were *Chaofa* (Lord of the Sky), cor-
rupted in Burmese to *Sawbwa*. These were princes, brothers or sons
of the monarch, who ruled over a *muang* (principalities). Immediately
below the *Chaofa* was a *Kem-Muang* — the heir of the *Chaofa*, who
is usually the brother or the eldest son. Other brothers and sons were
given districts to rule with the title of *Chao Khun Muang* (or *Myoza*, a
Burmese word adopted by the Shan). Under the *Chao Khun Muang* were
the *Paw-Muang*, *Tao Muang*, and *Pu Haeng* in charge of a large group
of villages; next, were the *Pu Muang* in charge of several villages, and
in charge of a village was *Pu Kae*, or *Pu Kang*. Directly attached to
the courts of the *Chaofa* were officials bearing titles of *Tao Sung*, *Pu
Seung*, *Phawng Muang*, *Tao*, *Paw Lam*, *Ho Bo*, *Bo*, and so forth. It is
difficult to give precise definitions of the various titles as Burmese or Pali
terms were introduced (particularly during British rule) such as *Myoza*,
Ngwekhunhmu, *Myo-ok*, *Myowun*, *Amat-choke*, *Banda-wun*, and others.[9]

The titles used for officers in the Tai or Shan royal courts were
no longer used after the fall of the Tai kingdoms of Ava (1555), and
Muang Mao (1604). However, the text of the *Ahom Buranji* in the Tai
Ahom script mentions such titles as: *Chao Seung Luang*, *Chao Phawng
Muang*, *Chao Ji*, *Chao Seng Luang*, *Chao Ching Luang*, *Chao Tao Luang*,
Pukon Luang, *Phukon*, *Chao Seng Muang*, *Tao Muang Luang*, *Phu Kae
Luang*, *Maw Seng Muang*, *Niu Muang*, *Ru Ring*, *Ru Pak*, *Ru Shao*, and
so forth. In the English text only Indianized titles such as *Borgohein*,
Gohein, *Barua*, *Sakia*, and so forth are given (Barua, 1930).

From historical and political evidence one can argue that the Tai,
known by others as Shan (or more correctly, Siam) constituted a state
as the Shan had probably achieved a very high form of political organization. This shatters the theory that the Shan-Burmese conflict is
one of "tribalism" against the modern nation-state. In fact from the
fall of Pagan (1286) to the rise of a new Burmese power centre under
Burinnong (1551–81), the Shan or Tai dominated all Burma, with the
exception of Arakan and some Mon areas. The Burmese were confined
to small principalities such as those at Toungoo, Prome (Prae) which
paid homage to the Shan-dominated court at Ava.

After Pagan, there were two centres of Shan or Tai power — one
at Ava as mentioned, and another, the Tai Mao kingdom. It seems that
Ava comprised both Shan and Burmese, though it could well be that
in the early years the Tai were the majority.[10] Or perhaps, they like the
Mongol and Manchu in China constituted only a thin top strata.

In contrast, the Tai Mao kingdom was wholly Tai or Shan and it included the eleven Yunnan Shan states,[11] Muang Yang (Mohnyin in Burmese) and Muang Gong (Mogaung) which covered all of Upper Burma north of Shwebo; and the principalities of Muang Mit, Hsenwi, Hsipaw (Ongbong), Muang Pai,[12] Muang Nai, Yawnghwe, and Kengtung, the original components of Shan state.

Of the two Thai centres, the Tai Mao Shan were not only more power-ful, they also had a say in who should rule at Ava.[13] The Ava kings in turn regarded the Tai Mao princes as allies and depended on these princes in times of trouble or war. It has never been determined why Ava and Muang Mao did not merge into a single kingdom or why scant attention is accorded to the Tai Mao kingdom by all historians on Burma despite its close links with events and developments in Ava.[14] Shan dominance in Burma Proper ended with the fall of Ava to the great Burmese conqueror Burinnong in 1555, and in 1604, Shan cohesion was shattered when the Muang Mao kingdom fell to an invading Chinese force.

Regardless of the destruction of their power centres, the Shan, far from being dispersed, prevailed as forces to be reckoned with under their respective *chaofa*. Burmese chronicles such as the *Hmannan Maha Yazawintawkyi* [The Glass Palace Chronicles], frequently mention the presence of Shan ministers in Burmese courts, of Shan elephants and horses in wars, of Shan spearmen, and of Shan princes participating in wars against the Mon and in foreign wars, not as nameless subjects or tribal cannon fodder, but as princes who obeyed only the king and owed personal loyalty.[15] In addition Shan princes and Shan women war-riors fought the British during the First Anglo-Burmese War (1824) at Prome with so much valour that their foes were impressed. Major J.D. Snodgrass, a participant, had this to say:

> Eight thousand men of his [Maha Ne-myo, a Burmese prince] *corps d'armee* were Shans ... accompanied by three young and handsome women of high rank, ... These Amazons ... rode constantly among the troops, inspiring them with courage and ardent wishes for an early meeting with their foe, ... The grey-headed Chobwas of the Shan ... swords in hand ... attacking all who offered to approach them with humane and friendly feelings, they only sought the death which too many of them found.[16]

One the other side of the coin however, rebellions by Shan *chaofa* were frequent. Though submitting to exceptional Burmese kings such as Burinnong (1551–81), Alaungpaya (1752–60), and Hsinphyushin

(1763–76), rebellion was never far from their minds. Even during the reign of King Burinnong, the greatest of Burmese monarchs, Shan princes of Muang Nai, Yawnghwe, Kengtung, Hsipaw, Muang Mit, Muang Yang, and Muang Gong, rebelled repeatedly. There was also a Shan rebellion, a rare one not led by princes.[17] It occurred in Hanthawaddy (Pegu), the Burmese capital in 1564 involving tens of thousands of Shan, who not only burned down the capital, but also took several provinces.[18] It was quelled only when Burinnong returned from Ayuthia and personally put it down.

Despite countless rebellions by patriotic Shan princes, the Shan did not succeed in overthrowing what they saw as a foreign overlord, which also meant, conversely, that Burmese kings were never able to really control the Shan.[19] From time to time, certain Shan principalities were able to free themselves, but according to Harvey, "whenever a recalcitrant *Sawbwa* gave trouble, other *Sawbwas* would answer the royal summons and put down the wicked member" — this characterized all Shan struggles for freedom, revealing "a fatal want of coherence" in the Shan psyche, which not surprisingly led them to more grievous plights.[20] That is, their rebellion achieved nothing but more loss of Shan life, more so since both loyalists and rebels were Shan. And because they were disunited, they were dragged into foreign wars of Burmese kings against Chiangmai, Lan-Chang, the Yunnan Shan states, and Ayuthia. Not only that, in the "Great Chinese Invasion" (1766–69), in the reign of Hsinphyushin, tens of thousands of Shan must have died in this war waged on Shan soil. Chinese accounts of the war say that while Burmese troops manned the stockades, Shan troops were used as shock troops.[21] It must also be assumed that Shan troops serving with the Chinese (under the princes of Yunnan Shan states, Muang Gong, and Muang Yang) fared no better.[22]

Due to the lack of a national focus, and manpower losses in rebellious and foreign wars, the Shan were by the 1830s much weakened, and made weaker by the carrot-and-stick, policy of cleverer kings of the Konbaung (or Alaungpaya) dynasty such as Bagyidaw and Mindon. Loyal *chaofa* were lavishly bestowed with rewards and favours, treated almost on a par with Burmese princes of the blood, while those whose loyalties were suspect were undermined.[23] That is, younger brothers or subordinate rulers were encouraged to seize the throne or rebel, and rebelling *myoza* or *ngwekhunhmu* were recognized as separate entities by the Burmese court. Thus the original nine Shan states[24] were reduced in size and power,

MAP 3.1
Twelfth Century Shan Principalities

Source: Compiled from *Shan State and Karenni List of Chiefs and Leading Families* (1946), Scott and Hardiman (1900), and other Shan sources.

and by the 1870s, there were in what is now the present Shan State, forty-one principalities. Likewise, the two major Shan states, Muang Yang and Muang Gong, covering all Upper Burma north of Shwebo, were similarly splintered.

Even so, contrary to claims by Burmese nationalists that the Shan State was, by virtue of Burmese conquests, particularly dating from

Alaungpaya (1752 onwards), an integral part of the Burmese empire, control by the court at Mandalay over the Shan was never firm. Relationships between the Burmese power centre and the Shan were never based on total domination or complete submission, but rather resembled the relationship between rushing waves at a stretch of rocky coastline. Strong winds and high tides would bring waves in, covering the coast, but there were rock formations or some pieces of high ground, here and there, above the foaming and eddying current, defying the sea, the waves, and the winds.

The Upsurge of Shan Nationalism and the British Annexation

Earlier kings of the Konbaung dynasty were certainly vigorous and singularly martial. They not only eliminated the Mon and maintained some control over the Shan *chaofa*; but also defeated a Chinese invasion commanded by the redoubtable Mingjui, the Manchu emperor's son-in-law, and conquered all Tai/Thai kingdoms or states including Chiangmai, Ayuthia, Lan-Chang, Sipsongpanna (in the east). However, the Burmese, powerful as they were, could not hold on to their eastern conquests due to two Thai heroes, King Taksin and Chao Phraya Chakri (later Rama I, 1782–1809, founder of the present Thai dynasty). It is interesting to speculate what the outcome would have been had the Burmese been completely successful and collided with another expanding power, France. Thwarted in the east, the Burmese moved westwards and "fought and died by hundreds and thousands leaving their bones to bleach from Junkceylon to the banks of the Brahmaputra".[25] By 1817, Burma's boundary in the west included Manipur (1758 and 1813), Arakan (1782), and Assam (1817), which brought the kingdom in direct contact with a similarly vigorous power, Britain.

Without doubt, Burma was then a great power, but only a regional one, and a medieval one at that. However, Burmese military successes against the Chinese (1766–69), the various Tai/Thai states (the Shan principalities, Ayuthia, Chiangmai, Lan-Chang, Sipsongpanna or Chiangrung, the Yunnan Shan states), the Mon, the Arakanese, the Assamese, and the Manipuri, had reinforced the belief of the Burmese court that their kings were rulers of even the universe. Unlike the kings of Siam, Burmese monarchs could not bring themselves to treat European powers seriously, and thus in every encounter with the

British in India, acted as if the "white men" were of no account.[26] Consequently, within a span of twenty-eight years and two wars (1824 and 1852), the Alaungpaya dynasty lost all its coastal provinces, and as well the whole of the Mon country (Lower Burma), and Assam and Manipur to Britain.

Just as disastrous for the Konbaung dynasty was the royal blood-letting prior to and following every accession, and in the interregnum. Not only royal princes but anyone close to them was executed by the new king, particularly in the event of successful palace conspiracies. The most bloody were when the Mingun prince attempted to seize the throne from King Mindon in 1866, and at Thibaw's accession in 1875 where princes were sewn up in velvet bags and beaten to death with sandalwood clubs while *zat-pwe* were staged to distract the public and drown out the screams.[27] As a result, many capable princes and experienced ministers lost their lives.

In the Konbaung period, during the first half of the dynasty, Shan princes and their subjects seemed to have been closely involved with the Burmese power centre, playing important roles in various wars, especially in repelling the Chinese invasion of 1766–69, and the First Anglo-Burmese War in 1824. However, in the later period, from accounts of the British who travelled in the Shan country such as Dr Richardson, and Captain W.C. McLeod in the 1830s, the princes and populace especially of Muang Nai, Kengtung, Mawkmai, Muang Pan were quite unhappy with Burmese rule which in some southern states, such as Muang Nai and Yawnghwe, was in the form of a Burmese garrison under an agent of Mandalay.[28]

The smouldering Shan resentment finally burst into rebellion in the northern state of Hsenwi in 1845. It arose from the execution of an influential minister, Tao-Sung Toon Kham, his wife, and seven sons, by the *chaofa*, Seng Naw Hpa, an appointee of Mandalay. This led to an uprising under the leadership of another minister, Tao-Sung Kham Mawn which caused Seng Naw Hpa to flee to Mandalay whereupon King Mindon sent a force to reinstate him. This was done and the ringleaders were executed. However, the rebellion did not die out and was given a new impetus with the return of Tao Sanghai from the Shan-Siamese wars of the 1850s in Kengtung who took charge of the rebellion.

Few Shan today are aware of the victories of the Shan over the Thai (Siam) in Kengtung. This may be because most Shan learn of their past only through oral history based on chronicles, or from memories of old people since Shan history has never been taught in schools even during British rule. As such, the victorious wars with Siam were never mentioned probably because they were waged against a brother group, and hence were nothing to be proud of.

In these wars, a combined Shan force beat off three attempts by Siamese armies equipped with relatively modern weapons to capture Kengtung.[29] Apparently, the monarchs of Siam (Rama III and Rama IV) did not intend to incorporate the Shan into the kingdom. These incursions were aimed essentially at carrying away people to re-populate the deserted cities of north Thailand which was the practice of the Siamese (Thai) until the early years of the fourth reign.[30] Had the Siamese monarchs any unification aims, they would probably have tried other methods instead of launching invasions, and would have succeeded.

Through victories the Shan felt more confident of themselves. This is evident from the fact that Tao Sang-hai and his Hsenwi veterans of the Kengtung campaigns managed to put up a sustained resistance against Burmese troops as well as fellow Shan (*chaofa* of Muang Mit, Hsipaw, and Yawnghwe). However, the rebellion gained more vigor when Tao Sanghai's son-in-law, Khunsang Ton-huung took over. For his successes in defeating one Burmese army after another, he is considered by all Shan as a folk hero. By the time the British set foot in the Shan hills in the late 1880s, he was in control of all of Hsenwi (an area of over 8,500 miles).[31]

Without doubt, the protracted and increasingly successful resistance by Hsenwi against Burmese control beginning in the mid-1840s which continued to the 1860s and 1870s, greatly inspired the Shan to overthrow the "active and oppressive reality" of the Burmese presence.[32] Thus in Kengtung, upon his accession to the throne, Chao Kawng Tai (1881–87) proclaimed himself independent, and furthermore, spread a welcoming mat to all fellow princes who dared challenge Burmese authority.

In 1882, Chao Khun Kyi of Muang Nai, angered by the imprisonment of his sister, the Muang Nai queen (of King Mindon) by Thibaw (1878–85), and the appointment of the Kengtong *myoza* without prior consultation, rebelled. He put to death the Burmese agent and soldiers at Muang Nai. As was usual, Mandalay summoned the princes of Yawnghwe, Lawksawk, Muang Pawn, and the *myoza* of Hopong, Lai-kha, Samka, and Khesi to attack Chao Khun Kyi who consequently fled to Kengtung.

However, the rebellions appeared contagious and other states —
Muang Pan, Muang Pawn, Lawksawk, Muang Piang-Laisak, Mawkmai,
Muang Sit, Muang Loen, Sa-Tuung, Ban Yen, Namkhok, Nong Bon, and
Muang Hsu, joined in. There is insufficient evidence to ascertain whether
Mandalay's difficulty with Britain was a prominent factor in prompting
Shan princes to rebel but it is clear that they were conscious, if only
dimly, of the outside world.

One of the main actors, Chao Ohn of Yawnghwe, asked in one of his
letters to Pilcher (1886), then Deputy Commissioner of Kyaukse (following the fall of Mandalay at the end of 1885), "whether we ought to join
the chiefs of the 57 states of Siam and so obtain British protection".[33]
Letters exchanged between rebel Shan princes, mentioned the possibility
of welding Shan principalities "into a congeries of independent states
like Germany".[34]

The most enlightened among Shan princes then was the Hsipaw
prince, Chao Khun Seng. When the Muang Nai prince rebelled in 1882,
the Burmese court suspected him of being somehow involved. He was
not, but did harbour thoughts of an independent Shan homeland.[35] Fearing
some harm would come to him if he remained, he fled to Siam, spending
some time in Bangkok and Chantaburi, and eventually settling down in
British Lower Burma. He was imprisoned by British authorities for the
murder of two men from his home state of Hsipaw on a misunderstanding that they were assassins sent by Mandalay. Not long after he was
freed and deported (due to his status, good conduct in prison, and the
pleas of his consort to Crosthwaithe, the British Chief Commissioner).
After some time spent with Saw Lapaw, the Karenni chief, he returned
to Hsipaw and resumed his position as an independent ruler in 1886.
It was Khun Seng who suggested a confederation of independent Shan
states as in Germany.

However, the Kengtung prince, Chao Kawng Tai, who had become
the leader of the rebel princes in the south, disagreed. This may have
been because he understood Shan nature better — that they "would per-
ish rather than submit to their own kind even for the sake of unity", and
were more willing "to accept a powerful arbitrator from the outside".[36]
As such, concluding that Shan princes must have a suzerain, he together
with other major rebel princes, namely, Chao Khun Kyi (Muang Nai),
Chao Weng (Lawksawk) and Khun Hti (Muang Pawn), formulated a plan
whereby a prince of the House of Alaungpaya, the Limbin prince, was
invited to head the League of Shan Princes, known historically as the

Limbin League or Confederacy. They would then march to Mandalay, dethrone Thibaw (who was part-Shan), and Limbin would be proclaimed king. In return, the new king would revoke the *thathameda* tax;[37] would not interfere in Shan affairs; and Shan princes would pay obeisance only once every three years.

It was indeed a good plan, but its implementation was less simple due to the complexity and confusion of Shan politics. Firstly, in such states as Lawksawk and Muang Nai, rival claimants had been appointed by Mandalay when the rightful ones rebelled, and these naturally opposed the Limbin Shan League. Secondly, as in Yawnghwe, the league became involved in local politics. What happened in Yawnghwe had important bearing on subsequent developments especially the coming of the British into the Shan hills.

One of the leading lights of the league (Chao Weng of Lawksawk) favoured a certain Chao Chit Su (a member of the Yawnghwe ruling house), and the league therefore appointed him the Yawnghwe *chaofa*. At this juncture, the rightful *chaofa*, Chao Mawng, who was in Mandalay at the time of its fall to the British, returned with the Laikha Queen (of King Mindon) in 1886, and was attacked by the league.[38] He received a leg wound in one of the many skirmishes, and after appointing his half-brother Chao Ohn as caretaker, returned to Mandalay for medical treatment. However, Chao Ohn proclaimed himself *chaofa* which incensed Chao Weng,[39] who did not like Chao Ohn, and referred to him thereafter as a "dacoit and usurper".

Chao Ohn's high-handed action not only alienated Chao Mawng, the rightful *chaofa*, but made an enemy of the very powerful Shan League. However, being, by all accounts, a consumate schemer, he was able to work his salvation. From May 1886, he sent the new powers-that-be, the British, letter after letter urging them to restore peace and order, and also requesting protection and recognition for himself.

Had the British not come up to the Shan country (which they did in January 1887), the Shan League (Limbin Confederacy) might have achieved control of all the Shan states since its opponents — Laikha, Muang Kung and Khesi were not powerful and would have eventually been defeated. Moreover, the league was in touch with the extremely capable and far-sighted Khun Seng of Hsipaw who, in turn, was allied to the Khunsang Ton-huung of Hsenwi. It is very likely that all Shan princes would have united, and it is probable too, that this united Shan force would have succeeded in dethroning King Thibaw. Most certainly, with the dynasty weakened by royal blood-letting, the court riddled with suspicion and intrigue, the King himself under the thumbs of two commoners (Queen Supayalat and her mother, the Dowager Queen), and the Burmese themselves fed up with misrule — the Burmese centre would be in no position to resist the league. At the very least, it would have had to surrender all claims to the Shan homeland. Thus the Shan League was steadily growing into a rival centre of power in Burma since nothing precluded the possibility of the Shan setting up a new Burmese power centre.

When the British took over Mandalay, the Shan League presented some awkward problems. Firstly, though the Shan League had potential, it had in 1886, as yet to fully unify all Shan. The fluid situation was worrying, since external influences could come into play. There was the risk that the Shan League might persist in their aim to capture Mandalay or that the more reputable and able Burmese princes such as the Chaunggwa, Myinzaing, or Mingun princes, the last named then taking refuge with the French in Saigon, might win over the Shan.

The French too posed a threat. For a time they were believed to have designs on Burma and Siam. It therefore made sense to do something in the Shan homeland. This, and the hope of opening the "Golden Road to Cathay" through the Shan country to Yunnan, and beyond — propelled the British to step onto the Shan stage.

Their task was made easier by welcoming letters from Chao Ohn of Yawnghwe and Khun Seng of Hsipaw (whom the British liked and admired), and in 1886, the Commissioner at Mandalay, Sir Charles Bernard, drew up "Plans for Establishing British Influence in the Shan States during the Open Season of 1887". Generally, the plan called for bringing the high Shan plateau, overlooking the Burmese plains, under some form of control as quickly and quietly as possible and that avoidance of conflict was imperative.

British presence was established by means of flag marches by armed columns which followed on the heels of friendly letters to the princes and chiefs promising recognition and the protection of the Queen. Consequently, agreements or treaties were signed with Shan *chaofa* and rulers who were recognized as ruling powers in exchanged for, among others, acceptance of British supremacy: avoidance of contacts with external powers; surrender of forest and mineral rights; and the undertaking to administer or rule in accordance with British "standards of civic discipline".[40]

The *chaofa* and rulers were also required to pay annual tribute in money in the manner they once paid to Burmese kings. The vassal relationship of Shan princes to the Burmese king was specifically included in the *sanad* (grants) bestowed upon them by the British. This was an important political point as it re-established Burmese suzerainty over the Shan. The princes signed it because they were unequipped to grasp the full implications of this political sophistry. But for the British, it was a political imperative in their future dealings with the French, Chinese, and Siamese. They had to re-establish the Shan country as part of the Burmese empire, if not Burma, which now lay at their feet.

This particular British action in 1888 by which the Shan unwittingly re-accepted Burmese overlordship negates accusations by Burmese nationalists, past and present, that the British dismembered the country. Ironically, the Shan looked upon the British as their friends and protectors.

The position of the Shan princes was, in the late 1880s, like that of a team of comparatively fine soccer players suddenly finding themselves in an American football game. Mandalay, their goal, was no longer the tottering and intrigue-ridden capital within their grasp, but the power base of an altogether different and most powerful "race" of men — the brightest and the best of the nineteenth century world.

Besides, while the British were at Yawnghwe, frantically dispatching messages of friendship right and left, and at the same time pondering the dismal prospect of a long and messy Shan war, the "leader" of the league, the Limbin prince, offered to surrender in exchange for a pardon and pension, and did so in June 1887.

By April 1888, the task which the Chief Commissioner at Mandalay set himself — the coralling of Shan *chaofa* as tributaries of British India — was completed. The southern Shan *chaofa* had in January in a durbar at Muang Nai been granted their *sanad* in which was outlined their powers and obligations; and the northern *chaofa* were granted theirs in March.[41]

The Shan under the British Umbrella

The history of the Shan under British supervision is essentially the study of the relationship of the British at various levels in a bureaucratic labyrinth with the Shan *chaofa* and rulers. As far as the common people were concerned, contacts with the "pale-faces" (a literal translation of the Shan word, *na-poek*), or *kula-khao* (White Indians) in both rural and urban areas were minimal. Yet most were aware of and thankful for the British presence since, firstly, it rid the land of predatory and cruel Burmese soldiery; and secondly, it did away with the wars, not only between Shan and Burmese armies, but also the ceaseless fighting among the Shan arising from rivalries and often at the behest of the Burmese overlord.[42] This total absence of strife was novel and cherished. For those who experienced life under the British umbrella, that period remained etched in their minds as a "Golden Age".

As soon as the British got the Shan *chaofa* and rulers to sign the *sanad* in the late 1880s and early 1890s, they immediately set out to draw boundaries which was confusing since all adjoining land was inhabited by the Tai/Thai races whose rulers paid tribute, at various times, or simultaneously, to Siam, China, and Burma, and sometimes operated independently. The British claimed or rejected areas according to the needs of the moment. This was done by the simple expedient of trotting out Burmese claims whenever it suited them, or ignoring such claims whenever necessary. An example was their disposal of the Tai/Thai areas such as the Yunnan (Chinese) Shan states, Sipsongpanna, and Muang Sing (which belonged to Kengtung). These areas, despite their generally favourable reaction to British presence and being sometimes vassals of Burma, were handed over to foreign powers, the former two to China, and the latter to France (as part of Laos).[43]

Until 1922, there was no such entity as the Shan State. Shan *chaofa* were separately recognized as almost sovereign rulers under British protection, and were placed under the direct rule of the Governor of India. In the late 1880s, they made the Shan *chaofa* unwittingly re-accept Burmese suzerainty when in fact there was then no Burmese suzerain as Burma had legally become a part of India since 1886.[44] The British, however, squared the circle by placing the Shan *chaofa* under the Governor of India, and put other peripheral areas (later to be known as Excluded Areas, Scheduled Areas, and Frontier Areas) under "indirect rule".[45] In retrospect, it must be recognized that a grave injustice was done to the Shan by thus retroactively re-asserting their vassalage to Burma.

Under this arrangement, the Shan *chaofa* and rulers were bestowed "full" power in internal matters. To this day, a large number of Shan and Burmese still regard the *chaofa* as having power over "life and death", and as such are judged as having ruled according to their whims and fancies. However, the "life and death" power is merely a ceremonial phrase, because in reality the princes had to defer to the resident British officer, that is, the political agents, the supervisors, superintendents, residents, and commissioners, who were seconded to the Shan principalities, and after 1920, specifically recruited into the Burma Frontier Service.[46] Relationships between British officers and Shan princes varied according to which level of the British hierarchy the former belonged. Officers in the field got along fine with the princes and were charmed by the latter's dignity; but in the later period, some of the British officers came to resent the Shan princes' lack of servility and they worked to promote the disunity of non-Shan sub-rulers and for the further division of Shan principalities along ethnic lines.[47] The British at higher levels, such as at the Burma office, and Delhi, however, were more interested in Burma and the Burmese, as will be seen as this chapter unfolds.

From the late 1920s onwards, British administration in the colonies, especially in India (of which Burma was a part), underwent some changes. There was a move towards greater self-rule by the Government of India Act 1919. In the process, the Burmese homeland was constituted as a province under the Government of Burma Act 1921. Consequently, the British were confronted with the question of the status of the Shan principalities and other Excluded Areas and whether they were to remain under the direct control of the Governor of India. Clearly, from the viewpoint of the bureaucracy, it was more expedient to transfer these areas and the Shan principalities to Burma, since they were at one time or other under Burmese kings.[48]

In order to facilitate the transfer of Shan principalities on to the Governor of Burma, a bureaucratic entity named the Federated Shan States was set up in 1922. A British Commissioner appointed by the Governor of Burma took charge of the central budget (to which each Shan state contributed 50 per cent of its revenue which was later reduced to between 27 per cent and 35 per cent), and also of common departments such as public works, medical administration, forest, education, agriculture, and to some degree, the police. In a nutshell, the Federated Shan States was a sort of sub-province (of Burma) but with finances "distinct from those of Burma Proper and under a distinct form of administration".[49]

Under this arrangement, the Shan *chaofa* and rulers had only advisory roles in the federal government despite the fact that they had to contribute 50 per cent of their revenue to the central fund. Since they did not enjoy any executive or legislative power in the federation, their status was severely reduced from that of semi-sovereign rulers in the late 1880s, to that of poorly paid but elevated native tax-collectors in 1922. Politically, it meant that the Shan as a whole had no say whatsoever in their fate since their representatives, the *chaofa*, had no voice either.[50]

The federation scheme was carried out without a hitch because the *chaofa* then were unaware of the political implications of this move. However, as the years went by, there appeared a new set of princes who had some education, had travelled outside their homeland to Burma, India, Siam, Ceylon, and in rare cases, to Britain and Europe. Many had served in the military or the paramilitary Frontier Forces, while some trained under the British as administrators. As such, they became increasingly aware of the political implications of past, present and future actions and the impact on the status and the future of their homeland and people.[51]

Though not as strident as Burmese leaders of the same period like U Chit Hlaing, U Ba Pe, U Pu, Dr Ba Maw, U Saw, and so forth, the Shan princes of the 1930s nevertheless saw what the federation of 1922 meant — that it had not only reduced their status, but had negated all the political significance inherent in the situation in the late 1880s. The Shan country was no longer a political entity but a mere administrative appendage of a colonial set-up, no different from other tribal areas, such as the Somra Tract. This, the *chaofa* of the 1930s tried to remedy by requesting that the British restore to them and their homeland, the status enjoyed in the late 1880s, that is, as semi-sovereign rulers and entities under British protection, or having the executive and legislative power in the federation devolving to them. The *chaofa* were not politicians and had been conditioned all their lives by the British to view politics as "ungentlemanly" and dangerous. As such, when the British "played politics" against them, they did not know how to respond politically. Their request for the restoration of the status enjoyed by the *chaofa* of the 1880s which in political terms meant the upgrading of the political status of the Shan nation and homeland was, therefore, intentionally construed by some British colonialists — and, of course, deliberately interpreted by their opponents, the Burmese élite (past and present), and by revisionist historians — as beggars aspiring to be kings in the interest of narrow self-interest.

Repeated reminders that the Shan had come into the British orbit only by virtue of political contracts in the late 1880s between the *chaofa* and the British all fell on deaf ears. From the late 1920s to 1941, Sir Chao Khe (from Hsipaw), Chao Khin Mawng (from Muang Mit), and Chao Shwe Thaike acted as the main spokesmen for the *chaofa* and the Shan as a whole. They even went to the series of Round Table Conferences in the early 1930s, held in London, to present their case, but all in vain. The situation remained the same till the Japanese invasion.

Contrary to allegations by Burmese nationalists that the British favoured the non-Burmese, particularly the Shan, and encouraged separatism, the British goal was the eventual amalgamation of all Excluded Areas with Burma and the bestowing of a dominion status to this new and unified entity.[52] Further proof that this was the case was provided when Burma, under the Government of India Act 1935 (Schedule X–XV), was separated from India and constituted as Ministerial Burma. Consequent to this, when the Shan *chaofa* once more requested the British to review theirs and their homeland's position in the light of increasing self-government being envisioned for Burma, the British simply ignored the Shan.[53]

There were great changes in Burma during British rule — lands reclaimed, agricultural output boosted, schools established, technical and higher education introduced and encouraged, roads and bridges constructed, buildings erected, hospitals and dispensaries set up everywhere, ports opened, and trade promoted.

Progress in Burma was but the by-product of British colonial imperatives. The British had to put something into Burma in order to get something out of it, and the resources of Burma Proper were easier and cheaper to exploit than the less accessible potential of the Shan and other hill areas situated further inland. Thus various support structures had to be developed in Burma. It was simply a question of colonial priorities. There was enough in Burma to occupy British bureaucrats and keep British trading houses happy. The backwardness and stagnancy in the Shan states was, like the progress in Burma, the result of British colonial imperatives and priorities.

The *chaofa* had little power beyond local matters and affairs — upkeeping religion, supporting monasteries-cum-schools, keeping trade routes open, the upkeep of market-places, apprehending criminals and suppressing banditry, upkeeping and initiating rudimentary irrigation systems, encouraging cottage industries, maintaining and managing administrative offices (recording tax, revenues, expenditure, and routine administrative matters), maintaining schools not under federal control, and native courts.[54] Even in local matters, they had to defer to the nearest British officer. Moreover, in the Federation (1922), the Council of Chaofa had no executive or legislative power, its function being merely advisory. Considering the *chaofas'* lack of power, and limited resources, it is surprising that they were able to bring some rudimentary improvements to the life of their people.[55]

It is pertinent here to say something about the *chaofa* and their rule. In the 1960s, it was fashionable (and even now among foreign scholars interested in Burma) to portray them as living lives of opulent luxury while peasants lived from hand to mouth, groaning under both feudal and colonial oppression. The fact is that even under the "feudal" scheme of things, Shan peasants were, in the European sense, freemen, and in village and local matters, governed themselves. Moreover, if a man did not like a particular rule or taxes levied, he was free to resettle elsewhere (many people in Sankampeng district, Chiangmai, Thailand, are descended from those who moved away from one of the Shan states about eighty years ago because they did not like the tax then imposed by their *chaofa*). It must be noted that Shan princes were not landowners like the British or European nobility. Land was owned by the state, in the modern sense of the word. There was very little room for despotic misrule since British Residents were always at hand to prevent excesses. As for the "opulent" life-style of the *chaofa*, they had more money, it is true, than the average Shan farmer and lived better as all élites everywhere and through the ages do. But they had to fulfill personal, social, and ceremonial obligations out of their own pockets (that is, from the personal allowance which was 10 per cent of the revenue and the amount varied from state to state). As an example, take an average state such as Yawnghwe. With a gross revenue of Rp379,129 it contributed Rp132,695 to the Federation at Taunggyi. Thus, nett revenue was Rp246,434 annually, or Rp20,533 monthly. Out of this, monthly salaries for judges, ministers, officers, clerks, policemen, guards, some categories of teachers, upkeep of religious institutions and edifices, expenses of local administration, and jails and court-houses had to be met. The prince was given an allowance (about 10 per cent), from which he had to support numerous relatives, the palace or manor, entertain state guests, donate to monasteries, monks, bright students, pay his personal retinue and staff, and meet other obligations expected of a prince.[56] Further the prince could not take a major share of the state revenue or spend as he pleased since he had to strictly abide by accounting practices instituted and supervised by British officers.

The most noticeable feature of the tail end of British presence in the Shan states is the hardening of the British colonial bureaucracy against the Shan and the princes. No less noticeable is that despite British studied ignorance of Shan aspirations, the Shan as a whole continued to highly esteem and admire them. The *chaofa* and their people even collected between £57,000 to £60,000 for British war efforts in the early 1940s which was described thus: "Proportionate to their numbers and wealth, the Shan states were the largest contributors of voluntary funds to the British".[57]

World War II: A New Set of Circumstances

The war reached Burma and the Shan states with the thrust of the Japanese 55th Division from the Isthmus of Kra to Victoria Point, then north to Mergui, and Tavoy on the Tenasserim coast at the end of 1941.[58] In opposition were two British Divisions, and various locally-raised units such as the Burma Rifles (composed of Karen, Kachin, Chin, and some Indians and Burmese), the paramilitary Frontier Forces, some Shan battalions, and a 50,000-strong Chinese contingent for defence of the Burma Road which joined Rangoon to Kunming via Mandalay, Lashio, Hsenwi, Wanting (Pangsai in Shan), Chefang, Paoshan, and Tali-fu.

The fighting that ensued was of a kind never seen before by the natives. Buildings were reduced to charred debris, bridges were blasted into twisted scraps, and roads, cart-tracks and foot paths were obliterated. The destruction wrought was almost total as the fighting never really ceased. Though by May 1942, the Japanese controlled important towns and strategic points, Allied aeroplanes kept up the pressure throughout the war. In addition, secret agents, many of them Karen, Kachin, Shan and Burmese were air-dropped whilst resistance groups such as Forces 101 and 136, were organized.[59]

Battle and destruction, of course, caused widespread dislocation as people from towns fled to villages and villagers into the jungle and reduced the people to extreme want and poverty. At the same time, among the active strata of the populace, attempts by the Japanese to win native support for the "Asia for Asian" ideology, and the Allied cries of "freedom and democracy" — both urging the natives to fight for their "motherland" — served to arouse and heighten nationalist feelings. More important, the war demonstrated with terrifying clarity especially to the Karen, Kachin, and Shan, the danger of putting one's destiny into the hands of others, no matter how powerful or invincible they were.

For the Burmese however, the war at least gave them some political rewards. The Japanese granted them "independence" in 1943 (August), but more important, it put a new set of leaders — the fiercely nationalistic Thakins — in control of the administrative machinery and of a national army of sorts called the Burma Defence Army. Burma was given by treaty, nearly all Shan states except for Kengtung and Muang Pan which were given to Siam. (This is quite significant as it indicates that the Japanese then viewed the Shan states as a separate entity. Notable too is the fact that Burmese units were forbidden to enter the Shan hills.)

The relationship between the Japanese and the *chaofa* was marked by Japanese prohibition of armed Burmese into Shan states. Though "belonging" to Burma, it is clear that the Burmese government of Dr Ba Maw had almost no say in the Shan states.[60] Yet there was much manoeuvring and activity. The Burmese government under the Japanese (headed by Dr Ba Maw) and politicians expended much effort to get the Shan to agree to bringing their homeland into Burma. It was a two-pronged attempt. On the one hand, senior ministers and civil officers met often with prominent *chaofa*, the most influential at the time being the Yawnghwe prince. He often had to make hazardous trips (due to Allied bombings) from Yawnghwe to Rangoon by car over cratered roads and makeshift bridges (no bridge escaped Allied bombers, it is believed). However, nothing came out of all this since neither Shan nor Burmese leaders were in control of anything and the future was most uncertain. On the other hand, politicians, the Thakins particularly, tried to achieve the unconditional incorporation of the Shan states through links with young Shan radicals.[61] These were graduates or former students of Rangoon University who greatly admired Aung San, U Nu, and other Thakins (most of whom won their political spurs as leaders of the Rangoon University Students Union in the pre-war years). The young Shan radicals heartily embraced Marxism and socialism and agitated against the *chaofa*, demanding among other things, the immediate joining of Shan State to Burma and the overthrow of the princes.

In contrast, however, in parts of the Shan homeland given to Siam, Kengtung and Muang Pan covering about 15,000 sq miles, the Siamese were in real control. However, the Thai fired by the modernization zeal of Field Marshal Pibul Songkram prohibited the chewing of betel nut (or *paan*) and the keeping of top-knots (practised among other men). This, and the attitude that the Tai were less civilized, the bombing of the Kengtung market on bazaar day,[62] and the lack of seriousness (as compared to British starch and drill) of the Thai military, impaired their image. The Thai certainly had all the right intentions and sincerely wished to bring progress to the Tai (Shan), but were too inexperienced, and hence needlessly antagonized the people of Kengtung, and Muang Pan. Had they perhaps been able to stay longer, a shared common language would have brought about mutual adjustment and respect. But Thai presence on Shan soil was but a wartime phenomena which ended whilst the Shan were still resentful, and puzzled by the actions and behaviour of their ethnic brothers.

From a political angle, destruction, death, dislocation, impoverishment, and terror suffered by the Shan in the four years of war only provided for the Shan leaders like their Kachin, Chin, Karen and other counterparts, a bitter lesson. The Shan especially were determined not to become anyone's dependents or subjects.

At the end of the war, the situation in Burma was radically altered. Like the French in Indochina, the British were faced with a new set of men in control of the capital. They had two alternatives: to attempt to displace these interlopers by force or to try to work out a settlement, and failing that, withdraw gracefully. Faced with this new set of circumstances, what loomed largest in the British mind was the fact that Britain's rule in India would soon end. Moreover, Britain was impoverished and this was why it agreed to India's independence in the first place. Also, the Labour Party led by Clement Atlee did not subscribe to the idea of an empire "over" which the sun never sets". These realities dictated that colonies which wanted to leave the empire would, and could not be prevented from doing so.

There was therefore no obstacle to Burma's independence except for the fact that the pre-war British Governor of Burma, Sir Reginald Dorman-Smith was against hasty withdrawal, and insisted on sticking to the Simla Plan drawn up by the Government of Burma in exile. The Simla Plan called for a period of rehabilitation, a return to the 1935 constitution, and in time, the constituting of Burma as an entity enjoying full equality with the dominions and with Britain. It also stated that the Shan states and the tribal areas would continue under the governor's rule until their amalgamation with Burma with the consent of their inhabitants.[63] However, the Thakins or the AFPFL under Thakin Aung

San disagreed and insisted on independence as soon as possible.[64] Since there was no real objection to the Thakins' stand from the Labour government in Britain, the only important question left was when and how the amalgamation of the Shan states and the Frontier Areas with Burma was to take place.

There has been in currency for some time, the surprisingly popular notion, particularly among Kachin, Shan, and Chin leaders that the British favoured their aspirations for self-government under British protection or even outright independence. Another version is that the Shan were given a choice of either joining with China, Siam, or Burma, or opting for independence (in some versions after a few years under Britain as a self-governing dominion). Yet another story is that Britain encouraged the Frontier Areas to demand independence, or encouraged the Shan princes to oppose union with Burma.[65]

The truth is that the tales sprang more from wishful thinking than facts, or from the psychological need of the Shan, Kachin, and others, to soften the pain of being abandoned by an esteemed and trusted "friend", the British. What is probable too is that some Frontier Service officers, Conservative politicians, army officers who had commanded Kachin and Karen soldiers during the war, had discussed with the Frontier Areas' leaders various hypothetical situations. A case of misunderstanding is possible since Britain did say on many occasions something about separate government for the Frontier Areas prior to their merger with Burma.[66]

In reality however, the Labour government and Lord Louis Mount-batten could not give much attention to the fate of the Shan and other Frontier people since there were enough problems in India (the Hindu-Muslim conflict, the status of Indian princely states, the issue of non-Indian Northeast territories, particularly the Naga among others). Nothing made so obvious Britain's lofty indifference as London's passivity to the Karen appeals for special consideration in view of their long loyalty and service which had caused them to be branded by the Burmese as "running dogs of the British".[67] Consequently, when Burmese nationalists in their turn became protégés of another imperial power (the Japanese), the Karen were severely repressed, even massacred.[68]

After twice sending delegations to London in 1946, all that the Karen gained from the British was a bitter speech against the Labour government by the powerless Winston Churchill, accusing it of betraying loyal friends and repudiating Britain's responsibility to "primitive peoples for whom British justice and administration had guaranteed peaceful livelihood".[69]

The feelings of apprehension and foreboding felt by the Karen at the prospect of life under Burmese domination was shared in varying degrees by other ethnic groups as well. For instance, there were people still alive in the Shan States who remembered the oppression under Burmese kings. The attitudes of Burmese politicians that their ethnic group was superior to all by virtue of their intelligence, their past conquests and present level of achievements, and the atrocities committed by the Burma Independence Army against the Karen, did not give any reason for the Shan and Frontier peoples to trust them. The Shan were in fact entirely sceptical of the Burmese and not very happy about the prospect of joining Burma. Further, the general attitude among the Shan was that it was senseless to exchange one yoke for another.

On one of my travels in the late 1950s I happened to lodge myself in a *sala* or *zayat* — a kind of pavilion in the grounds of a monastery in Muang Kung town. It being a day during lent, several elderly men joined him and they started a conversation which turned to politics. They grumbled about the Burmese and one of them asserted that all the mess was due to the *chaofa*, "especially the Chaofa of Yawnghwe", for joining the country to Burma. Quite stung by this accusation, I wanted to retort, but my Shan language skill being then quite limited, I had to remain silent.

Notes

1. Shan chronicles have as yet to be properly translated and compiled. At present, they are scattered in various works such as Scott and Hardiman (1900), Chao Saimong Mangrai (1965), Milne (1910), Cochrane (1915), and Colquhoun (1885). The English translations are unsatisfactory as the chronicles were read by a Shan person, recorded in Burmese by an Indian (whose knowledge of both Shan and Burmese could not have been perfect), and then, translated into English.

2. This includes most of present day Northeast Frontier Areas of India. In 1820, the Assam kingdom was "liberated" from the Burmese by the East India Company. It evolved into a part of British India and after 1947, became an integral part of India.

3. The date of founding of the Mao Kingdom varies with chronicles, but fell to the Chinese in 1604. During the reign of Hso Khan Fah, it held Assam, Arakan, the Chinese (Yunnan) Shan states, Upper and Central Burma,

present North Thailand, Laos, parts of Vietnam. The Tai Mao kingdom apparently did not enjoy good relations with China and had to face numerous invasions beginning from 1343 A.D. (namely in 1343, 1393, 1445, 1461, 1479, 1495, 1515, and 1604).

4. Ava was established by the three Shan brothers based in Kyaukse. They apparently were allies of the Mongols who conquered Pagan, and for a time ruled as uncrowned kings of Pagan in 1287, later establishing capitals at Pinya (1312), Sagaing (1315). Their descendants then founded Ava in 1364.

5. Martaban was established in 1281 (Harvey 1925), and recognized by Sukhothai in 1293, and China in 1298. Wareru was responsible for the *Wareru Dhammathat*, which according to Harvey (1925), was the earliest surviving lawbook in Burma. After his death the capital was shifted to Pegu or Hanthawadi, and his kingdom survived until 1539, but as a Mon power centre.

6. As narrated to Dr Kraisri Nimmanahaeminda by Colonel Ba Shin, of the Burma Historical Commission in the early 1960s, and related to the writer. The writer uses interchangeably the terms, Tai, Thai, Shan, and Siam. This is because both the Shan and the Siamese or Syam are one and the same people, and speak the same language except for variations in tones and accent, and of course, loan words from Chinese, Burmese, and Pali in the case of the former, and Sanskrit, Cambodian, and Chinese in the latter case.

7. Some scholars interpret *Siam* as "Gold", or "Guardian of the South". Modern Thai interpret *Thai* or *Tai* as meaning "free". In Shan usage the term simply means "native of". For example, *Tai Kengtung*, means "native of Kengtung".

8. For non-Tai kings, the Shan term is *Khun Haw Kham*, denoting a lower rank. Royal ranks in Shan are as follows: *Chao Haw Kham, Chaofa, Chao, Khun*, and *Kham*. The sons of the *Kham* are commoners, as are daughters of the *Chao*. However, if such a woman marries a *Chaofa*, her children will be of *Chao* rank. If she marries a *Chao*, her sons will be of *Khun* rank, but not the daughters.

9. Some southern principalities such as Baw, Pindaya, Sa-muang-kham, and to some extent Yawnghwe whose population were Danu, adopted Burmese terms since the 1820s. However, usage of Burmese terms became widespread only during the British period arising from British encouragement of Burmese language usage in Shan State and other Frontier Areas. Burmese was a compulsory subject in schools.

10. This can be deduced from the fact that there are still large Shan settlements in the Burmese plain at Pyinmana, Thazi, Toungoo, Pyu, Pegu, Prome, Rangoon, and even in the delta. A substantial number of Burmese everywhere quite proudly claim to have Shan blood in their veins. During Burinnong's time

there was a major revolt by the Shan in and around the capital, Hanthawadi, in 1564.

11. These Shan are collectively known as the *Tai ty Khoang* or "Tai of the lower Khoang"; and the Tai of Sipsongpanna, living further south are known as the *Tai nua Khoang*, or "Tai of the upper Khoang".

12. There are at present two Muang Pai. One is in Thailand in Mae Hongson province, and the other in Southern Shan State adjoining the Karenni State. Which Muang Pai was part of the Tai mao kingdom? It is very probable that the original Muang Pai included both. By the time of the British arrival (late 1880s) there were seventeen states under the *chaofa*, seventeen independent *khun muang* (or *myoza*) states, and eight independent *tao muang* or *ngwekunhmu* states.

13. The Chaofa of Muang Gong (Mogaung), Muang Yang (Mohnyin) and Hsipaw (Ongbong) were kingmakers or were kings of Ava. In fact, the penultimate king of Ava was also the Chaofa of Muang Pai, known in history books as Mobye Narapati (1546–52), and the son of the Hsipaw Chaofa. The last Ava king, Sithukyawhtin (1552–55), was also a Shan.

14. History books used in Burmese schools only note the Shan period of Ava as that when Tho-Han-Bwa (Hso Harn Fa) desecrated pagodas and killed more than 300 Buddhist monks. While the Shan Tho-Han-Bwa's dastardly deed is known to every student, Alaungpaya's greater cruelties against the defeated Mon, and the massacre of Mon monks are not mentioned in history text books, and are forgotten or glossed over by many Western scholars.

15. See Harvey (1925), p. 270.

16. Quoted in Chao Saimong Mangrai (1965), p. 53.

17. See Harvey (1925), p. 177, and U Kala Yazawungyi (1960).

18. It is unclear how a large Shan population came to be settled near Pegu and adjacent provinces regarded today as predominantly Burmese. Harvey and others infer they were prisoners. However, the possibility that they were natives (since the Pagan period) cannot be overlooked.

19. Surely the Shan cannot be accused of being feudal tribesmen rebelling against a modern state. They rebelled because they saw Burmese kings as alien overlords, and were clearly conscious of Shan identity. If such feelings do not constitute nationalism — then what is nationalism?

20. See Harvey (1925), p. 166. R.H. Pilcher as quoted in Chao Saimong Mangrai (1965), p. 84.

21. Harvey (1925), p. 255. See also Chao Saimong Mangrai (1965), p. 52.

22. It is surprising how the Shan gained the reputation among Westerners and others as an unmartial race. Throughout history, they fought the Chinese, Burmese, Mon, fellow Tai/Thai (more than others), Kachin, Karenni, Pa-O, Lahu, the Karen National Defence Organization (KNDO), PVO (Burmese leftists), White Flag communists, and KMT stragglers. During the Vietnam

war, Shan mercenaries fought the Pathet Lao and North Vietnamese Army (NVA) units in northern Laos. In the 1970s, they fought the communists in Thailand as part of the Chinese Irregular Force. At present in Shan State, close to 5,000 Shan are serving with the CPB.

23. Chao Saimong Mangrai (1965), p. 54.

24. Muang Gong, Muang Yang, Muang Mit, Hsenwi, Muang Nai, Yawnghwe, Muang Pai, and Kengtung. For a list of the 41 states in Shan State see Chao Saimong Mangrai (1965), Appendix IV.

25. Christian (1945), p. 2.

26. This interpretation is contrary to the views of revisionist historians who maintain that the wars with the Burmese kingdom and the final annexation were the result of British imperial motives and that whatever the Burmese kings did or did not do was irrelevant. This view is too dogmatic. Annexation by Western powers is not inevitable or preordained. The policy of the early kings of Thailand, from the first to the fifth reign, argues against the inevitability of annexations by Western powers. Wisdom, foresight, acceptance of realities, and attempts at good government accompanied by various reforms — these were the reasons which kept Thailand free, and in the post World War II era, put her on the path of development, progress and stability.

27. As related to the Yawnghwe children by Gyidaw Khin whom, we were told, was a kin. I do not know how this was so because she was of the House of Alaungpaya, through the Limbin line. The Yawnghwe and the Limbin family were very close somehow.

28. See Chao Saimong Mangrai (1965), pp. 59–79.

29. For details of the re-population of the north during the period in question, see Dr Kraisri Nimmanahaeminda (1965).

30. According to Kengtung natives, one such siege of Kengtung town was beaten off through the defenders' use of giant "rockets" (*nu fai* in Shan, and *bong fai* in Thai) which stampeded the Thai war elephants.

31. At the Conference of Muang Yai, March 1885, the British recognized Khunsang Ton Huung as the *chaofa*, but not before dividing up Hsenwi and giving the smaller segment to Chao Naw Muang of the original House of Hsenwi. This southern sector was known as South Hsenwi, but in the time became Muang Yai state.

32. Chao Saimong Mangrai (1965), p. 55.

33. Ibid.

34. Ibid., p. 111.

35. Ibid., p. 117.

36. Ibid., p. 147.

37. A household income tax introduced by King Mindon in Burma Proper in 1862, and later (1868) introduced in parts of Shan country.

38. He was recognized as the Yawnghwe Chaofa in 1897 after Chao Ohn's death. He received the KSM decoration in 1901, the CIE in 1908, was knighted in 1916 as Sir Chao Mawng and died in 1926. My father, Chao Shwe Thaike, the nephew of Chao Mawng become prince in 1927. (In 1928, another prince who was knighted was Hsipaw's Chao Hke.) According to my family, he was then in Mandalay because the new king, Thibaw (1878–85), did not trust him. Chao Mawng was also adopted by King Mindon.

39. He was one of the few Shan princes who did not submit to the British, and fled to Muang Che in Sipsongpanna (now part of Yunnan, China) and died in 1896. One descendant of Chao Weng, Chao Mya Sein (married to a Chinese nationalist general) fled to Thailand with two daughters. In the late 1950s, she re-settled in Rangoon, and again had to flee to Thailand following the anti-Chinese riots in Rangoon in the mid-1960s.

40. Chao Saimong Mangrai (1965), pp. 243–46.

41. Chao Saimong Mangrai (1965), see Appendix VII.

42. Cady (1958), p. 41.

43. See Chao Saimong Mangrai (1965), pp. 217–39, 275–99.

44. Cady (1958), p. 132.

45. Apart from the Shan and Karenni states, other Frontier Areas were (1) Shan or Tai areas of Song-Hsup, Singaling Khamti, and Khamti Luang; (2) Arakan Hill Tracts; (3) Chin Hill Districts; (4) Kachin Hill Tracts; (5) Somra Tract; (6) the area known as the Triangle; (7) Hukawng Valley; (8) Salween District, and (9) all unadministered tribal areas.

46. In fact between 1888 and 1920 the Tao-Muang of Loilong; the Myoza of Keng-kham, Muang Nong; the Chaofa of Laikha and Mawkmai were deposed by British authorities. In the period 1920–40, the Myoza of Sa-Tuung, Ban Yen, Namkok and Nong Bon were deposed for various reasons. In 1927, Chao Pomlue of Kengtung was declared ineligible for the title. (Compiled from *Shan States and Karenni: List of Chiefs and Leading Families*, 1945).

47. An example of this being the separation of the *Kao-Kang* or "Nine Village Tracts" (now known as Kokang) from Hsenwi, and its recognition as a *chaofa* state after World War II. Another example was the creation of a "Kachin sub-state" by the British.

48. "Burma" prior to independence refers only to the Burmese homeland, and does not include Shan and Karenni states, or other Frontier Areas.

49. *Shan States and Karenni*... (1945), p. 3.

50. For better or worse, the *chaofa* represented the people. Despite not being elected, Shan society is not rigidly stratified, and interaction between the ruler and the ruled was not too formalized. The kinship system in which in-laws were related to other in-laws, further extended the family of the *chaofa*. *Chaofa* were never landlords in the individual ownership of land.

51. For example, the Yawnghwe prince served in several units of the British Army in Burma and in the Frontier Force from the age of about fifteen to thirty. His brother-in-law, the Hsenwi prince, my maternal uncle, also served for some time in the military. The Kem-Muang of Hsenwi, the heir apparent, Chao Mun Pha, also an uncle, participated in Wingate's campaign against the Japanese, was captured, and sentenced to death. Due to the intercession of his wife, the Hsenwi prince, and others, he was spared.
52. Christian (1945).
53. In 1937, the Hsipaw prince, Chao Ohn Kya, presented a memorandum to the Secretary of State for India and Burma, again reminding the British of past pledges, and complained of the lack of interest displayed in Shan representations to British authorities (Taylor 1983, p. 25).
54. Each principality had a tradition of self-sufficiency and division of labour according to villages. One village may specialize in iron-work, another in weaving, the third in pottery. But some states were famous for certain crafts. For example, Muang Kung for pottery; Muang Nong for bamboo craft; Yawnghwe for "Bangkok" and "Chiangmai" silk and silver-ware; Kengtung for lacquerware; Hsenwi for "Namkham" bags; Muang Nai for woodcarving and stone sculpture, and so forth. However, all states, to varying degrees, had villages engaged in paper-making, iron-ware, cloth weaving, and so forth.
55. Compile from *Shan States and Karenni...* (1945). On this point, it would be helpful to look into the annual gross revenue (1939), of some Shan states:

Townships	Area (sq mi)	Gross Revenue (Rp)	% to Federation
Kengtung	12,400	427,879	$27\frac{1}{2}$
Muang Nai	3,100	111,524	35
Yawnghwe	1,393	379,129	35
Lawksawk	2,362	76,353	35
Baw	741	14,872	35
Hsa Muang Kham	449	67,742	30
Hsipaw	4,591	775,590	35
Hsenwi	6,422	690,889	35

56. Monthly allowance of the Hsipaw prince being Rp5,000 (out of Rp64,000 monthly revenue); Namsan prince, Rp4,000 out Rp53,802; Hsenwi prince, Rp4,000 from Rp57,573; Muang Loen, Rp1,100 out of Rp2,640, and so forth. Compiled from *Shan States and Karenni...* (1945).
57. Taylor (1983), p. 26.
58. For an authoritative but concise account of the war in Burma, see Christian (1945).
59. One of them was Mahn Win Maung, a Karen, and the third Union President. See Chapter 5.

60. Dr Ba Maw agreed to serve the Japanese and was appointed Head of State, but was eclipsed by Aung San and the Thakins (AFPFL) in the post-war period.

61. Among whom was my uncle, U Tun Ohn. These men educated in Rangoon became great admirers of the Thakins and embraced "socialism". Their programme was immediate unconditional union with Burma, and the removal of "feudalism". However by the late 1950s, they had become disillusioned with Burmese arrogance and the undisciplined Burmese soldiers in Shan State, and supported the move for constitutional reforms in the early 1960s.

62. According to the natives, two Thai aeroplanes appeared out of the blue and strafed the market-place though British units and installations were nowhere near.

63. Cady (1958), p. 507.

64. Formed in early 1944 to expel the Japanese with Aung San and the communist Thakin Than Tun as the leading lights (incidentally their wives were sisters). At that time, the Thakins, though allied to Japan had secretly contacted the Allied Forces in Ceylon and India. Since the communists were the first to resist the Japanese, the AFPFL in its early days was dominated by them. The communists lost out in an internal struggle with Aung San and other elements in 1946.

65. Like all Shan and non-Burmese natives I did not even think of questioning these tales until the early 1960s when I had to write background papers on Shan and Burmese policies on behalf of the Shan State Army (SSA). (Surprisingly, Steinberg 1982, p. 33.)

66. British policy statements concerning the Frontier Areas in 1931, 1935 and as per the Simla Plan during the war.

67. The Karen teams were led by Saw Ba U Gyi, a well-to-do British-trained lawyer, and the undisputed leader of all Karen in peace as well as in war. His death while in action in the early years of the now thirty-five year old Karen rebellion deprived the nationalist movement of much cohesion and political direction.

68. For a comprehensive and rare account of the Karen-Burmese relationship, see Cady (1958).

69. Cady (1958), p. 540.

4

Shan-Burmese Relations from 1948

The Spirit of Panglong and the Union

There is a Burmese saying, "A bad beginning makes for an uncertain ending", and this certainly applies to the creation of a new nation-state in 1948 — the Union of Burma.

The one significant factor which overshadowed everything else was the fact that neither the British nor the Burmese nationalists (whose burning ambition it was) were prepared for the swift unravelling of British power. The Shan and the Frontier peoples were even less prepared, since under British rule they had — except for a few individuals — almost no contact with the outside world.

The Japanese war changed all that overnight, and the need by both the Japanese and the Allied Forces for native support and the subsequent barrage of propaganda, awakened in the Shan and Frontier peoples an awareness of such things as love for one's homeland, the duty to repel foreign occupiers and aggressors, and to stand for one's rights.[1]

During the war, the Burmese nationalists sided with the Japanese while most of the Frontier peoples sided with or secretly sympathized with the British, and thus, with their return to Burma, the leaders of the non-Burmese ethnic groups, especially the Karen, naturally expected some favourable considerables from Britain regarding their future. Instead, the British began establishing relations with the Thakins, whilst pointedly ignoring the people who had fought for them as regular soldiers or as guerillas behind Japanese lines.

The Shan were particularly dismayed by the Simla Plan since it further reduced, in the name of democratization, the status of the *chaofa* to that of non-princely native tax-collectors.[2] This, in effect, further lowered the political status of the Shan states from that of a sub-province (as in the 1922 federation) to that of a tribal area under direct bureaucratic rule. It, however, would not have been too bad if there were British guarantees regarding the future position of the Shan states whatever the status of the *chaofa*, but this was not forthcoming.

In 1945–46 there existed a dichotomization in the British position. On the one hand, there was the Governor (Dorman-Smith) and the colonial bureaucracy which insisted on following the British timetable which by the 1931 Act would lead to eventual dominion status for a unified Burma. On the other hand, there was London and the formidable Mountbatten, and important Labour figures such as Tom Driberg, who favoured in varying degrees, the AFPFL's demands of immediate amalgamation of the Frontier Areas and independence.

Not unnaturally, the Shan and Frontier leaders were thoroughly confused, and there was the danger that they would sold cheaply and willy-nilly thrown into the "Burmese cart" like so much unwanted baggage. If the Shan and Frontier leaders remained passive, and if it so happened that London over-rode the Governor and acceded to the demand for immediate independence of Aung San and the AFPFL, what guarantee was there that the Shan and the Frontier people would not be thrown to the Burmese lion? There was certainly no British policy with regard to the future of the Frontier Areas in the event of Burma being immediately granted independence.[3]

In this crucial period, the Shan princes and other leaders were engaged in much politicking. The most active and prominent among the Shan were the Yawnghwe prince, Chao Shwe Thaike; the Muang Pawn prince, Chao Sam Toon; and the Sa-Tuung prince, Chao Khun Kyi. These three Shan statement were not only instrumental in bringing together all the princes including Shan administrators, community leaders, tribal chiefs, intellectuals and politicians, but also Chin and Kachin leaders who were in a similar predicament.

It could here be argued, as it has been done by Burmese leaders and nationalists, and obliquely by historians such as Trager (1966), and Steinberg (1982), that the actions of the *chaofa* during this period were damaging and destructive, and retarded the process of nationhood. If left to themselves, the Shan, Kachin and Chin would have willingly opted for unconditional amalgamation with Burma (and hence, everyone would live happily ever after). It was also suggested that the *chaofa* were active only on their own behalf, and at any rate did not represent the people.

Some scholars even go so far as to claim that the activities of the *chaofa* and consequent constitutional arrangements prevented or sabotaged the "traditional pattern of accommodation" *vis-a-vis* the Burmese and other ethnic groups. This argument is rather puzzling when even Burmese history reveals that the only type of "traditional accommodation" has been Burmese domination by force of arms and frequent rebellions as has been resumed in the Shan hills these past twenty or more years, and more than thirty years in the case of the Karen.

Hence, in the light of historical facts and current realities, that is, widespread strife and instability, and socio-economic regression, actions by the *chaofa*, in particular the three Shan statement, must be seen as, in the main, constructive. They provided both the Burmese and the non-Burmese with a framework within which both the major and the minor components of a newly established nation-state could work out their differences and finally attain a common nationhood. It must be noted that if a similar arrangement for the accommodation of the differences (ethnic, historical, political, administrative, and socio-economic development) between the Burmese and non-Burmese peoples had been the creation of the Burmese elite along it might have been viewed in a more positive light.

During this bewildering period, the *chaofa*, various Shan, Kachin, and Chin leaders met frequently to discuss the situation in which enemies had become fast friends and friends were fast becoming "nobodies".[4]

As 1946 was ending, the lame-duck Governor of Burma, Sir Reginald Dorman-Smith was recalled. This signalled the victory of Aung San and the AFPFL and heralded the fact that Burma would soon become independent. In January 1947, Aung San was invited to London, resulting in the London Agreement (or the Aung San-Atlee Agreement) by which Britain agreed to Burma's independence "either within or without the Commonwealth as soon as possible".[5] Clause (8) provided for the "early unification of the frontier Areas with Ministerial Burma", and among others, the setting up of a Frontier Areas Commission of Enquiry (FACE) to determine the wishes of the non-Burmese ethnic groups. This provision was made without any consultation with the Frontier Areas, despite a cable by the *chaofa* to London stating that Thakin Aung San did not represent the Shan and the Frontier Areas.[6] The London Agreement of 1947 clearly refutes the contention that "the *Sawbwa* [the princes] were forced to fight a rear-guard action to protect their position with the assistance of the British between 1945–48".[7]

When the princes were informed of this, they were naturally stunned, as were all Frontier leaders. The princes had no recourse but to take the formal position they had prepared in 1946, in which the purely advisory 1922 Chaofa Council or Federal Council was rejected in favour of a Shan State Executive Council composed of princes and representatives of the people, vested with executive, legislative, and financial powers.[8] This was in fact a mini-revolution, an assertion by the Shan of their national identity and independence, which was politically an essential measure as British action had made it imperative for the Shan to act on their own.

At this juncture, one is led to wonder what would have happened if the AFPFL, in particular Aung San, had refused to recognize the Shan State Executive Council and refused to negotiate with Frontier leaders on the basis of equality. Perhaps this was what the British had hoped for as the ensuing confusion or even armed conflict between the Burmese and others would necessitate British presence in the area for quite some time.[9] If this was the case, it failed because of Aung San's pragmatism and foresight and because the British in their own craftiness had alienated the people who sincerely admired them.

Even though Aung San could, if he had wished (by virtue of the 1947 London Agreement), dismiss the negotiations among Shan and Frontier leaders and undermine them by using FACE, he did not. He went to the Shan states in 1947, and at Panglong on 12 February signed an agreement with Shan and Frontier Areas leaders in which Ministerial Burma essentially recognized the right of self-government and autonomy of the Shan states, and agreed to the autonomous status for the Kachin and Chin areas in the approaching unification of Burma.[10]

Though this was perhaps the best that could have been achieved under prevailing circumstances, it was far short of the *de facto* political position the Shan had attained in the 1880s, that is, as entities free of tributary ties to the then Burmese king (King Thibaw), and even a rival power centre in Burma (as members of the Limbin League). However, the Panglong Agreement of 12 February (celebrated as Union Day since 1947) was a good beginning for the building of a new relationship based on equality and mutual respect with the Burmese state.

Another important outcome of this period was the setting up of the Supreme Council of the United Hill Peoples (SCOUHP), as umbrella organization covering the Shan, Kachin, and the Chin. It would have been the most effective political force in their dealing with the new Burmese power centre and politicians had it been consolidated, but no reference was made to it after independence.[11] An attempt to revive it by the Shan government in 1961 was cut short by the coup of March 1962.[12]

Following the signing of the Panglong Agreement, a constituent assembly to draw up the constitution of the new state was convened in June 1947. However, on 19 July 1947, Aung San and the whole interim cabinet, including Chao Sam Toon, one of the three Shan statement, were assassinated. U Saw, who was prominent in the pre-war politics of Burma, and Prime Minister of British Ministerial Burma in 1940 was in the post-war era eclipsed by the rise of Aung San. He was found guilty of master-minding the assassination, and hanged.

The death of Aung San disorientated the Shan and Frontier leaders who trusted him not only because he was a man of his word, but because he could get things done. Moreover, they believed that Aung San did not subscribe, as most Burmese politicians appeared to do, to the concept of the Burmese as a conquering and superior race. Added to the loss of their anchor, Aung San, there was the bewildering political jargon, terms, definitions, and laws, that emerged while framing the constitution. Furthermore, they were made to understand that the constitution was only an interim one which had to be completed by September for presentation to the British Parliament, implying that whatever changes that were desired could be made after independence.[13]

What the feelings of the Shan are towards the aftermath of the Panglong Agreement and subsequent conditions and events is best described by a popular song (*The Promises of Panglong*) which first appeared in the early 1970s:

> A free homeland for the Tai
> This, we agreed on at Panglong
> The vows and promises so solemnly made
> And now, though it has never been told
> By whom the promises were broken
> We know who betrayed whom
> But the Tai have always been true
> Where are the vows and promises of Panglong
> Have they all gone, I wonder, with Aung San.

Shan-Burmese Co-operation during the First Decade

Despite the hasty nature of the graft which brought together the different components of the Union of Burma, the bonds which linked

the Burmese, Shan, Kachin, and Chin — the signatories of the 1947
Panglong Agreement — remained strong from 1948 to the late 1950s.[14]
A surprising phenomenon considering the fact that the new Burmese
power centre (the AFPFL government of U Nu) was buffeted on all
sides by the storms and squalls of rebellion and dissension following
independence.[15]

In the three or four years following independence, there was a
communist uprising (led by Thakin Soe of the Red Flag communists
and Thakin Than Tun of the White Flag communists); rebellion by the
AFPFL's own militia, the People's Volunteer Organization (PVO); mutiny
by major components of the 1st, 2nd, and 3rd Burma Rifles; uprising by
Muslims, the Mujahid in Arakan, and by a certain monk, U Sein Da, also
in Arakan.[16] There was too an armed insurrection by the Karen National
Defence Organization (KNDO) which enjoyed the support of almost all
Karen communities and Karen army units; and a mutiny by some Kachin
Rifle units led by a war hero, Captain Naw Seng. It certainly looked as
if U Nu's AFPFL government would be toppled since it held only the
capital, Rangoon, while the rebels, then called "multi-coloured insurgents",
held not only important towns such as Moulmein, Pegu, Prome, Insein
(really a suburb of Rangoon), Prome, Meiktila, Taungoo and Mandalay,
but they straddled all the main north-south communication lines — the
Irrawaddy, railways, and roads.

The Shan State too had its share of rebels, in particular Kachin
mutineers under Captain Naw Seng, Karen rebels and their allies, the
Pa-O of Southern Shan State.[17] Those rebels for a time held various
Shan towns such as Lashio, Hsenwi, Kutkai, Muse, and Namkham in
the north, and others in the South including the capital, Taunggyi. In
addition, the White Flag and leftist PVOs were active mainly in areas
bordering Burma, from parts of Lawksawk up to parts of Muang Kung,
Hsipaw, and even Namsan. No sooner had these armies been contained,
Chinese nationalist (KMT) forces retreating from China encamped on
Shan soil in Kokang, Vieng Ngun, Muang Loen, Muang Hsu, almost
over-running Kengtung, and at one time they occupied Tachilek, just
across the river border from Maesai (Thailand). In keeping with the
American aggressive defence stance against communist China in the
1950s, Taiwan proceeded with U.S. assistance to reinforce and build
up these stragglers into a formidable force. Soon these KMT divisions,
further strengthened by Tai Nua and Tai Lue recruits from both sides of

MAP 4.1
Positions of Shan Rebels and Kuomintang (KMT) Forces in Shan State (1949–51)

* BCP (Burmese Communist Party) or White Flag communists now known as CPB

* Pa-Ō rebels allied to the Karen National Defence Organization (KNDO)

Ⓟ PVO (People's Volunteer Organization)

Ⓚ Kachin army mutineers and rebels under Captain Naw Seng

⊡ KMT (Chinese stragglers under General Li)

Source: Compiled from various reports of Shan State Council (legislature), Taunggyi, 1952–53.

the border, as well as Wa and Lahu tribesmen, began launching attacks into Yunnan. The Taiwan-U.S. strategy was to use the Shan State as a base and establish redoubts in Yunnan, after which Taiwan would launch the long awaited sea-borne invasion. This was an ambitious plan which if carried out whole-heartedly would have succeeded, but would perhaps embroil the whole of Southeast Asia in a bloody and meaningless war. Like the earlier rebels, General Li Mi, the nationalist Chinese commander in Shan State, attempted to enlist the support of Shan princes but was politely rejected.[18]

Had the Shan princes made common cause with the rebels, the Kachin and Karenni leaders would have joined in. However, the *chaofa* though naturally sympathetic to the Karen, saw clearly that the victory of the rebels would deliver the country into the hands of the communists, particularly the White flag of Thakin Than Tun since it was the most well organized, and at that time had a substantial following among the Burmese. The Shan and the Kachin who had kith and kin across the China border could not help but be aware of what life under communism meant as tales of communist barbarities had been carried to them by Shan and Kachin refugees. This strengthened their determination to prevent a similar occurrence in their homelands.

It must be said that it was fortunate for the Union that Shan, Kachin, and Chin leaders were far-sighted. If they had joined the rebels, the AFPFL would have had no choice but to call in the British, or perhaps, the United States would have been forced to intervene, which in turn would draw Mao's China in on the side of a very strong rebel force. Subsequently, we would perhaps have seen the division of the country into the North and South as in Korea or in Vietnam prior to the American defeat in the early 1970s. That such a fate was avoided is due to the wisdom of the Shan and other non-Burmese leaders. Such a scenario is not as far-fetched as it seems given the lack of real unity and rapport between the ruler and the ruled in Burma today.

Another factor which influenced the Shan princes, Kachin, and Chin leaders in favour of the AFPFL was the cordial personal relations which the then Prime Minister, U Nu, established with non-Burmese leaders. They admired his principles, humanity, and intellect, and knowing that he was not deceitful, they trusted him. As regards the Shan, U Nu liked and trusted the Muang Mit prince, Chao Khun Khio, the Head of Shan State during the 1950s (and 1960–62) and at different times, Foreign Minister and Deputy Prime Minister. U Nu also gained the goodwill and respect of the most influential Shan leader, the Yawnghwe prince, Chao Shwe Thaike.

The third factor was that the 1948 constitution (actually completed in 1947), though not federal or in line with the wishes of the non-Burmese or the promises given by the late Aung San, at least provided the constituent units with some say in internal administration and affairs. At any rate, it was accepted for the time being because of the implicit understanding that changes could be made in the near future as soon as some peace and stability was restored.

Yet another factor binding Shan princes, Kachin and Chin leaders to the government of U Nu was the mental and political orientation of these men. They were by nature conservative and traditional men who feared more than anything else the chaos of rebellion and revolution. The Shan princes particularly understood the very anarchic nature of the Shan and the propensity of many of their compatriots to, if given the change, assume princely airs and fancy trappings which only fostered greater disunity and created more disorder. Moreover, their experience under the British as soldiers and administrators had conditioned them to give their loyalty to whoever was the constitutional authority. If there were any changes to be made, they could be affected, the princes reasoned, through appeals and petition, and by constitutional means.[19] And besides, neither U Nu nor the AFPFL had violated the constitution in any way then, and therefore deserved a fair chance to run the country.

Hence in the civil war between the AFPFL under U Nu and the various formidable rebel armies, the Shan, Kachin, and Chin leaders not only rejected overtures by rebels and others (such as KMT generals) but actively assisted the government of the day. Young Chin, Kachin and Shan recruits swelled the ranks of the Burma Army and the Union Military Police, and they fought extremely well. In the Shan State, the *Chaofa* raised levies, out of their own pockets and state treasuries to fight the rebels and KMT irregulars.[20]

By the mid 1950s, thanks to the support of the Shan, Kachin, and Chin, all immediate dangers to the AFPFL of U Nu had faded — the military strength of communists and leftists had been broken, and the Karen movement was losing steam and coherence after the death of its undisputed leader, Saw Ba U Gyi.

Thus one would have thought that the AFPFL's victory would bring to the Union a long period of stability, peace, and hopefully, some prosperity. There was however, a falling out among national leaders characterized by petty accusations, slander, juicy gossip, and a general washing of dirty linen in public. This squabbling at the very top gave the general impression that the fate of the country lay in the hands of dishonest and petty-minded men who were alleged to be more sensitive to their wives' complaints and the interests of numerous "hangers-on" than to national problems and issues.[21] To be fair however, this break-up was perhaps inevitable since the AFPFL was, in the first place, a collection of disparate elements — various trade unions and guilds, different shades of socialist groups, religio-ethnic groups, ethnic organizations, various youth and social associations, peasant organizations, and prior to 1946 included both the Red and White Flag communists.

The unravelling of the AFPFL led to many cabinet crises, but most damaging was U Nu's weak leadership, judgement, and sense of direction. Finally, in 1958, the new Burmese power centre, the AFPFL, split into two, the "Stable" AFPFL of Ba Swe and Kyaw Nyein (a contemporary and close friend of Burma's hero, the late Aung San) and the "Clean" AFPFL of U Nu. Worse still, each half splintered into cliques revolving around Ba Swe, Kyaw Nyein, Thakin Tin, Bo Min Gaung, Thakin Tha Khin, Kyaw Dun, and others.

Even before the AFPFL began to lose its coherence and direction, however, another group of men was slowly establishing their strength and influence — the Burmese military establishment. The civil war during the early years of independence had not unnaturally given the military not only a larger share of the budget and other privileges but much freedom of action and power. In unsecured areas such as in some parts of southern and eastern Shan State which were placed under martial law, military men enjoyed sweeping powers as military administrators. Significant too, is the fact that the army's top brass were, strictly speaking, not military professionals, but "half" politicians arising from the fact that they were veterans of the BIA which in essence was a political organization engaged in a military role. As such they had close connections with politicians (for example, Ba Swe and Kyaw Nyein within the ruling AFPFL) and other political groups (for example, a shadowy group known as the "Red Socialists"). Being thus politicized, the army saw itself not just as the sword-arm of the state, but an embodiment of the will of the nation, that is, the Burmese "race", for in their mind, the "race" they belonged to was the nation, all others being subject peoples.

However, no matter how much power and influence the army had managed to reap, it would not have emerged as a rival power centre had it not been for the genius of one man, General Ne Win.[22] Despite his early reputation as a playboy more interested in horses and pleasures, he was very ambitious and read much, especially books on history and politics. (It is said that he particularly immersed himself in Chinese history, and is one of the handful who can really be called an expert on China.) Ne Win also worked hard to make the Burma Army not only united but obedient to his every command. This he achieved by creating a controlling body within the military staffed by absolutely trustworthy men — the MIS. Its personnel were like political commissars in communist armies, and like the American FBI, the MIS also kept detailed dossier on all army officers and civilians. Furthermore, because the army enjoyed extra-legal authority in the Shan State and other non-Burmese homelands, the MIS became effectively a secret police force answerable to no one but itself.

Thus, by the late 1950s and early 1960s, the army under Ne Win, ably assisted by Maung Maung, Aung Gyi, and Tin Pe,[23] had become a centre within a centre, with its own embryonic political party (the National Solidarity Association with branches nationwide, run by the Psychological Warfare Department), businesses and industries (the Defence Service Institute under Brigadier Aung Gyi) and a parallel police apparatus (the dreaded MIS, controlled in effect by General Ne Win).

The squabbling among leaders which broke the AFPFL, made governance such a farce that the army was "invited" in 1958 by U Nu to step in as the caretaker government.[24]

Ne Win and his brigadiers and colonels quickly got down to work in the manner which has been praised by Western scholars.[25] They cleared Rangoon of squatters, kept the streets clean, made trains run on time, swept noisy leftists and rowdy students to off-shore detention (on Cocos Island), silenced rebellious tribesmen and stripped feudal and troublesome Shan princes of their power (*sic*).[26]

Regardless of the army's successes however, their efforts were, it seemed, not appreciated by the people who in the 1960 election returned U Nu to power. The Stable AFPFL (Ba Swe–Kyaw Nyein alliance) considered by voters to be the army's obtained only 41 out of 250 seats. It was an overwhelming victory for U Nu, and for democracy as well, because U Nu's campaign theme was the continuance of parliamentary democracy and the rejection of dictatorship.

The theory of many Western scholars was that U Nu's victory was due to his image as a good Buddhist and the support of the clergy.[27] This does not provide an adequate explanation since U Nu had made it very plain to the voters that the election was of crucial importance for democracy, and anti-dictatorship was the main theme underlying his campaign speeches. The Burmese voters may be many things, even superstitious and unworthy of democracy, but they nevertheless chose democracy and U Nu in 1960.

There is, it seems, a basic contradiction in Western thought concerning Asia, particularly Southeast Asia, pertaining to politics. On the one hand there is the argument that Western democracy with its periodic elections, parliaments, and so forth, is an alien transplant and therefore unsuitable for the East — which gives rise to the question of what then is a suitable form of government and politics in Asia? Are the people of Asia therefore to be condemned to living forever in political squalor and barbarity? It certainly would seem to be the case, if the West and Western governments had their way.

Conversely, and in the same breath, after saying that such things as elections, parliaments and civil rights are Western transplants, the West (both the governments and scholars) insist on the sanctity of the concept of the nation-state as if this was indigenous to this region, while in reality it is, like democracy, a transplant pure and simple.

Regardless of whatever conclusions were later reached by outside observers and scholars concerning the 1960 general election, the feelings of the natives, both the Burmese and the non-Burmese, was that the military had been resoundingly rebuffed and that whatever problems there were would henceforth be solved in a democratic manner through parliament or within the legal framework of the constitution. Everyone was therefore optimistic for the future, forgetting that for democracy to really work, those forces prejudicial to open government would have first to be curbed — a task easier said than done since the Burma Army had by then established itself as a centre within a centre.[28]

U Nu and the Clean AFPFL (renamed the Pyidaungzu or Union Party) were, however, unequal to this crucial task since the bickering among the champions of democracy began soon after the election over allocation of posts and spoils of victory. This must have deeply affected U Nu for he lost all sense of proportion altogether and became, according to the Rangoon cocktail circuit, peevish, hectoring, petty, and worse, turned his mind and energies to irrelevant and unnecessarily divisive issues such as making Buddhism the state religion, proposing the construction of grand shrines on Mount Popa for the *nats* (Guardian spirits), a modern dog-pound for Rangoon's strays and so forth.

A belief widely held, especially by the non-Burmese, up till now is that U Nu did nothing against the army because he had contemplated the use of force against the constituents states if and when the time came; and that U Nu was aware and approved of the 1962 coup by General Ne Win so as to avoid a constitutional amendment giving the states more power and responsibilities. This argument seems unfounded. Although U Nu was personally against a federation on the American model, which the Shan and others favoured, and though he might have used force against them if they proved intransigent, he certainly would not have killed democracy in order to keep the non-Burmese in line. And as regards the belief that U Nu did nothing to curb the army, it was, firstly, not possible since his own colleagues were disunited. Secondly, he was lulled by General Ne Win who had retired Maung Maung, Tun Shein, and others who had been very prominent in the caretaker government, thus giving the impression that the army had purged itself of anti-democratic elements.[29]

In the years following the 1960 election, renewed squabbling amongst the leaders of the ruling Union party accompanied by slander and insinuation naturally impaired the image of politicians, and U Nu's erratic performance as Prime Minister, played into the hands of the military. It was given the opportunity to strike when the constituent or subordinate states led by the Shan government called for a reform of the Union constitution. Given the complexities of the issue, and the general Burmese understanding that the Shan, Kachin, Chin and Karen were subject peoples, the move for the structural reforms of the constitution (or the federal movement) was not well received by the politicized sector of the Burmese population, especially the Rangoon press. Soon, the federal movement became, as it were, a diabolical scheme hatched by feudal and reactionary Shan princes in league with foreign enemies — Chinese nationalist warlords, the Taiwanese, Thai, and Americans (even the Southeast Asia Treaty Organization [SEATO]) to dismember Burma, and destroy the Union among others things.[30] In March 1962, the army struck, giving as its main reason the danger posed to the very existence of the Union by secessionists plotting to dismember it.[31]

The Military and the Shan

Studies dealing with Burma, particularly on the period after independence, lead one to believe that Burma's disunity and woes stemmed mainly from the unreasonable and illogical intransigence of the non-Burmese minorities, especially on the part of the privileged Shan princes.

The Union of Burma was, before its inception, considered by the Shan as a voluntary partnership of peoples and a union of equals.[32] This was what Aung San had said to them time and again in all their meetings with him at Panglong in the Shan State, and elsewhere.

However, Aung San died a martyr's death on the eve of independence before the constitution was reviewed and adopted. Without Aung San, the Shan and others had to deal with a new and less far-sighted set of leaders — U Nu, U Kyaw Nyein, U Ba Swe, U Tin Tut, whom they did not know as well as they did Aung San (who, in fact, was a stranger to them until 1946).[33] This must have been traumatic for both the Burmese and the non-Burmese. However, in drafting and reviewing the constitution, the Burmese had all the advantages as they all understood constitutional matters, were politicians, and had experienced civil servants and legal experts, trained by the British and educated in Britain at their service.

The constitution which was finally completed was contrary to what the Shan and other minorities wanted for it was, in essence, unequal. It was not a union of equal states but colonial in structure with Burma Proper constituting a mother state while the others were subordinates. There was no federal government because all federal power was vested in the government of Burma Proper. What was worse was that though the constituent (in reality subordinates) states could legislate on local affairs, state laws could be nullified by the Union (that is, Burmese) government. Matters pertaining to forests, minerals, oil, and so forth were under Union jurisdiction. And to add to this imbalance, Burma Proper was represented in the Upper House by 53 members while the five component states sent only 72 members, which meant, in principle, that there was unequal representation.[34] This was bad enough, but it was made worse by the fact that the Upper House, or Chamber of Nationalities, did not have much power. For example, it had no power to initiate a financial bill, or reject such a bill passed by the Lower House or Chamber of Deputies.

Whatever the inequalities in the constitution and regardless of what they felt, the Shan and others did not raise any objections at the framing of the document out of respect for the late Aung San who had worked so hard for independence and unity among the different ethnic groups. Secondly, they were told that this was an interim constitution and any changes desired could be made after independence. But after independence was granted in January 1948, the new government of U Nu was confronted by unrest stirred by the communists and PVO (which originally was the AFPFL's army, but after Aung San's death it leaned more and more towards the communists). Then came the civil war which plunged the whole country into chaos.

The Shan rallied to U Nu's AFPFL government and stemmed the tide of rebellion. But no sooner had indigenous rebels been contained in Shan State, fleeing KMT units poured in, and with assistance from Taiwan and the United States, re-organized and proceeded to transform the eastern Shan State into a spring-board for the invasion of China. Consequently, more Burma Army units had to be sent into the Shan State to deal with the KMT. The Shan government and people at first welcomed the Burma Army but before long it became just another foreign occupation force no better than the KMT, especially in the eyes of the rural people.

Here we come to a very controversial point: the behaviour of the Burmese soldiery. As a Shan who has travelled widely in his home-land and having had close contact with villagers in the course of his work in the nationalist movement, I have no cause whatsoever to doubt the tales concerning atrocities by the Burma Army, especially units pre-dominately Burmese. In this respect, my Burmese friends say that the brutality of Burmese soldiers were not directed against the Shan *per se*, but that they were just as rough on the Burmese population in Burma Proper — which may very well be the case. However, since the Shan are as different from the Burmese as Frenchmen are from the Russians, and whatever one might say about the Shan, Burmese and Karen belong-ing to one nation, the poor behaviour of Burmese soldiers made the Burma Army in local eyes a foreign army of occupation, thus giving rise to anti-Burmese feelings. In comparison, though the Chinese KMT were exploitative, they rarely brutalized villagers nor did they go out of the way to express contempt for things Shan, as did Burmese soldiers.

One would have thought that the top military brass in view of the army's role as the guardian of the nation and as a "unifying factor" (a definition popular among Western analysts), would have demanded good behaviour from the Burmese in the army especially when in non-Burmese homelands. However, it was not the case, and never has been. Why?

The kind of indiscipline referred to is not a matter of a rape case here, some looting there, but mass pillage and plunder, wanton killings, taking women along on operations (using them as coolies by day and raping them at night), forcing whole villages into coolie service (tying them five to a length of rope at night, frequent beatings without reason, abandoning them when sick or wounded), using these coolies as human shields and human mine detectors, and other horrors. Such descriptions should not be taken as anything other than a presentation of what the Shan and other non-Burmese (Karen, Kachin, and others) believe to be true, since they are difficult to verify.

After a period of indecisive clashes with the KMT intruders, the AFPFL government of U Nu protested the aggression to the United Nations. By the end of 1954, due to prompt U.N. response and the co-operation of Thailand, over 10,000 KMT troops were air-lifted to Taiwan, thus officially ending the KMT issue.[35]

Following the removal of immediate danger from rebels and foreign forces, the Burmese power establishment became more and more preoccupied with and anxious about Chapter 10 of the Union constitution, which provided the Shan and Karenni the right to secede from the Union after ten years.

For the Burma Army, particularly, this was a hot issue since its creed, "One Blood, One Voice, One Command", precluded the concept of a multi-centred structure for Burma. Such things as autonomy, state rights, federalism, and so forth, were perceived as utter rubbish and tolerated only because Aung San, the father of the army, had decreed them in 1946–47. With the end of ten years approaching, Burmese leaders in general and the army in particular, became increasingly convinced — perhaps because this was what they would have done had they been in a similar situation — that the Shan would secede. Consequently they reasoned others would follow suit, and thus Burma would once more be dismembered. That this was Burmese reasoning is borne out by various speeches and writings of Burmese leaders of that period, including U Nu who even threatened to fight a war, as Lincoln did, to prevent secession.

To pre-empt secession it therefore became imperative to destroy the credibility, prestige, and authority of Shan *chaofa* — the traditional rallying point of the Shan. Hence the princes were increasingly portrayed in the media — newspapers, magazines and journals, short stories and novels — as despotic, indolent, exploitative, disloyal, and feudal reactionaries who plotted with KMT opium warlords, SEATO agents, Thai pimps, American war-mongers and British neo-colonists to destroy the Union.[36] In addition, local anti-*chafa* politicians such as Namkham's U Toon Aye, Kyaw Zaw, Tin Ko Ko and fellow-travellers were given ample assistance by the army and some AFPFL leaders.[37] According to many Shan nationalists, the self-styled anti-feudalist Pa-O rebels were secretly aided by the army (but there is no real evidence of this, though it is not impossible).

What was the general attitude of the Shan to the anti-*chaofa* campaign by the Burmese establishment? In quite a number of states, for example, Muang Loen, Kengtung, Muang Nawng, and Laikha, where the Shan were predominant, or where the population whatever its composition, had little or no contact with the Burmese except as marauding soldiers, the attacks were deeply resented. Elsewhere too, however, the campaign was not favourably received not out of sympathy for the princes, but because it was regarded as undue Burmese interference in Shan affairs. Moreover, tales of army atrocities, and the basic differences between different peoples — in habits, outlook, food, clothing, norms, behaviour — did not improve matters, and was made worse by Burmese arrogance and scant respect for Shan customs and sentiments.

As the anti-*chaofa* campaign progressed and intensified, there was due to the abovementioned factors, a counter-reaction. This in turn led the army to conclude that the princes were organizing the people in preparation for an uprising.

From the standpoint of the Burmese establishment, the sullen antagonism of the Shan and the profusion of weapons and firearms in Shan State were indeed alarming. It is important to note that the owning and bearing of arms is a tradition in the Shan State with which the British never interfered as they were rarely used by natives to settle disputes or quarrels. This differs from Burma Proper, where the carrying of arms was banned. For the Burmese however, an armed and hostile population posed a grave threat. Consequently, the disarming of the Shan population became imperative. The military therefore dispatched its first columns in 1956 into the countryside to disarm the populace whom they saw as potential rebels, and to seek out hidden arms caches, disrupt the alleged preparations by the princes for an uprising, and strike terror in the hearts of the Shan so that they would not even dare think seditious thoughts. In the process, village leaders, an important political segment of any rural society, were alienated since hundreds of them were taken away for questioning, and were beaten and tortured. Many died under torture, and quite a number were maimed and some were mentally scarred for life.

The military's reign of terror put the Shan government at Taunggyi, MPs, civil servants, political parties, and the *chaofa*, in a most awkward position since nothing could be done to curb the army's excesses as matters pertaining to the defence were the jurisdiction of the Union government. Many Shan MPs, ministers and civil officers who tried to redress the situation — by quietly approaching Union Ministers or local army commanders — were not only rebuffed, but accused of slandering the army in repeating harmful and seditious gossip, creating disunity, dancing to be the tune of American war-mongers and British neo-colonialists, and even of plotting rebellion. Naturally, this effectively silenced what one would call the responsible and moderate sector of Shan society.

Consequently, the leaderless and desperately unhappy people turned more and more to those who preached armed rebellion — namely, all manner of hot-headed patriots, self-styled messiahs, even recuiters for ex-KMT warlords. Given the situation then, armed uprising did indeed seem the only alternative.

Despite all the fiery talk of armed resistance however, there was actually very little preparation for such a serious undertaking. In fact, no one had any idea on how to organize a unified armed movement, or worried too much about the finance for or the costs of fighting a war. The general attitude was that the Free World, the United Nations, the Americans and the British would not look on passively since the Shan cause was just, and the Burmese were grossly oppressive.

Such rosy optimism was due in part to total Shan ignorance of the ways of the world, and partly stemmed from memories still fresh of arms and ammunition, rations and radios, all floating down from the skies (during World War II). In part, it was due, ironically, to Burmese propaganda accusing foreign powers of involvement in plots by the princes (the logic and implication being that there is no smoke without a fire), and to some degree due to tales drifting in from the border which were the imaginative product of a man named Saw Yanda. In May 1958, he raised the banner of revolt — a white eight-pointed star above a crossed spear and sword on a blood red background. Word soon came of brand new carbines and machineguns still in crates; of tanks, artillery pieces, even aeroplanes, all lined up at warehouses and camps on the Thai border.

Thus in 1959, bouyed with hope, and bursting with bitterness and anger, the Shan, La ("Shan-ized" Wa) and Wa warriors led by an illiterate paramilitary police (UMP) officer, Bo Mawng, and a Rangoon University student, Chao Kyaw Toon, attacked and captured the town of Tangyan in Northern Shan State. Several towns such as Muang Gao and Mang Seng, and some army outposts in Muang Loen also fell. It took the Burma Army supported by the air force and artillery almost ten days of hard fighting to drive the rebels out.

The Tangyan battle ignited the flames of rebellion, and everywhere small bands, armed with swords, spears, muskets, and a few bolt action rifles of assorted makes, sprang up. These were led by former village heads, ex-policemen, adventurers, even monks — men who had no connection with the princes or politicians; men such as Bo Kang Yoom, Bo Nga Muang, Bo Deving, Bo Paan, Pao Yung, Kan Hawk, Sai Hla Myint or Bo Farang, Bo Hso-lum, Bo Wi, Bo Hso-lae, and Bo Toon Hla. In other words, peasant leaders who did not know anything but how to fight, and how and when to run, might have swept the enemy from their homeland if the uprising had been centrally planned and enjoyed outside support — which would have been the case had the princes been involved.

We now come to the question of the inactivity of the princes at a time when it was clear that the Burmese establishment had no intention of honoring Aung San's promises at Panglong. Since they, the *chaofa*, were responsible for the linkage with Burma, was it therefore not their duty to undo this mistake?

The charge levelled against the *chaofa* by the nationalists, who had like the horsemen of the Light Brigade flung themselves into the mouths of hell, that the princes dishonoured their obligations is difficult to refute. However, it must also be remembered that long before all this, the British had in 1922 stripped them of princely power in all but name, reducing them from being semi-sovereign rulers to a class of native chiefs on a stipend. And with independence in 1948, despite their loyalty to the government during the height of the civil war, their names had been dragged by the Burmese establishment into the mud and slime. They were vulnerable to anyone with stones to throw.

The princes had long ago concluded that the division of the Shan State into principalities was no longer viable, and had given their support to the Shan government at Taunggyi which would henceforth serve as a national focus for all the Shan — the first of its kind following the end of the Tai Mao kingdom in 1604.

Therefore in 1952, the princes announced their intention to surrender whatever was left of their powers to the new Shan power centre, Taunggyi, and by 1957 they had accomplished this.[38] The 1958 "surrender of power" of which much political capital was reaped by the military (that is, the transfer ceremony taking place during the caretaker government in 1958–60) was but a formal finalization of the princes' arrangement with the Shan government.

In a way, the latter period of the 1950s was a transition period in the Shan State, a time when power was devolving from the princes to Taunggyi, and the princes were engaged in shoring up the new Shan power centre. As such, though they were still princes, with some prestige and moral authority, they had no power, and were closely watched by the MIS.

Even if the *chaofa* had had the power to act, it is doubtful if they would have plotted armed rebellion because of their British training as administrators and their conservatism. Rather than take up arms to bring about changes, they were more inclined to seek redress within the framework of the constitution.

The armed outburst at Tangyan in 1959 shocked the princes and Taunggyi as much as it did the Burma Army. However, the Shan government did not, as did the army, see the application of more force as the solution. The cause of the uprising was the heavy-handed action of the army and the Shan government's inability to help or protect them. Therefore, the Shan government and leaders reasoned, some changes were in order — namely, changes in the structure of the Union which would give the states some control over defence and bring about a more equitable balance of power between the Burmese and the non-Burmese. The important thing was to win the hearts and minds of the people, and this could be done only if Taunggyi had the power to protect them. Thus was born the movement to amend the constitution, popularly known as the federal movement since it called for the re-structuring of the Union along the lines as practised in the United States. These were equal representation in the Upper House (as in the U.S. Senate) and elevation of its power; a state legislative list like that of the United States; a different status for the Burmese State from that of a Mother State; and a genuinely federal government.

The federal movement, rather than being a plot by the *chaofa* to take the Shan State out of the Union as alleged by the Burmese establishment and Western scholars, was the handiwork of a legally constituted Shan government in co-operation with prominent individuals (such as U Kya Bu, Dr Ba Nyan, Panglong Khun Htee, Thaton Hla Pa, Loong Sang Sam, Chao Khun Sam, U Toon Ohn, U Toon Myint Lay, and U Toon Pe); politicians and MPs (including Nankham U Toon Aye, the anti-*chaofa* leader regarded widely as in league with the army); and princes (the most prominent being the Yawnghwe prince and former Union President, Chao Shwe Thaike).[39]

The federal movement (1960–62), must therefore be seen as an act within the legal and constitutional framework undertaken by the responsible and moderate elements in Shan society and politics aimed at circumventing a civil war situation and defusing the armed rebellion. It had nothing to do with alleged secession plots or the discontent of the *chaofa* over the loss of power. Moreover, it was not an ultimatum since the movement's steering committee merely pointed out the clauses in the constitution which, in effect, made the Shan State a subordinate state — rather, it was a format for further discussion, and was not in any way sinister or seditious.[40]

It is most incredible that those from the West writing about Burma should, like parrots, repeat the charges made by the coup-makers of 1962, and other Burmese, against the federal movement. It reveals in these otherwise scholarly men a distressing lack of intellectual curiousity and a sad disregard for realities. One would have expected that historians and scholars should as far as it is possible study both sides of the coin, and, if that is impossible, as in the case of Burma due to restrictions imposed by Rangoon, then they should at least be suspicious of the "facts" presented by the one side involved in the conflict.

The support that the federal movement enjoyed from all the governments, leaders, and politicians of other non-Burmese states must also be examined. Some reservations were expressed by three persons at the Taunggyi Constitutional Conference in June 1961, namely, U Aye Soe Myint, a Karen; the Kachin elder statesman, Samma Duwa Sinwa Naung; and Zahre Lyan, a Chin delegate.[41] They were three out of 226 delegates which included the Kachin, Karen and Chin teams. Even then, the three did not oppose the movement *per se* but urged caution and called for more diplomacy, no doubt prompted by their apprehension of the military.[42]

The federal movement thus cannot be criticized on ideological or political grounds but perhaps validly on practical grounds. That is, the Shan government and other non-Burmese badly timed their plea to U Nu for constitutional reforms, and in this connection, failed to take into account the qualitative changes that had taken place at the Burmese power centre. Notwithstanding the rejection of the voters in the 1960 election of the military, power no longer rested with the politicians, much less with the Clean AFPFL of U Nu. In fact, the 1960 rebuff by the voters had not only angered the military but had made it close ranks. The renewed bickering among politicians, especially within U Nu's camp, had made the civilian establishment in the army's eyes, no longer necessary or useful. It can be said that the 1960 rejection by the voters of the military made it all the more imperative for the military to act as soon as possible because U Nu would certainly, sooner or later, clamp down on the army. Hence, the army had to strike before U Nu became any stronger. The federal movement coming at a time when U Nu was not even in control of himself, therefore confused many people, and was cleverly exploited by the more chauvinistic Burmese elements. With or without the army's encouragement, the movement came to be seen as an evil conspiracy. Thus the Shan and other non-Burmese leaders unwittingly played into the hands of the military.

Certainly the non-Burmese, in particular the Shan, failed to see the military as a hidden but growing rival power at the Burmese centre, and the overwhelming victory of U Nu at the 1960 poll led them to believe that the army would accept the supremacy of the ballot over bullets, or they believed that it would be forced to do so by U Nu.[43] What the reformists did not know was that U Nu and his government, whose members were enmeshed in intrigues and quarrels, had lost the control and confidence of the military.

The Burma Army being the product of Burmese nationalism, a national sentiment revolving around racial pride and memories of the imperial glories of Burinnong. Alaungpaya and Hsinphyushin was very much enraged by the federal movement. They were desperate too, since a successful constitutional reform would undermine the army's supremacy in the non-Burmese areas, and make it subordinate to the state governments, and moreover, extinguish the army's dream of a kind of national unity or "one-ness" which the Burmese had achieved with Burmese swords and courage prior to the ascendancy of foreign imperialism. The Burmese would be on the same level as those subordinate peoples — and this certainly was unthinkable.

Hence in March, when all non-Burmese leaders were gathered in Rangoon for a seminar to discuss the federal proposal, the military struck. In the early morning of 2 March, army units were dispatched to detain all non-Burmese leaders and delegates, Union or Burmese ministers, important politicians, and seize key points in Rangoon. All those tasks were achieved without a single shot being fired except at the unguarded home of the Yawnghwe prince, Chao Shwe Thaike. There was intense firing in the dark and early hours, and the Yawnghwe prince's favourite son, Chao Mee who was then seventeen, was killed. Despite the coup-makers claim that there was resistance, no proof was offered, or claim made of firearms found or confiscated in the house.

In the Shan State, not only were the remaining princes taken into captivity but everyone who was anyone — politicians, community leaders, prominent businessmen, senior civil servants, even police officers — were detained and then imprisoned for four to six years without charge or trial. One prince, the Hsipaw Chaofa, who was at Taunggyi and who had, at one time or other, incurred the personal displeasure of some senior army officers, simply disappeared. According to eyewitnesses, he was stopped at an army checkpoint outside Taunggyi and taken away, but the army denied any knowledge of this. To this day, no one knows what became of him.

The Shan Resistance: Trials and Ordeals

The fighting in the Shan State between what one would call Shan nationalists and the Burmese power centre has now entered its twenty-fifth year with no end in sight. On the contrary, from the late 1960s, another war has been added to this Shan-Burmese conflict, namely, the struggle between two Burmese centres — Rangoon and the CPB.

Initially, the Shan uprising in 1959 was largely nothing more than an outburst of anger and bitterness by the peasants who had suffered mistreatment and atrocities at the hands of Burmese soldiers. Such being the case it appears that this uprising could have, and would have been contained by the mid or late 1960s had the federal movement not been squashed by the 1962 army coup. In other words, within a genuinely federal Union, the Shan government with its power enhanced, especially with respect to the Burma Army in the Shan State, would not have found it too difficult to wean the bulk of the rural population and the politicized elements away from the path of armed struggle — the former because they would no longer suffer atrocities, and the latter because it would have been meaningless to wage war against a real national government in the Shan State at Taunggyi, or against a Union in keeping with the spirit of Panglong and the promises of Aung San. Without these two important elements — the rural population and the politicized elements — the rebellion would have gradually petered out.

However, since the 1962 coup not only crushed the reform movement, but terrorized and removed the traditional leaders and politicians from the political scene for four to six years, a socio-political vacuum was created in the Shan State. This situation was made worse by the new regime's implementation of the Enterprise Nationalization Law in 1963, and the Socialist Economy Protection Law in 1964 (that is, demonetizing of 100 and 50 kyat notes and making illegal all private trade and businesses) which brought about a general economic collapse throughout the country. Thus an economic vacuum was added to the socio-political vacuum in the Shan State.

The inflicting of such grave damages upon the political, social, and economic infrastructure of Shan society led to its disintegration. This collapse, however, benefited neither the Burmese regime nor its number one enemy in the Shan State, the nationalists. Whatever gains there were to be reaped from the chaos were harvested by others and not the main antagonists.

Despite the post-1962 Burmese claims about its successes in the Shan State, Burmese control and presence in this area were, at best, tenuous. The regime may have been able to set up party and administrative organs (such as the branches and units of the Burmese Socialist Programme Party [BSPP], and peoples' councils at various levels), but these do not function as support-generating dynamos for the Burmese. Even in "white" areas, that is, areas under the shadow of major Burmese army garrisons, there is no feeling of loyalty, only an apathetic form of submission. How incomplete and shaky the post-1962 Burmese control was, can be seen from the fact that the army was able to get only 60 per cent of the population to vote in the 1974 constitutional referendum (as opposed to 92 per cent in Burma Proper).[44]

Another indication of Rangoon's lack of control over the Shan State was the resounding failure of its "Burmese Way to Socialism" programme and economic policies. There is today no socialism in Burma except in the sense that there is, officially speaking, no "exploitation" and private business. In reality, however, Burma's economy is kept afloat by a highly capitalistic blackmarket that involves trade with neighbouring countries based on narcotics and Burmese goods and commodities.[45] The inflow of electrical and other appliances, tools, utensils, garments and footwear, toilet articles and detergents, foodstuffs, mechanical parts, plastic products, and so forth come from Thailand, China, and India.

At the opposite end of the political spectrum, the Shan nationalists, like the Burmese centre, spent most of their energy fighting the forces of anarchy brought about by the collapse of Shan society. Consequently, despite the difficult and long struggle now in its twenty-fifth year, they are nowhere near their goal which basically is the removal of oppressive Burmese presence from Shan soil.

Their most urgent task was moulding the armed bands which had mushroomed across the length and breadth of the Shan country into a sort of politico-military instrument with which the Shan nation would expel the unwanted foreign oppressors. However, those who appreciated the need for a comparatively modern organization with proper command and control structures, division of responsibilities and labour, financial and civil administration — were in the minority. Therefore, the laying of this basic groundwork took up most of the time and energy of the politicized elements (university, high and middle school students, and intellectuals). It was in the late 1960s that the university students were able to establish a properly constituted and relatively modern resistance organization, the SSA and the SSPP. However, since the SSA/SSPP did not control the Thai-Shan border and the trade routes, this vanguard Shan resistance organization did not have the resources to bring about the unification of all Shan armies. For example, both the SUA of the alleged "drug king" Khun Sa and the SURA of Moherng by virtue of their close association with the Chinese commercial complex of Southeast Asia were superior in resources to the SSA/SSPP — a situation which ruled out the unification of Shan armies under the leadership of any of these armies.[46]

The Shan nationalists were seriously hampered in their war with the Burma Army by the fact that even before the actual first shots were fired (Battle of Tangyan in 1959), there was already entrenched on Shan soil an invisible opium and trade-oriented empire controlled by former KMT merchant-warlords and armies. These foreign elements had by then established bases which served many purposes — as listening posts (for

Taiwanese and American intelligence from which agents were sent into China); opium storage and refining centres; opium buying stations; storage and distribution points for contraband goods; and private fiefdoms of local commanders — in an area covering about one-third, or approximately 20,000 sq miles of the Shan State.[47] They were organized into two armies in Thailand, the 3rd Army headquartered at Tun Ngop, and the 5th Army with headquarters at Mae Salong in Chiangrai province. Furthermore, both armies, thanks to the Taiwanese and Americans, enjoyed a special status in Thailand as the CIF (Chinese Irregular Force), a special anti-communist force allied to the Royal Thai Army.

The Shan uprising of 1959, the 1962 army coup, and the subsequent chaos (caused by the collapse of Shan society bereft of traditional leaders), and the economic vacuum (due to the coup-makers blanket nationalization measures) in the Shan State suited the former KMT. The Shan uprising kept the Burma Army busy, and the economic collapse in the Shan State and Burma Proper resulted in a serious shortage of all manufactured products and consumer goods, thus boosting the cross-border trade controlled by the former KMT. It made tycoons of these Chinese generals and colonels, and of course, their trading partners, the network of Chinese merchants and finance-houses. Added to this good fortune arising out of Burma's woes, was the boom in heroin demand following the increased American presence in Indochina.

Given therefore the military and economic predominance of the ex-KMT merchant-warlords to whom the Shan State had become a happy fishing ground, Shan rebel leaders had two options. The first was to dislodge or impose some control over these alien and exploitative elements. The second was to submit. Many rebel bands and leaders chose the latter course since they were in no position to challenge the ex-KMT merchant-warlords, and these soon became, in effect, auxiliary units (if the band was small and unorganized) or front organizations (if the band was better organized and large) for the ex-KMT and other Chinese commercial interests. Under such an arrangement, Shah armies and bands obtained in return, limited amounts of arms and ammunition, and some funds from the former KMT for the continuance of the war against the Burmese. Thus, while Shan rebels and the Burma Army traded shots, whatever money or profit there was to be made from the socio-political and economic vacuum then prevailing flowed into the pockets of warlords and merchants in Thailand, Laos, Burma, and Hongkong. Only the university students who commanded the SSIA, and later the

MAP 4.2
Kuomintang (KMT) and Major Shan Armies in
Shan State (1965–66)

CHINA

Pangsai
Muse
Namkham
Kutkai
Kunlong
Hsenwi
Muang Mit
Nawnghu
Muang Goot
Namsan
Muang Long
LASHIO
Vieng Ngun
KYAUKME
Hsipaw
Tangyan
Muang Yai
Maymyo
Pangyang
Pangsang
Khesi
Muang Hsu
Muang Yang
Muang Sang
Muang He
Muang Nawng
Muang Ma
Muang Kan
Muang Kung
Muang Ping
KENGTUNG
Lawksawk
Laikha
Kunhing
Takaw
Loimwe
Muang Yong
LOILEM
Pa Liao
LAOS
TAUNGGYI
Namsang
Muang Pyak
Shwenyaung
Hopong
Kalaw
Yawnghwe
Muang Nai
Tachilek
Muang Hsat
Muang Ton
Maesai
Mawkmai
Muang Pan
CHIANGRAI
LOIKAW
THAILAND

Not drawn to scale

☆ Kuomintang (KMT) forces or bases

⊛ Shan State Army (SSA)

☆ Tailand National Army (TNA)

⊛ Shan National Independence Army (SNIA, formerly Noom Suk Harn)

* Note how well protected KMT bases are by the Shan Parties.

Source: Compiled from "Situtation Reports and Intelligence" data, SSA GHQ Office, 1966.

SSA/SSPP, attempted to curb the unrestricted license of the Chinese to economically exploit the Shan State. However, the SSA/SSPP did not make much headway in this direction since it was unable to unite other Shan rebels, and thus stood alone. It also had to bear the brunt of the Burma Army offensives, and in the early 1970s, there emerged a threat from another quarter — the CPB.

Politically, the CPB constituted the most serious threat to Rangoon. Prior to the decision by the Chinese Communist Party to actively aid the CPB in 1966, the latter operated exclusively in the Burmese lowland and the delta region.[48] However, when the CPB's bases in Burma were destroyed in intensive Burma Army operations, thanks to large numbers of defectors who not only provided invaluable information but co-operated with the army, it became necessary for the Chinese to rebuild the CPB.[49] The Chinese radicals proceeded to build up a Burmese communist movement around a nucleus of about a hundred or so Burmese China-based communist cadres including Thakin Ba Thein Tin, the longtime party representative in China.[50] The army was commanded by the Naw Seng, a Kachin captain of the Burma Army who mutinied in 1949 and was driven into China. Its officers were Naw Seng's veterans and Kachin and other non-Chinese officers seconded from China's People's Liberation Army, and made up largely of Kachin, Wa, La, Lahu, Lisaw, Kokang Chinese recruits and volunteers from both sides of the Kachin and Shan border with China. Soon the rank of the Burmese communist army was swelled by young Chinese from Rangoon, Mandalay, and other towns of Burma who had fled to China following the bloody anti-Chinese riots in 1967.[51]

Beginning from late 1968, the CPB began its operation from its bases in China, and by the mid-1970s, it had occupied the border town of Kiu-khok or Wanting (on the Shan-Chinese border); part of Namkhan and Muang Si-Muang Tam areas (in Hsenwi); all of Kokang except Kunlong town (for which town a two-month battle was fought in the early 1970s causing the Burma Army more than 2,000 wounded or dead); Vieng Ngun and the whole of Wa state; all Muang Loen east of the Salween up to Pangsang (which the CPB made their headquarters); in north Kengtung, the areas of Bet-Kang, Muang Bawk, Muang Ngyen, Muang Yang, and Muang Ma; in east Kengtung, the areas of Muang He-Muang Khan, Muang Yawng (the towns changed hands several times, but were retained by the Burma Army) and Pa Liao-Keng Lap — altogether more than 15,000 sq miles of the Shan State.

During the upsurge of communist military activities in Shan State, the Burma Army suffered high casualties. Clearly, there was a need to win the support of the local populace in the Shan State, and to neutralize the Shan rebels. Instead of embarking upon a radical change, such as sharing power with genuine representatives of the people or with the natural leaders, or negotiating with the politicized rebel elements who were, in view of the danger posed by the CPB, willing to explore alternative solutions,[52] the Burmese came up with a non-political, and somewhat cheaper solution. This was the *ka-kwe-ye* (KKY) Policy — the raising of local defence auxiliaries to fight the communist and other insurgents, and in return, these auxiliaries would be permitted to engage in cross-border trade with Thailand and Laos. Rebel bands were also promised this lucrative opportunity if they surrendered.

The KKY programme of the Burma Army hurt the politicized rebel elements, greed being much stronger than patriotism, and many units of the SSA defected. However, a much greater damage was caused to humanity as a whole as KKY units,[53] in time, became auxiliaries for the complex of Chinese merchants, finance-houses, and warlords who controlled the trade of several countries and had access to the international narcotics markets and other facilities. The KKY forces bought opium from the growers for the Chinese shareholders and narcotics network, and escorted the merchandise to the border. The smaller units did this by mule caravans, while the larger ones by truck convoys either to Tachilek on the Thai border, or to Muang Nai. Once the consignments reached the border, the KKY rank and file had only to enjoy themselves and prepare for the return trip since this end of the operation lay with the Thai or Laotian part of the Chinese network. On the return journey, the KKY units would transport consumer goods and other products back to depots in Kengtung, Muang Nai, Taunggyi, Tangyan, and Lashio. A KKY unit would make on the average two trips a year for which it would earn from 10 per cent (in the case of small and medium bands) to 50 per cent (in the case of the Kokang KKY of Lo Hsin Han, and Loimaw KKY), of the value on opium and contraband handled.[54]

As can be seen, the impetus given to the international heroin trade by the Burma Army's KKY programme between 1963 and 1973, is incalculable as is the human misery stemming from this trade. Opponents of Rangoon claim that such trade and the transportation of opium in bulk (by eighty-mule pack or four to six-truck convoy) just could not be carried out without the knowledge of the Burma Army. Burma is not a "free" country, and particularly in the Shan State, there are checkpoints at the entry and exit points of every town. How then, could thousands of kilograms of raw and refined opium be transported or stored in Lashio and Tangyan and elsewhere under the shadows of Burmese garrisons without the knowledge and consent of the Burma Army?

The decision by Rangoon to scrap the KKY programme in 1973 may have stopped the open dealings in opium by the government's own auxiliaries, but it is figuratively nothing less than the act of a murderer throwing away the gun after killing someone.

More apalling and incomprehensible is the American advocacy of chemical spraying from the air in the Shan State, a notion which Rangoon has so far resisted. This would have effectively amounted to condemning the Shan people to slow poisoning and the destruction of the ecological environment of the Shan country.[55] It would appear a drastic and cruel measure especially in view of the fact that no serious and in-depth field study of the socio-economic factors and issues underlying the problem of opium cultivation has been carried out by any "internationally accredited" researchers. Surely, the Shan people deserve some hearing before being subjected to chemical warfare operations by the most powerful nation in the world?

While the resurgence of the CPB and its military successes in the Shan State caused the Burma Army to embark on a course which launched an "opium and heroin boom" between 1968 and 1973, the politicized element within the Shan resistance (SSA/SSPP) found itself in an awkward position with regard to the CPB.[56] Its aim certainly did not appear friendly. Its ideology differed but also its aim in the Shan State was clear, that is, turning the Shan country into a battlefield and using local manpower as cannon fodder. Besides, the CPB did not possess any clear policy on the structure of the country in the event of its victory. On a political and ideological level, the CPB was an enemy. However, on a pragmatic level, it was Rangoon's enemy and was fighting and hurting the Burma Army very badly, thanks to Chinese aid. It even offered the SSA/SSPP "free" gifts of arms.

The question of what to make of the CPB sowed doubts and confusion especially among the middle and lower levels of the SSA/SSPP. Not only were the CPB's battle performance and weapons admirable, but communist successes in the Indochina war and the growing communist movement in Thailand at one time, favoured the CPB's argument that communism was the wave of the future before which all opponents would

MAP 4.3
Communist Party of Burma (CPB) in Shan State (1971–73)

☆   CPB forward areas

✪   Shan State Army (SSA)

▨   CPB liberated areas

Source: Compiled from "Situtation Reports and Intelligence" data, SSA GHQ Office, 1973.

fall like so many dominoes (which reveals that not only the West, but the communists too subscribe to the domino theory). Given such a favourable international climate it was not difficult for the CPB to undermine the non-communist leadership of the SSA/SSPP.

Despite such a bleak overall picture, the SSA/SSPP leadership refused (until 1974) all CPB's overtures or offers of gifts of arms "without any strings attached". Since Rangoon was no help in stemming the communist tide due to the Burma Army's practice of forcibly taking villagers into coolie service which further alienated the populace, the SSA/SSPP leadership concentrated on setting up a non-communist united front of all non-Burmese (Karen, Kachin, Karenni and Mon) resistance. It was hoped that this front would also politically isolate the CPB, and in time develop into a "third force" in the politics of Burma.

At the same time, the SSA/SSP endeavoured to build Shan unity, one of many such attempts. However, as in the past, unity proved as elusive as the mythical pot of gold at the end of the rainbow. SURA set up in 1959 by the breakaway SSA chief-of-staff, Moherng rejected the overtures on the ironic grounds that the SSA/SSPP was contaminated by the CPB. However, the real reason was that the SURA's support elements — the profit-orientated complex of apolitical Chinese merchant-warlords and finance-houses — did not like the idea since a united Shan entity would spell the end of the freedom from taxation and regulations they had hitherto enjoyed.

At this point it would be pertinent to turn briefly to the SSA and its role in the struggle for the realization of Shan aspirations. With the reader's indulgence I will present some of my own personal observations.

My tenure (1969–72), as commander of the 1st Military Region of the SSA was eventful. This was the time when the Burmese unleashed their newly formed 77th, 88th, and 99th Divisions in the Shan State — troops flushed with victory over the communists in the Burmese lowland. Moreover, the SSA was fighting almost alone since the other major Shan army (SURA) was occupied with consolidating its position on the Thai border with the help of the Chinese merchant-warlord army of General Li (and the ex-KMT 3rd Army). This meant that there were few clashes there with the Burmese since these two groups were interested only in making money and carrying on a trade which did not pose any political or military threat to the Burmese presence. The creation of the KKY units by the Burmese — which were permitted to engage in opium-contraband trade — freed more Burmese units for sweeps against the SSA, and the CPB.

Despite constant military pressures and the isolation of the SSA, I was nevertheless able to firm up the army and upgrade its performance — through organizational reforms and closer co-ordination of subordinate organs, such as military units, administrative (civil) network, and political teams. Most effective was the mobilization of local youths (aged 16–40) of both sexes in resistance work. They were organized into youth associations (one in each "village circle"), and given more voice in local and village affairs through self-help associations, parents-teachers associations, village government, religious committees, and the village militia. The participation of the youths greatly facilitated not only our war efforts, but improved the life of the people since it enabled us to set up a network of primary and night schools, basic health care, and to improve roads, bridges, wells, sanitation, and personal security in the region.

The awakening and participation of local people in resistance work in turn helped me to curb latent dictatorial tendencies within the army which were particularly serious in the accusations of spying for the enemy. Deserters seldom received fair hearings, but were summarily executed by local units. Needless to say, many of those accused were but victims of local spite and jealousy. I feel that my happiest achievement while commanding the 1st Military Region, was the passage of a general order stipulating that even if a person were guilty of treason, robbery, and desertion, that person shall be pardoned if guarantees of good conduct are forthcoming from kin or village elders. This put a stop to summary execution within SSA areas, at least until 1977 when I left the nationalist movement.

The day-to-day performance of the SSA was further enhanced as a result of the setting up of a leadership school in 1969 to which all NCOs and officers (below the rank of major) were required to attend. Participants were taught basic geography and history, basic government, the fundamentals of military organization and operations, intelligence gathering and reporting, political systems and theories, and a smattering of international politics. For administrative (civil) officers, a security and administrative council was set up which not only supervised the work of administrative units and personnel, but gave periodic courses in politics, governments, and leadership.

As a result, the SSA gained the reputation of being a well co-ordinated, disciplined, and dedicated outfit. Internally however, things were not as it seemed due to squabbling among leaders — more pronounced among the Shan somehow — which was made worse by subversive activities of the CPB to undermine non-communist Shan leaders and unity.

Another large Shan army, the SUA (Shan United Army, formerly the Loimaw KKY, pre-1970) was politically paralyzed as its leader, Khun Sa,

Shan State Army (SSA): leaders and officers at Muang Tung Camp, Northern Shan State, 1970. Back row (left to right): Sai Pan (Colonel Boontai) SSA GHQ Office, died 1983; Sai Nyan Win (Major Seng Han), co-ordinator, civil administration department, SSA 1st Military Region, died 1983; Sai Nyunt (Lt.-Colonel Muang Kon) deputy director, intelligence department, SSA 1st Military Region, died 1973; Sai Myint Aung (Colonel Ongbong) SSA GHQ Office, died 1978; Bo Ngaa-muang, director, military department, SSA 1st Military Region, retired in 1976; and myself, commander 1st Military Region, retired 1976. Front row (left to right): Bo Hso-gyam, sub-district officer, 1st Military Region, died 1972; Sai Tun Hlaing (Major Oum Muang), chief co-ordinator, civil administration department, 1st Military Region, retired 1976; 2nd-Lt. Chao Zoi, special aide, civil administration department, retired 1976; Sai Kyaw Myint (2nd-Lt. Kwan Muang), special aide, civil administration department, 1st Military Region, currently with TRA; Captain Sai Naw Muang, chief radio officer, 1st Military Region, currently with the SSA faction allied to the CPB.

was still in jail in Mandalay. (He rejoined the SUA as president only in 1976.) It co-operated with the SSA/SSPP in some areas, such as during the operation to disrupt the opium-heroin business of the Burmese-sponsored Kokang KKY force (under Lo Hsin Han) and others.

However, at one juncture, it seemed that the SSA/SSPP would succeed in setting up an umbrella organization when Lo Hsin Han's Kokang KKY and other auxiliaries faced disbandment by the Burma Army in 1973 due

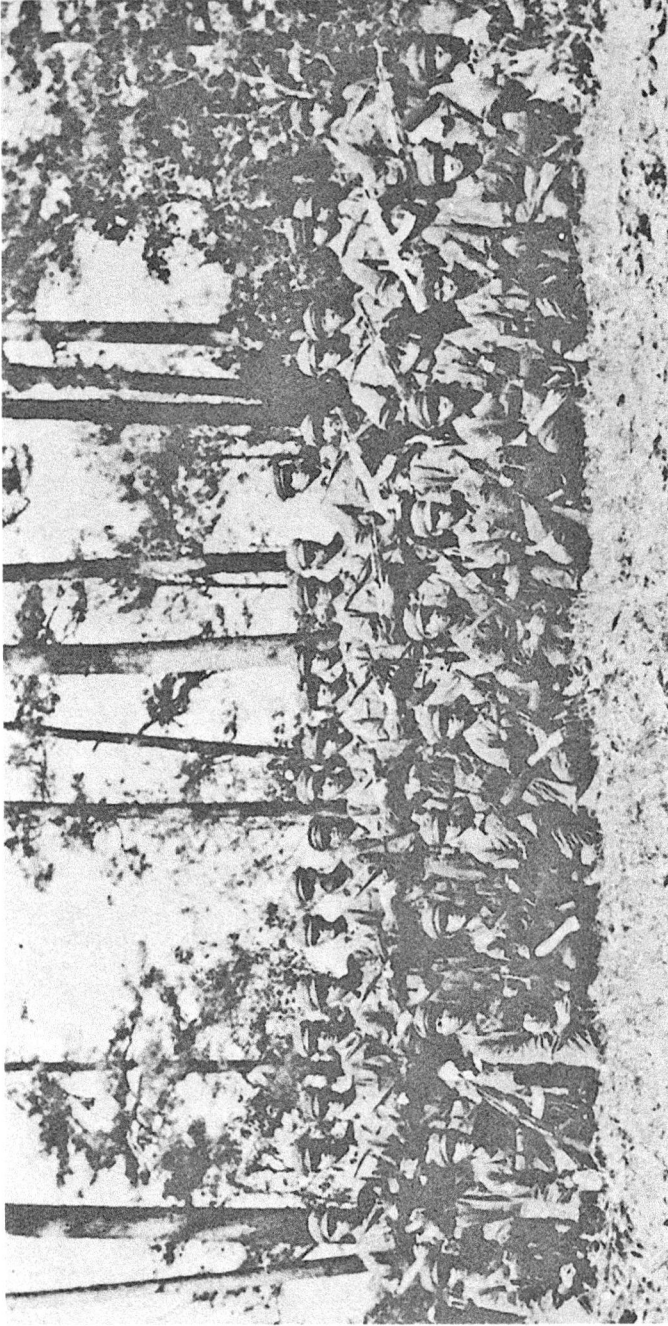

Shan State Army (SSA) troops with weapons and uniforms supplied by the CPB in 1974.

Shan State Army (SSA) troops attending a briefing before an operation (c. 1974). Addressing the troop is Colonel Zam Muang, SSA chief-of-operations.

to unfavourable international publicity and furore over Burmese narcotics — a clever political move since it overnight established Rangoon as a front-runner in the war against narcotics. Lo Hsin Han approached the SSA/SSPP and agreed to fully back the plan for unity and to co-operate in the eradication of opium in the Shan State, putting his signature to one of the several SSA/SSPP proposals to the international community for ending the opium problem.[57]

But before plans for unity could be implemented, Lo Hsin Han arrived at Muang Mai, the SSA southern headquarters, was enticed into a Thai helicopter and whisked to captivity, and then sent to Rangoon via Chiangmai and Bangkok. It was a well-planned operation involving Americans, Thai, and Burmese authorities. Rangoon benefited most since it got Lo Hsin Han before he was able to reveal too much about the intricacies of the Burmese-sponsored "heroin and opium boom" of 1968–73. Presumably, Thai and American officials benefited too, perhaps in larger budget allocations. Yet the opium and heroin trade continued to flourish as never before without Lo Hsin Han — naturally, since he was the "king" and linchpin of the world's narcotics industry only in the minds of those who thus crowned him.

Politically, the "Lo Hsin Han affair" dealt the non-communist leaders of the SSA and SSPP a severe setback from which they never recovered. They could offer no defence against communist-inspired attacks accusing the West and the United States in particular of perfidy and travesty of justice.[58] Hence after 1973, the faction within the SSA/SSPP which advocated military co-operation with the CPB gained increasing influence, resulting subsequently in the SSA/SSPP's acceptance of arms of some 200 assorted pieces from the CPB in 1974.

By then, the SSA/SSPP had split into two factions although a formal break would not come about until 1976. The southern faction which was still under the firm control of the non-communist leaders tried to counteract the CPB's growing influence and expansion into the areas west of the Salween (with the help of the SSA northern faction) by attempting to establish closer relations with the KIA which was facing a similar problem in the Kachin State *vis-a-vis* the CPB. At the same time, they attempted to get the United Nationalities Democratic Front (UNDF) composed of the Karen, Karenni, Mon, Arakanese, and the SSA/SSPP to send a joint force into the Shan State to reinforce the position of the southern SSA/SSPP.[59] However, the KIA president, General Zau Seng, his brother and chief-of-staff, the chief-of-operations (another brother), and the general-secretary of the KIO (Karen Independence Organization, the political arm of the KIA), all lost their lives in 1975.[60]

With regard to the question of establishing a UNDF military presence in the Shan State proposed by the non-communist leaders of the SSA/SSPP, this too did not materialize as the KNU were wary of becoming involved in Shan politics, and regarded the CPB as a remote secondary threat. To cut a complex story short, the political vanguard of the Shan resistance, the SSA/SSPP, collapsed from external pressures, and internal dissensions in mid-1976.

The Restoration of Peace and Stability in Burma and the Shan State

Though the collapse of the SSA/SSPP, the political vanguard of the Shan resistance, spelled the end of a force which gave the uprising strong political overtone, the war is far from over and could drag on for years, given Rangoon's insistence on the military defeat of the rebel armies in the Shan State and elsewhere.

With due respect to the determination of Rangoon and the courage and fighting skill of the much vaunted Burma Army, it still appears that the defeat of the rebel armies — the CPB in the Kachin and Shan States, the KIA, the SUA,[61] the Thailand Revolutionary Army (TRA);[62] the Karenni Army, the Kawthoolei Armed Force (Karen), the Mon Army, to name but the major ones — numbering between 35,000 to 40,000 battle-hardened jungle fighters, is quite far-fetched.

Perhaps with massive influx of military assistance from outside, and many millions of US dollars, Rangoon could destroy at least the non-communist rebels since these do not enjoy any outside support. However, the collapse of these non-communist rebels would most likely not benefit Rangoon in any way as can be seen from the fact that rather than surrender, the SSA/SSPP numbering about 4,000 switched loyalty to the CPB upon the crumbling of the non-communist leadership. It is quite obvious that the only winner within such a scenario would be the CPB, besides which it would be impossible to determine what might happen, or what China's reaction would be, if and when the CPB gained control of these non-communist rebel armies and the rural population of the non-Burmese homelands.

If Rangoon's aim is to impose its control over the Kachin, Shan and Karen, and their respective homelands, it is most obvious that a different approach is needed. The twenty to thirty years of ceaseless fighting has not improved Rangoon's position in any way on the question of its control over these peripheral areas, and has gravely damaged the country. Even though Burma, in terms of natural and other resources ranks way above Thailand, the country's per capita income of US$90, is way below Vietnam (US$160), slightly lower than Ethiopia (US$91) and equals Cambodia (under Heng Samrin) and Mali. Those countries below Burma are Laos and Bangladesh (US$35), Upper Volta (US$75), Chad (US$73), and Bhutan (US$70). Surprisingly Nepal enjoys a higher per capita income than Burma, at US$104. The members of ASEAN (Association of Southeast Asian Nations) all have a higher standard of living than Burma, namely, Indonesia (US$289), Thailand (US$379), Philippines (US$412), Malaysia (US$716), and Singapore (US$2,292).[63] The low per capita income of Burma makes it one of the ten poorest countries of the world despite its abundance in natural wealth, and speaks volumes against those in power — a point which has not been, oddly enough, commented upon by various experts and analysts writing about Burma.

In terms of benefits gained however, it can somewhat be discerned that the war in Burma has benefited the military top brass (and counterparts in the ruling BSPP) and immediate circles in terms of personal comforts and opportunities. The armed forces, have benefited though marginally, by way of receiving the largest slice of the national budget. However, on closer examination, one finds that even this marginal gain is of doubtful value because whatever arms or military hardware the armed forces have been able to obtain, these — rifles, mortars, artillery pieces, shells, vehicles, aircraft, and others — are not standardized,[64] stemming from Rangoon's dread of dependency on any source or supplier. Consequently, Burma's armed force compares very unfavourably with the Thai or Malaysian army, and it most certainly would not perform at all well in a real war situation. Hence, it can be said that the protracted fighting in Burma has in actuality greatly reduced both the defensive and offensive capabilities of the national armed forces.

Economically, the war has not only bled the country dry and wasted its abundant natural resources, but has caused Burma to be kept afloat by blackmarket activities controlled by alien (mainly Chinese merchants and financiers). Unlike colonial wars waged by European powers in the eighteenth and nineteenth centuries, Rangoon's war against its non-Burmese minorities has neither generated any economic or trade advantages nor improved in any way the quality of life of the Burmese or Burman themselves in their homeland.[65]

What we have in Burma is the case of a potentially rich country wasting its time and energy in a senseless war. The Shan, Kachin, Karen and others are not fighting to seize power at the centre from the Burmese, or to oppose *in toto*, the control of the Burmese centre over the country as a whole. What they are fighting for is the degree of autonomy within their own homelands. This is the crux of the conflict.

I have for some length of time been involved in a rebel army and believe that bringing about a political defeat of ethnic rebellions is not as difficult or as wasteful as trying to inflict a military defeat. To clarify, these ethnic rebel organizations being guerilla armies, are dependent on the "grassroot factor" for their existence and operations. Without the support of the local populace, guerillas are helpless. For example, as an officer responsible for, among others, the upkeep of law and order, I had to pacify rural bandit gangs which were naturally poorly armed and unsophisticated. In places where we had not as yet won the trust and confidence of the local peasants, there was nothing we could do except run around in circles though we were comparatively better armed, better trained, and moreover equipped with wireless sets.

It seems that Burmese leaders in Rangoon and the political élites of Burma are either unaware of the political vulnerability of ethnic rebels, or are deadly fearful of politicizing the war — that is, refusing to consider and recognize the political nature of the conflict, preferring to treat the various ethnic rebellions as nothing more than common banditry.

Therefore, given Rangoon's unwillingness to politically attack the Kachin, Shan, Karen rebels, these rebels will continue enjoying the support of their kinsmen, and the politics of violence will continue, further weakening national cohesion, and in the final analysis, creating a political vacuum. There is already a political vacuum is Burma, and this certainly does invite, at the very least, foreign meddling, and further disunity and instability in Burma.

There is little basis for optimism about the future because in so far as Rangoon is concerned, it will probably continue to treat ethnic rebellions as common banditry and will continue trying to wipe them out militarily as it has been doing all these years since 1949. And the ethnic rebels, enjoying some degree of legitimacy among their groups, and more significantly, occupying Burma's border areas with India, China,

Laos, and Thailand, will as a matter of course find it not too difficult to fight on regardless of whatever military weight Rangoon is able to throw against them.

This tragedy can be traced to the very strong distrust on the part of the Burmese élite of the Shan and other non-Burmese tinged with a large measure of belief in past Burmese imperial glories, and a condescending paternalism adopted from the British. Hence, the Burmese elite and policy-makers have not been able to perceive of the non-Burmese as anything other than conquered peoples, or, at best, ignorant and irresponsible natives. As such, one could interpret Burmese efforts at nation-building, especially after the 1962 coup, as campaigns of conquest and subjugation characterized by the destruction of the native leadership structure and their political cohesion.

Consequently, what we have in the non-Burmese homelands are forcibly imposed control structures totally alien and unresponsive to the aspirations and needs of the local populace, and a complete breakdown subsequently in communication between the rulers and the ruled — a situation that only encourages trends favourable to rebel armies or foreign agents. Clearly, within such a political vacuum and climate of alienation, the creation of a sense of nationhood is well nigh impossible, and whatever degree of control Rangoon is able to impose will be dictated solely by the degree of military presence and efforts the Burmese centre is able to apply in these non-Burmese homelands. Therefore, even given the massive superiority of the Burmese military in the event that Rangoon is able to obtain generous military aid from, say, the West (stemming from Rangoon's linkage of rebel armies to the outflow of opium and the international trade in heroin, for example), Rangoon's control over the Shan State and other non-Burmese homelands will still be as uncertain now as it has been in the past since such rule or control is not based on the consent of the ruled.

It seems that Rangoon has lost sight of its goals, and the war like Frankenstein's monster has acquired a will and logic of its own, blinding Burmese leaders and policy-makers to any other consideration except fighting and winning a military victory at all cost.

In view of the fact that the three decades of fighting in Burma has not to any perceivable extent strengthened the control of the Burmese centre over the non-Burmese entities, and considering the depth of poverty to which the country has sunk it certainly is time for Rangoon in particular, and rebel leaders in general, to do some very serious thinking.

MAP 4.4
Communist Party of Burma (White Flag Faction) in Shan State (1982–83)

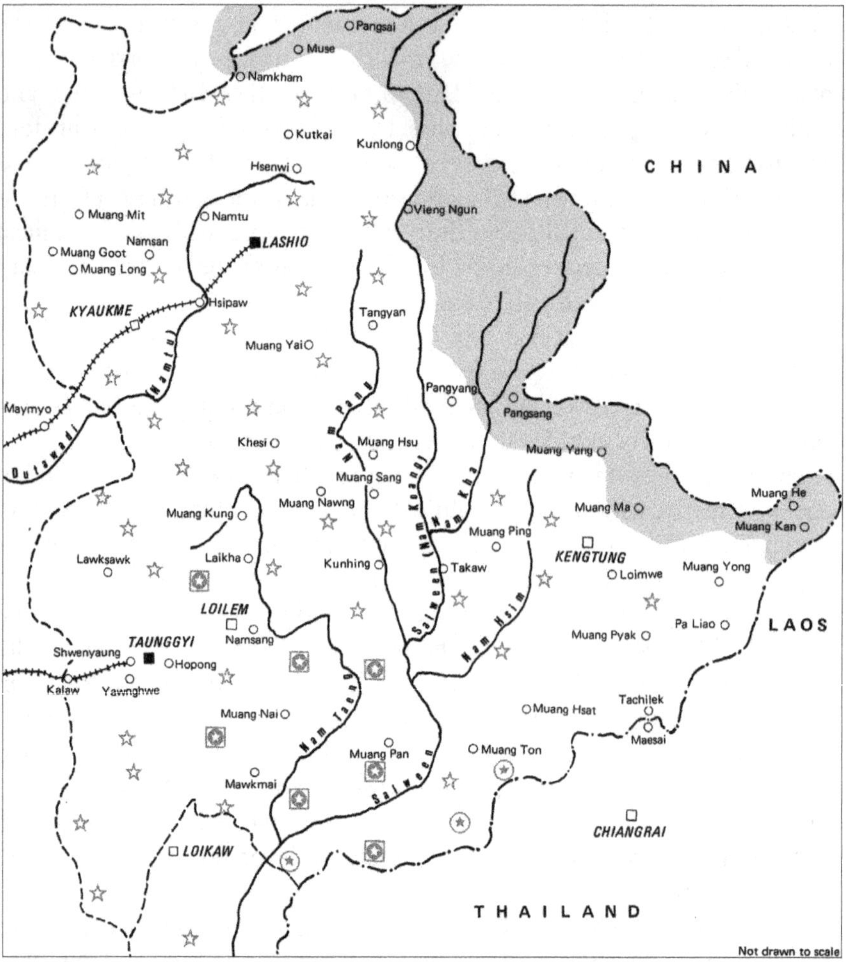

CPB's liberated area (which has contracted)

☆ CPB forces and forward areas

Tailand Revolutionary Army (TRA -- merger of SURA and an SSA faction)

Shan United Army (SUA) of Khun Sa

Source: Compiled from Intelligence data obtained from Shan State Army (SSA), Shan United Army (SUA) and Shan United Revolutionary Army (SURA), 1983.

In reality, military victory is not only elusive, but even impossible perhaps, given the gap between the non-Burmese and the Burmese military and other Burmese instruments of control in the non-Burmese areas. A military victory will not bring about any kind of nationhood, or lasting peace and stability. Uprisings will end and rebel armies disappear if and only if Rangoon accepts objective realities and gets down to the real business of providing the peoples of Burma, both the Burmese and the non-Burmese, with the kind of leadership which the country badly needs in the spirit that was displayed before independence was gained.

In the absence of such leadership, it seems likely that the protracted war will continue because of the failure of Rangoon or the Burmese power establishment to provide them with peaceful and constructive ways to preserve their historical identity, culture, language, traditions, and way of life.

The crucial question to ponder is what will happen after the Burmese leader, General Ne Win, now in his seventies, leaves the scene? Will the Burmese-dominated central authority be able to contain the CPB to a mere military presence without national political significance in the Shan and Kachin homelands?

In all probability, and ruling out a sudden warm cordiality in the now cool Beijing-Rangoon relationship, the ethnic rebels, particularly the Shan and Kachin (whose combined homelands cover almost 99,000 sq miles)[66] will be increasingly influenced and eventually absorbed by the CPB (and therefore China), to pose for Rangoon a serious political and military danger. At such a time, Rangoon would find it very difficult to gain even a political victory as the political demand of the armed opposition would then be quite different. Instead of demanding autonomy it would demand the control of the centre itself, in keeping with the aims of the CPB. In short it would be altogether a new ball game.

For the sake of argument, even if the Beijing-Rangoon relationship becomes markedly warmer (excluding therefore the scenario stated), the situation facing Rangoon would not be very comfortable unless there developed a more comradely relationship between China and the Soviet Union (and by inference, Vietnam). Even then, a Soviet-Chinese *rapprochement* would certainly make the United States and some of Burma's neighbours most decidedly uneasy — all of which starkly underline the pitfalls facing the small nations of Southeast Asia, particularly Burma.

The time has come for Burma's leaders, both in Rangoon and in jungle headquarters to re-think seriously and practically their ambitions, and prejudices. For much too long, the people of the Union of Burma have been entrapped in a politics of violence. All efforts must be undertaken to break the vicious cycle which has made the Burman (or Burmese), Shan, Mon, Karen, Karenni, Kachin, Chin, and Arakanese, pitiable victims of war and violence.

Notes

1. Regarding nationalist feelings among the non-Burmese ethnic groups, Western scholars seem to subscribe to two conflicting theories: (1) that it was encouraged by the British to counter Burmese nationalism, a classic divide-and-rule ploy, and (2) that it was a by-product of Burmese nationalism, encouraged by Burmese nationalists. All ignore the impact of World War II on the consciousness of the non-Burmese. Indeed, nationalism in the Shan State owes much to Dr Ba Nyan of Hsipaw who organized a youth movement where members were taught Japanese, Shan, and Burmese, and Japanese marching songs were translated into Shan. Members also did military drills, marched, and shouted slogans.
2. This is cited in a speech by U Kya Bu, a signatory of the 1947 Panglong Agreement regarded in the Shan State as a senior statesman, and was prominent in the constitutional reform movement. See the *Records of Constitutional Reform Conference* at Taunggyi (1961), pp. 47–53.
3. See, *Resolutions of the Steering Committee (Shan State) for Constitutional Reform* (1961), p. 5 [in Burmese].
4. The Karenni stayed out of the discussions as they had a different status as a sovereign entity under British protection.
5. Maung Maung Pye (1951), pp. 103–10.
6. This was narrated by the Mahadevi of Yawnghwe, and was common knowledge to all involved in the politics of the period. The Yawnghwe prince was frequently branded as unpatriotic by Burmese politicians and the military for sending this cable.
7. Taylor (1983), p. 32.
8. Cady (1958), p. 546. See also the *Records of the Constitutional Reform Conference* (1961), speech by U Kya Bu, p. 47–53, and *Resolutions of the Steering Committee for Constitutional Reform* (1961), p. 36.
9. A feeling widespread even among the Burmese. In fact, the Burmese owe the British a great debt of gratitude for the way things shaped in their favour.
10. This was a face-saving gesture provided by the London Agreement of 1947. For an account of the report by FACE see Cady (1958), pp. 547–51. It is

a most curious document, since having recorded Karen objections to the merger of the Salween District with Burma Proper, it recommended just that. The Chin were similarly confused, but finally opted for either remaining within the Commonwealth or a statehood within the Union. The view of the Karenni who were against even statehood were recorded. In short, it was a rubber-stamp providing Britain with an opportunity to abdicate all responsibilities with respect to the Frontier Areas.

11. I am unable to say more about this body since I have no access to those involved, and because its key organizers — Chao Sam Toon (Muang Pawn prince), Chao Khun Kyi (Sa-Tuung prince), and Chao Shwe Thaike (Yawnghwe prince) — have long since died.

12. *Records of the Constitutional Reform Conference* (1961), pp. 37–39.

13. *Resolutions of the Steering Committee (Shan State) for Constitutional Reform* (1961), p. 15.

14. The review of the Union constitution began in June, and was completed in September 1947. However, work was interrupted by the assasination of Aung San and his interim cabinet on 19 July. This, and the ferment among the communists and the PVO (who obeyed only Aung San), must have quite distracted members of the constituent assembly.

15. For a comprehensive account of the early civil-war, see *Burma and the Insurrections* (1949).

16. Thakin Soe and the Red Flag have gone underground since 1947. They viewed independence as a transfer of power by imperialists to their lackeys, the AFPFL. To a certain degree, the White Flag of Thakin Than Tun shared this outlook. Than Tun served as the first general-secretary of AFPFL, but was expelled in 1946 for communist agitation (more likely, to dispel British fears). For a comprehensive account of the White Flag, see Yebaw Mya et al. (1970).

    The PVO is an auxiliary force raised by Aung San from the more unruly elements of earlier armed forces such as the Burma Independence Army, Burma Defence Army, Burma National Army, and Burmese Patriotic Forces in preparation for an armed uprising if Britain refused to meet the AFPFL's demand for independence. In the Burma Rifles Mutiny, a communist officer, Bo Zeya, one of the Thirty Comrades, played an important role in getting Burmese units to mutiny and make common cause with the White Flag. The rebellion in Arakan involved some Arakanese nationalist-cum-Red Flag communist activities until the early 1970s, ending with the surrender of a certain Kyaw Zan Shwee. The KIA also attempted in the same period to establish a non-communist Arakanese nationalist movement but failed. Presently there are a few hundred Arakanese serving with the KNU (Karen, under Bo Mya) organized as the Arakan Liberation Organization (ALO), which is a member of the National Democratic Front.

17. The Pa-O rebellion in Shan State was initially in support of the Karen
(KNDO), but by the early 1950s it became a movement against the Shan
princes which made it a natural ally of the Burma Army. Shan nationalists
see the Pa-O as being hand in glove with the Burmese military. Conversely,
the military frequently accused the princes of being in league with Pa-O
rebels. However in 1958 the Pa-O leader Thaton Hla Pe surrendered under the "Arms for Democracy" programme, and was active in the federal
movement. In 1975 part of the movement joined the CPB. The Pa-O movement then lost its political momentum. It is alleged by the pro-communist
faction that the non-communist White Pa-O are in league with Rangoon's
appointed Head of Shan State, Tun Yin Law, a Pa-O and former Burma
Army major.

18. The KMT in Shan State contacted various *chaofa* individually using inter-
mediates such as Olive Yang of the Kokang ruling house and members of
the ruling houses of Yunnan Shan states. However, as the KMT's plan for
re-conquest of China was too elevated for the individual *chaofa* to grasp,
nothing resulted from these contacts.

19. It was perhaps in 1961 that I smuggled an SSIA leader, Sai Kyaw Sein,
into Rangoon. When one day, I approached the Hsipaw prince, Chao Kya
Seng, and suggested a meeting with the SSIA representative, the prince
handed me a copy of the Union constitution and said: "Please read the
oath we have sworn as MPs." Ironically, the Burmese military disliked
him intensely and suspected him of being disloyal. On the day of the coup
(2 March 1962), he was stopped at a check-point outside Taunggyi and
that was the last anyone heard about him.

20. The levies were raised at the suggestion of U Nu according to the Mahadevi
of Yawnghwe on the understanding that the princes were to be reimbursed
(this never materialized). What the Shan wanted was the raising of several
more Shan Rifle units to be stationed on Shan soil (under the control of
the Defence Ministry). But the Burmese did not approve of this. Even the
existing 1st Shan Rifles did not see much service in Shan State but was used
in the Shwegyin area against the Karen. One of my nephews, Shwe Thaike,
a captain in the 1st Shan Rifles was killed in battle with the Karen. The
manner of his death was related to me in 1961 by the commander of the
Karen unit involved, Brigadier Lin Tin of the 5th Kawthoolei Brigade.

21. For a detailed account of the AFPFL split see Trager (1966). Rangoon was
brimming with tales of some wives instigating their husbands to push out
certain ministers.

22. See Chapter 5.

23. See Chapter 5.

24. No one in Burma at the time believed in the "invitation" story. The tale
was that Ne Win, Aung Gyi and Tin Pe went to U Nu and demanded power

be transferred to the army peacefully. This seems plausible due to U Nu's anti-army platform in the 1960 election.

25. Almost all Western scholars have high opinions of the caretaker government most probably because they saw the army as "modernizers" which unfortunately was proved false by the post-1962 performance of the military.

26. Contrary to credit taken by the army for the surrender of power by Shan princes in April 1959, the fact is that it had been planned since 1952 by the princes, and the Shan government in the interest of unity and uniformity. Power was transferred not to just anyone, but to the Shan government and the Shan people.

27. These allegations may perhaps stem from the need of these scholars to explain the rejection of the military as the agent of modernization by the people. Hence, the implications forwarded that the electorate was irrational and superstitious.

28. Any work on the history of post-1948 Burma will not be complete until there is included a study of the rise of the military in Burmese politics. In fact, nothing in-depth is known about the Burmese military establishment even now though volumes have been written about its actions and activities.

29. See Chapter 5.

30. The Southeast Asia Treaty Organization (SEATO) was a brainchild of the United States to counter aggression by communist China in 1954, and is now defunct. In Burma, it was seen as an instrument of American aggression and thought to be engaged in undermining Burmese sovereignty. Being accused as a SEATO agent was then regarded as the ultimate political insult.

31. Other reasons, such as that politicians were ruining the country, were also given. It is rare that coup-makers are able to solve the problems cited for the take-over. Hence, scholars and historians should not give too much weight to words of coup-makers or join them in finger-pointing exercises.

32. For detail of the Shan, Kachin and Chin position on the proposed Union, see *Resolutions of the Steering Committee (Shan State) for Constitutional Reform* (1961), p. 10. Also *Burma Frontier Areas Commission of Enquiry* (1947).

33. See Chapter 5.

34. Composition in the Upper House was as follows: Burmese 53; Shan State 25; Kachin State 12; Chin Hill 8; Karenni State 3; and Karen 24.

35. *Area Handbook for Burma* (1971), p. 192. For details see *Kuomintang Aggression against Burma* (1953). Unofficially however, the KMT remained on Shan soil as stragglers. They organized into merchant-warlord armies — ex-KMT 3rd and 5th Armies — and traded in opium with Laos and Thailand as part of the clan network of overseas Chinese merchants and finance-houses.

36. The most prolific writer in this genre was a certain Bo Ni, reputedly an MIS officer. The hero of his stories was usually a young Burmese officer who not only saved pretty Shan lasses from the clutch of corrupt, treacherous feudal lords, but foiled dark plots to dismember the Union.

37. After the 1962 coup, Kyaw Zaw became the ambassador to Indonesia. The main criticism of anti-feudalist Shan politicians was the gambling permitted (for a fee) by the *chaofa* at certain *poy* (festivities). Visitors to the Shan State in the 1950s were amazed that at these *poy* there were no broils despite the drinking, gambling and the carrying of some kind of arms by every male.

38. See the *Records of the Shan State Council 1957–58 Session* (1958), p. 106 [in Burmese].

39. See Chapter 5.

40. See the *Resolutions of the Steering Committee (Shan State) for Constitutional Reform* (1961) [in Burmese].

41. See Chapter 5.

42. See the *Records of the Constitutional Reform Conference* (1961), pp. 53–55, 60–44, and 67–69. Regarding this point, it is baffling how a distinguished anthropologist, Lehman, arrived at the conclusion that only the Shan and Karenni supported the federal movement. He sited as proof an incident he witnessed in which Samma Duwa Sinwa Naung, a Kachin leader, left in a huff after a furious argument with the supporters of the movement at the Kayah Guest-house. Lehman could not have read the record of the Taunggyi Conference printed and distributed by the Shan government in 1961. See Lehman (1981), p. 4.

43. Among Shan princes only the Hsenwi prince, my maternal uncle, and the Namsan prince made efforts to cultivate the army's favour, even matching nieces and daughters to army officers. Consequently both escaped imprisonment in the 1962 coup. The Hsenwi prince who was at one time strongly anti-Burmese was appointed Head of the Shan State during the military caretaker government (1958–60).

44. Steinberg (1982), pp. 87–88. Percentage of voters in Kachin State, 60 per cent; Karenni, 71 per cent; and Arakan, 80 per cent.

45. The resources "exported" include jade, rubies, sapphires, tin, wolfram, antimony, rubber, teak, livestock, forest products, such as animal skins, horns, bone carvings, and elephant tusks, cultural and religious artifacts, antiques, lacquerware, woodcarvings, coins and silverware, and even cash crops such as chillies, garlic, nuts and beans, and of course, opium which constitutes a cash crop within the context of economic collapse in the Shan State.

46. The SUA evolved from the Loimaw KKY. Since the mid-1970s, its leaders, Khun Sa, has been crowned "king" of the international heroin business by

the world's anti-narcotics bureaucracies, especially American drug-busters. The SURA was set up in 1969 by Moherng, then the SSA's chief-of-staff, and enjoyed the support of the former KMT 3rd Army.

47. The former KMT bases were in Kokang and Loi Tao in Hsenwi; Vieng Ngun and the large areas down to Pangsang, east of the Salween; Muang Hsu and Muang Sang, west of the Salween; and Bet-kang, Muang Bawk, Muang Nyen, and Muang Yang (northern Kengtung); Muang Ma, Muang He-Muang Kan, Muang Yong, Pa Liao-Keng Lap (east Kengtung); Muang Pu, Muang Hsim, Muang Hsat, and Mawng Palao in west Kengtung. Significantly, all areas mentioned are opium growing areas.

48. One of the reasons for this support was that Beijing suspected Rangoon of being more inclined towards Moscow, and according to sources within the CPB, actively in league with Liu Shaoqi and Chen Yi. In the 1963 peace talks initiated by Ne Win, the Chinese apparently attempted to get the CPB incorporated into the post-1962 Burmese power structure, but was rebuffed. Following this, the Burmese who had spent ten to fifteen years in China were "re-absorbed" into Burma and began attacking local leaders as being "revisionists" and "soft" on the Ne Win regime, and called for a hardline approach. Rangoon was branded as "fascist, reactionary, and revisionist". Beijing began praising the CPB as the heroic vanguard of the revolutionary Burmese peoples. The 1967 anti-Chinese riots in Rangoon and elsewhere probably tipped the scale in the CPB's favour.

49. The purges were initiated by the Beijing-returned cadres in the style of the Chinese cultural revolution. Top leaders like Goshal, Yebaw Htay, General Yan Aung, military commanders, and veteran cadres were humiliated at mass meetings and executed. Consequently, hundred of party veterans and thousands of villagers turned against the party. The chairman, Thakin Than Tun, was killed by a bodyguard, and the men who succeeded him, Thakin Zin and Thakin Chit were also killed in action. The Chinese who helped rebuild the CPB, included Marshal Lin Biao, and presumably Jiang Qing and the "Gang of Four". As a result, when Deng Xiao Ping returned to power, the CPB which owed its favours to Deng's mortal foes, suffered an eclipse.

50. Contrary to views among Western analysts, the rebuilding of the party was not carried out by remnants who retreated to the China border from the Burmese lowland, but by cadres who were in self-imposed exile in China for ten to fifteen years. Prior to China's decision to aid the CPB, these were not even recognized as members of a fraternal party, but as "special guests".

51. How the anti-Chinese riots in Rangoon and other Burmese cities came about is murky. But local opinions were that the mobs were incited by the regime's *agent provocateurs*.

52. As general-secretary of the Shan Unity Preparatory Committee (SUPC), I made overtures for exploratory talks with Rangoon in 1968, and in 1969 as commander of SSA 1st Military Region held informal indirect talks with Colonel Chao Saw Ohn of the Burma Army, a confidant of Ne Win. Since Rangoon could not offer anything except its willingness to accept the SSA as a KKY, the talks were discontinued.

53. The KKY units ranged from very small ones such as the Pangyang and Muang Gao KKY, to medium sized ones such as Muang Nai KKY under Sai Nong, the Namtu KKY, Bo Lai Oo KKY, Vieng Ngun KKY under Mahasang and Chu Hong Chai, Loisae KKY under Wu Chung Ting, U Sein KKY, Chin Chao Wu KKY, the Kengtung KKY of Lao Yang, and so forth. The biggest and the oldest (since the early 1930s) being the Kokang KKY under the internationally known Lo Hsin Han till early 1973, and of course, his successor Khun Sa of Loimaw KKY.

54. It is difficult to give detailed and exact figures on the earnings of the KKY units doing escort and transport work for the narcotics-contraband network. However, a rough estimate can be worked out. A medium convoy of eighty mules will carry about 4,000 kg of raw opium (three to four times more if refined). Say, that border price for opium is 1,000 baht per kg, the value of consignment being 4 million baht, the KKY unit will receive 0.4 million baht. This is from opium alone. The money received on contraband carried cannot be calculated as the amount and value varies.

55. The aerial spraying proposed by the United States may involve only "harmless" herbicides. However, who can guarantee that more toxic chemicals will not be introduced later? In any case how harmless are "harmless" weed-killers especially when sprayed in large quantities, frequently, and over a long period?

56. It was indeed a "boom" since it involved hundred of millions of baht on the border alone. Further, heroin price being twenty times higher than opium, and Bangkok price being ten times the refinery price, and New York price being astronomical, the profits made would amount to many fortunes even in US dollars. According to a seizure (1964) in Germany — 32 kg heroin was worth US$20 million, or 1 kg heroin was worth US$0.6 million. Compare this to US$43.66 to US$65.50 per kg of raw opium in the Shan State (the highest price obtained by cultivators). As such, to blame this multi-million international agro-industry on Shan rebels and the ragged cultivators is like blaming Japanese workers for the troubles of the American motor industry.

57. See Lintner (1984), pp. 403–50. A further account of the SSA/SSPP relationship with Lo Hsin Han is portrayed in the film, *Opium Warlords*, made by Adrian Cowell for Anglia Television, London (1975).

58. The extradition of Lo Hsin Han by Thailand to Burma raises many points since there is no extradition treaty between the two countries. And if Lo Hsin Han was involved in heroin, he did so under the KKY programme of the Burma Army. At the time of his detention by the Thai police, he was not as yet proved guilty — in fact there were only allegations by the media.

59. The UNDF was established in early 1974. The front still exists today, but remains as it was during its early years, more a political forum.

60. See Chapter 5.

61. The strength of the SUA is estimated by several sources including Thai officers at 3,000-strong.

62. TRA set up in 1934 by Moherng comprises SURA, and the anti-communist faction of the SSA under Zam Mai. Estimated strength is at 4,000.

63. *World Almanac 1980*, pp. 513–98.

64. Small arms for the Burma Army are largely of West German origin but include those from Yugoslavia, East Germany, Czechoslovakia, United States, Britain, Italy and Israel. Artillery pieces are mainly from the United States and Yugoslavia and some are from Sweden and Eastern Europe. The air force had vintage British jet trainers and aircraft but these are now American, French and Italian. For land transport the army is dependent on private World War II trucks and for inaccessible places, coolies, bullock or elephant carts.

65. Composed of fourteen administrative divisions, that is, the broad Irrawaddy River Valley, encircled by a horse-shoe of homelands inhabited since the beginning of Burma's history by the Arakan, Chin, Kachin, Shan, Karenni, Karen, Mon, and others.

66. Shan State: 64,346 sq miles (per the Shan State government, 1957), and Kachin State: 34,379 sq miles (present Burma Government 1983), Union of Burma: 261,218 sq miles.

PART THREE

WHO'S WHO IN SHAN POLITICS

5

Historical and Political Personalities (A Personal Perspective)

Alaungpaya

King; founder of the last Burmese dynasty which was named after him — (sometimes referred to as the Konbaung or Mandalay dynasty). A Burman, he ruled from 1752 to 1760. He was also known as U Aung Zeya, the headman of Moksopo village in Shwebo, Upper Burma. He defeated the Mon in Lower Burma, killing and burning mercilessly and indiscriminately. He put an end to the Mon as a political power in Burma, and in the process destroyed their culture and civilization. Like all "unifiers" of Burma, Alaungpaya invaded Siam but died while laying siege to Ayuthia.

Aung Gyi

Brigadier; Burman or Burmese. He was sacked from the Revolutionary Council which staged the 1962 coup. Though not a member of the famed Thirty Comrades, he nonetheless played an important role in building up the pre-independence Burmese armed forces, and the Burma Army. He was particularly prominent in the military government of 1958–60, and was the architect of the army's economic muscle (Burma Defence Industries). Aung Gyi was jailed in the mid-1960s for alleged involvement in a coup attempt against Ne Win. He was released after several years in prison and is presently running a popular cafe in Rangoon.

Aung San

General (pre-independence Burmese armed force, BIA and BDA); Burmese, native of Natmauk. He was regarded as Burma's founding

father, one of the four "unifiers". He gained prominence as a student
(Rangoon University) strike leader. He formed a group whose aim was
Burma's independence and together with Thakin Thein Pe Myint, Thakin
Hla Pe, Thakin Soe and Thakin Than Tun, informally established the
Burma Communist Party (BCP, which later split into the White Flag
under Than Tun, and the Red Flag under Thakin Soe). Just before the
Japanese war, on verge of arrest by the British for subversion, he left
the country. Aung San planned to contact the Chinese KMT for aid, but
diverted to Japan and was given military training with other Thakins or
nationalists (the Thirty Comrades) by the Japanese military intelligence
on Hainan Island. During the war he served as Defence Minister in the
puppet government of Dr Ba Maw, but managed through communist
leaders to contact the Allied Forces just before Japan's defeat. He
emerged in the immediate post-war years as a major political figure
(thanks to the rapport established with Lord Louis Mountbatten, the
Allied Far East Supreme Commander). As such, Aung San managed to
out-manoeuvre the pre-war British Governor of Burma, Sir Reginald
Dorman-Smith, and to by-pass the Simla Plan for Burma which envisaged
self-government in stages within the dominion. His greatest achievement
was to obtain the agreement of leaders of the Frontier Areas (Arakan,
Kachin, Chin, Shan homelands) to co-operate with the AFPFL which
he formed, and jointly demand independence — the instrument for
this being the Panglong Agreement of 1947. In July of the same year,
while the constituent assembly was in session, Aung San and members
of Burma's interim cabinet were assassinated. Aung San's widow, Daw
Khin Gyi, was ambassador to India at one time, and prior to the 1962
coup, was active in social welfare activities, and much respected. Their
eldest son, Aung San Oo, now in his late thirties, is a long-time resident
in Britain and so is a daughter.

Aung Win

Sai; Shan, native of Loilem, Shan State, and a cousin of my wife (Nu
Nu Myint). Since 1982, a member of the Central Committee of the CPB.
In the late 1950s and early 1960s he was active in Shan student affairs
(Rangoon University), but regarded as more Marxist than nationalist.
Following the 1962 coup, he was among those who organized a series
of student protests on campus, resulting in a massacre on 7 July 1962,
and the army's demolition of the historic Students Union Building. Sai

Aung Win went into hiding, ending up in the jungle as one of Thakin Than Tun's bright young men. He witnessed the bloody purges within the CPB leadership, a mini Chinese-style "cultural revolution", initiated by radicals who returned from exile (that is, those who had been in China since mid-1950s and returned to lead to communist movement in the mid-1960s). Aung Win's next assignment was as an aide to Thakin Tin Tun (a former civil-servant) who was in charge of the CPB's northeast (that is, Shan State) committee. He was a classmate of mine and of many SSA leaders, and was sent to persuade them to make common cause with the CPB, but failed. When Thakin Tin Tun fell in a clash with the Burma Army, Sai Aung Win again met with the SSA in the late 1970s to request a safe passage to the Shan-Chinese border. Upon arrival at the CPB headquarters (then at Pangsai or Wanting, Hsenwi area), he was put in charge of the Shan language radio programme, "Voice of the People".

Aye Soe Myint

U; Karen. One of the Karen delegates at the Taunggyi Constitutional Reform Conference in 1961. He did not oppose the reform proposals, but urged extreme caution. He participated in the Karen uprising in the late 1940s, but surrendered (most probably under U Nu's "Arms for Democracy" programme) in 1958. He worked closely with the Stable AFPFL (Ba Swe-Kyaw Nyein faction, pro-military) and with the Army's psychological warfare people.

Ba Maw

Dr; politician and lawyer, a Burmese of Armenian descent; deceased. He was educated in Britain and gained political prominence in the 1930s, serving in the Governor's Executive Council (following Burma's status as a province, and subsequent separation from India) at various times. Unlike old-time Burmese politicians such as Sir Paw Tun, U Ba Pe, Sir Maung Gyi, and others, Dr Ba Maw was in touch with the younger nationalists, the Thakins such as Aung San, and U Nu who served him well as they chose him to head the government during the Japanese Occupation. He obtained by treaty from Japan, the Shan homeland (known then as the Federated Shan States), but it excluded Kengtung and Muang Pan which were ceded to Thailand. In the immediate post-war period, Dr Ba Maw was eclipsed by Aung San, and by U Nu and AFPFL politicians in independent Burma. He was a charming and worldly man, and was a good friend of my father, the Prince of Yawnghwe. Dr Ba Maw's son-in-law, Bo Yan Naing (whose wife was a senior tutor in English at Rangoon University during the my undergraduate days), was one of the Thirty Comrades, and his son, Zali Maw, fled to Thailand in the mid-1960s and started an armed movement to overthrow Ne Win. When U Nu launched a movement to depose Ne Win in the early 1970s, Bo Yan Naing and Zali Maw joined him. But the movement collapsed due to a lack of direction and failure to win the support of the non-Burmese rebel armies. In 1981, like U Nu, both of them accepted Ne Win's amnesty and returned home.

Ba Nyan

Dr (medicine); Shan, native of Hsipaw; died 1970. He was one of the earliest medical school graduates of the Shan State, and was related by marriage to the ruling family of Hsipaw. He is regarded as the father of modern Shan nationalism since he founded various youth and patriotic associations during the Japanese Occupation. In the immediate post-war years, he was one of those who advocated outright independence for the Shan State regardless of the British policy concerning Burma. In the post-1948 period, he served as chief health officer for the Shan State government at Taunggyi. He was active in promoting Shan literature, culture, arts, traditions, and inspired Shan students at Rangoon and Mandalay universities in their nationalistic activities. With the advent of the 1962 coup, he was, like many prominent Shan from all walks of life, imprisoned for five years without charge or trial. His stepson, Khun Thawda, joined the rebel Noom Suk Harn movement in 1959.

Ba Sein

Thakin; Burmese, one of the founders of the nationalist Thakin movement. Prior to World War II, he had close and clandestine contacts with the Japanese, and was responsible for sending young Burmese nationalists (that is, the Thirty Comrades) out of the country for military training with the Japanese. After World War II, he was eclipsed by Aung San, U Nu, and the AFPFL, but continued in politics as a lone rightist and pro-West figure in a leftist environment, and was as such regarded as

an American and SEATO stooge. He also had some contacts with Karen
rebels, in particular Zau Seng (a Kachin serving with the Karen till 1960
who founded the Kachin Independence Army).

Ba Swe

U; politician; Burmese, native of Tavoy, Tenasserim coast. He gained
prominence in the strike by oil-well workers of Yennangyaung, Central
Burma, in the pre-war years. One of the vice-chairpersons of the ruling
AFPFL party, holding various cabinet posts — Deputy Prime Minister,
Mines, Defence, and just before the AFPFL split (1957–58) he was
Prime Minister for a short while. Within the AFPFL he controlled the
labour union bloc and enjoyed a close relationship with the military,
in particular, Brigadier Aung Gyi. In the 1960 general election held
by the military caretaker government of Ne Win, the Stable AFPFL of
Ba Swe and Kyaw Nyein suffered a massive defeat due to its army
connection. Contrary to expectations, Ba Swe was not invited to serve
in the government after the 1962 coup.

Ba Thein Tin

Thakin; Burmese, native of Tavoy, Tenasserim coast; currently chairperson
of the CPB. A member of the pre-war Thakin movement. Following
the communist general uprising in 1949, he was sent to China as a
representative of Thakin Than Tun's White Flag faction. However, until
the anti-Chinese riots that swept through the towns of Burma in 1967
(which Beijing believed was fuelled by Burmese authorities), Thakin
Ba Thein Tin and other Burmese communists in China were neglected.
After the riots in Burma and the rise of Marshall Lin Biao and other
radicals, the Burmese communists were treated as heroic revolutionaries,
and he played a vital role in building up a communist force on the Shan
and Kachin borders with China. Following a Chinese-inspired "cultural
revolution" within the CPB, leading to the defeat of the White Flag
on the Burmese plains, and the death of chairperson Thakin Than Tun,
followed by the deaths of the new chairperson Thakin Chit, and other top
leaders such as Bo Zeya, Thakin Zin, and Bo Pu, Ba Thein Tin became
chairman of the party. He is reportedly physically very frail, requiring
round-the-clock medical attention, but is indispensable because of his
close links with the Chinese.

Ba U Gyi

Saw; Karen leader and martyr, lawyer by profession. He died in a Burma
Army raid on his hideout not long after the Karen uprising of 1949.
He was from a well-to-do family and educated in Britain. He achieved
prominence in the immediate post-war years when feelings between the
Karen and Burmese were tensed following atrocities against the Karen
by the BIA during the Japanese Occupation. The Karen, traditionally
loyal to the British (serving in government, the military, and police)
were regarded as traitors when Burmese nationalists gained power under
Japan. After the war, Saw Ba U Gyi and other Karen leaders tried to
get Britain to grant them a separate homeland within the dominion.
However, Britain, anxious to leave Burma, refused to even consider the
Karen pleas though Saw Ba U Gyi and his colleagues went to London
twice to present their case. The British Labour government was content
to leave the Karen question (as well as the fate of the Frontier Areas
— Arakan, Chin, Kachin, and Shan — and the status of Karenni whose
independence the British had recognized in 1875) to be settled by the
Burmese (Aung San and the AFPFL). Accordingly, Saw Ba U Gyi, trying
to make the best of a bad position, negotiated with Aung San, and later
with U Nu. However, given bad feelings on both sides and the anarchy
arising from Britain's departure, fighting broke out in 1949. All Karen
units, the Karen Rifles, policemen, officials, and others joined the rebels.
Had Saw Ba U Gyi lived longer, the Karen rebellion would not have
dragged on until now since the Karen would have been a politically
cohesive force and the government would probably have had negotiated
a settlement. Instead, the Karen became politically disorganized — a
military force in a political vacuum. It could even be said that without
Saw Ba U Gyi, there was no one within the Karen ranks with whom U
Nu and the AFPFL could deal.

Bagyidaw

King; Burmese; seventh monarch (1819–39) of Alaungpaya dynasty. In
his reign Burmese expansion moved westwards, into Assam, Arakan, and
Manipur. Thus the Burmese came into direct conflict with the British
in Bengal over ethnic rebels. According to the British, the Burmese
marched into Bengal in 1824, and consequently Burma lost all her
maritime provinces.

Bayinnaung, see Burinnong

Bodawpaya

King; Burmese; sixth monarch of Alaungpaya dynasty; reigned 1782–1819. Like his father Alaungpaya, the founder of the dynasty, Bodawpaya failed in his attempt to conquer Siam. He however turned west and conquered kingdoms adjacent to British India — Arakan, Manipur, and Assam (the latter two founded by the Tai). However, there was constant rebellion in the new possessions which gave rise to border incidents with British authorities whom the Burmese suspected of aiding the rebels. In the reign of Bodawpaya's grandson, Bagyidaw, the Burmese attempted an invasion of Bengal, adjoining Arakan, which led to the First Anglo-Burmese War of 1824, resulting in the loss of Burma's western possessions and all coastlines.

Brang Seng

Kachin rebel leader; native of Myitkyina, currently president of KIO (which he helped found) and its army, the KIA. He was a teacher at a Baptist missionary school in Myitkyina, before organizing the Kachin armed movement. The deaths of Zau Tan, the chief-of-operations, killed in a clash with Burmese communists in Shan State (1974); his elder brothers, Zau Seng, president and commander-in-chief, and Zau Tu, chief-of-staff, both assassinated on the Thai border (1975) and the Pungshwe Zau Seng, general-secretary assassinated in the same year, Brang Seng was elevated to the top position in the KIO.

Bu-jong Luang

Respected holy man among the Lahu in Shan-Thai border area; died of old age (believed by Lahu to be more than 100 years old) in the early 1980s; of obscure origin. He became a revered figure among the Lahu, and was first recognized in the Muang Hsat area of Kengtung in the early 1960s. Due to the mistreatment of Lahu villagers by the early Shan nationalist army (Noom Suk Harn), Bu-jong Luang managed to rally the animist Lahu who came to revere him as a "divine deliverer". There were widespread clashes between Shan rebels and the Lahu all over Kengtung state with the Burma Army abetting the Lahu. Peace was restored when an SSA column (under Khun Kya Nu) captured an important Lahu village headman in 1964, and released him together with his men, arms, and opium. In the early 1970s there was friction between the Lahu and the Burmese, resulting in Bu-jong Luang fleeing to Thailand and raising a rebellion.

Burinnong or Bayinnaung

King; Burmese; founder of the Toungoo dynasty; reigned 1551–81; regarded as one of the greatest conquerors of mainland Southeast Asia — "Conqueror of Ten Compass Points", according to the Thai. King Burinnong conquered the Shan or Tai of Ava and Muangmao (in which was included the present Shan State); the Shan or Tai states of China (Chinese Shan States, and Sipsongpanna); Chiangmai and Ayuthia (also Tai), and devastated Lanchang or Laos (a Tai/Thai kingdom); the Mon kingdom of Hanthawaddy or Pegu (founded by a Shan, Wareru, in the thirteenth century), and the Arakanese kingdom. His later achievements notwithstanding, his origin was humble and obscure. His mother was a wet-nurse to Tabinshwe-hti, son of Mingyi-nyo, the ruler of Toungoo — a small Burmese kingdom under the shadow of the Shan-dominated Ava in the north, and fenced in by the Mon of Hanthawaddy in the south. When Tabinshwe-hti became ruler of Toungoo, he and Burinnong defeated Prome (a Burmese kingdom), Hanthawaddy (Mon) and Arakan, but he was unable to storm Ayuthia. Burinnong learnt a valuable lesson from this failure — that is, it was impossible to conquer Siam without first getting the Shan princes of Upper Burma and Shan State on his side, either through conquest or other means.

Chang Chu Chuan

Chief-of-staff of SUA; Chinese, a native of Manchuria. In his youth he served in the Nationalist Army of China, and after Mao's takeover, was among the KMT that retreated into Shan State. In the late 1950s, Chang jointed Khun Sa's Loimaw KKY which the Burmese had encouraged to fight KMT stragglers, and later, Shan rebels. Chang's first claim to fame was when he led Loimaw forces in a clash over the opium trade, challenging the ex-KMT's (General Li and Tuan of the 3rd and 5th Armies) monopoly. The pitched battle occurred on the Shan-Lao-Thai border and made international headlines in 1967. Also involved was General Ouane

Rattikorn of the Laos Armed Force who called in an air-strike to clear the battlefield. Chang's latest claim to fame was at the battle of Hintek in Thailand in 1982. Chang and two dozen followers held out against superior Thai police and paramilitary forces for nine hours, slipping away at nightfall. He was also featured prominently in Adrian Cowell's documenary, *The Opium Warlord*. Though a Chinese, he regards himself as a citizen of Shan State, and is loyal to Khun Sa.

Chaung Gwa

Prince; Burmese; member of the Alaungpaya dynasty; led a resistance movement after the fall of Mandalay in late 1885. He was an able leader and the British worried that he might manage to eventually win over Shan princes who were then preparing for war under the banner of another Burmese prince, the Limbin prince. The Shan aim was to dethrone King Thibaw (whom the British deposed instead) and put their puppet on the throne. According to British thinking then, had the Chaung Gwa prince succeeded in winning over Shan princes, the British would be bogged down in an unending war which subsequently would invite French, and to a lesser degree, Chinese and Siamese involvements. This fear, or foresight, of a long untidy war complicated by foreign meddling caused the British to enter the Shan states and, by peaceful means, quickly restore order. This was achieved by persuading Shan princes to accept the protection of the Queen, thus making the Shan principalities collectively the protectorate of Britain through treaties signed with the princes.

Chin Chou Wu

Chinese merchant. During the KKY period (1968–74), when the Burma Army allowed influential non-Tai figures (that is, Chinese or Yunnanese, Wa, Lahu, among others) in Shan State to raise armies and engage in cross-border opium-contraband trade, Chin Chou Wu was one such person. In these trading activities, the KKY leaders had extensive dealings with Burmese authorities, in particular the MIS at Lashio, Loilem, Taunggyi, Kengtung, and Tachilek. The KKY had headquarters and storage facilities (for opium, heroin, contraband, and arms and ammunition) in the above mentioned towns, and moved merchandise in truck convoys. The wealthier KKY leaders, such as Lo Hsin Han, who had close connections with the international finance-trade-kinship network, operated as semi-independent entities. The less influential ones acted as agents for the big cross-border syndicates or trading-houses in that they bought raw opium from peasants, stored and transported opium as well as contraband, for which they received commissions ranging from 10 to 30 per cent of the volume handled.

Chit

Thakin; communist leader; killed in action around 1970; member of the pre-war Burmese nationalist group, the Thakins. After the demise of Thakin Than Tun and the decimation of the party's leadership due to enemy action and internal purges (a cultural revolution in the Chinese mould), Thakin Chit became party chairperson. However, the fortune of the White Flag or BCP (Burmese Communist Party which was changed to Communist Party of Burma, after receiving Chinese aid) was at a low ebb due to mass defections by supporters horrified by the butchering of their leaders (Goshal, General Yan Aung, Yebaw Htay, among others) in the purges. These defectors co-operated with the Burma Army and helped it to liquidate communist bases and leaders, including Thakin Than Tun, the party chairperson, and also followers such as Thakin Chit and Thakin Zin.

Chit Su

Chao or prince; Shan, member of the Yawnghwe ruling family. In the early 1880s, he was the nominee of the Shan Confederacy or the Limbin League for the princeship of Yawnghwe. This was because one of the prominent leaders of the league, Chao Weng, Prince of Lawksawk (related to the Yawnghwe family) thought the rightful *chaofa*, Chao Mawng, was pro-Burmese (as he was at one time adopted by King Mindon as son). At that time, Chao Mawng was at Mandalay (retained on suspicion of disloyalty by King Thibaw who succeeded Mindon). When he returned, he was attacked by the league, and was wounded. He went back to Mandalay, leaving the state in charge of Chao Ohn, a half-brother. Chao Ohn declared himself *chaofa*, and resisted the league, and at the same time, repeatedly begged the British to intervene which they did in 1887. Chao Ohn was recognized as *chaofa*. Disappointed, Chao Chit Su went into exile in Siam. In 1966, the writer met an old man living in the Yanawa area of Bangkok who said his ancestors were from Yawnghwe.

Chu Hong Chai

Chinese merchant. During the KKY period, he was a leader of the Vieng Ngun KKY and closely affiliated to Lo Hsin Han of Kokang. In 1974, when the KKY programme was scrapped, Chu Hong Chai together with the Kokang KKY (under Lo Hsin Han) defected to the SSA. Around 1980, due to old age and ill-health, he retired and took up farming in Muang Mai, the southern base of the SSA. His first wife, a native Hongkong, still lives there. His present wife of more than thirty years, is the sister of the ruling chief (a rank lower than *chaofa*) of Vieng Ngun, Wa state. I found Chu Hong Chai to be a simple, kindly man, not at all a "typical" merchant-adventurer.

Clift, Tommy

Air Commodore; Burma Air Force. An Anglo-Shan (mother was Shan) who joined the RAF before the World War II. After independence, he served in the new Burma Air Force and became its chief till the 1962 coup. Soon after Clift together with his family came into Thailand, and with the help of Air Marshal Dawee Chullaspha, the Thai Air Force Chief (an old friend), he set up Tommy Tours which catered to American servicemen on R & R to Thailand. In 1970, when Prime Minister U Nu set up the PDP aimed at overthrowing Ne Win, Clift joined the movement. However, the PDP collapsed after a few years due to U Nu's inability to command his subordinates, the squabbling among top leaders, and lack of success in the field. Clift once again made a move, settling down in Australia. While with the PDP, Clift managed to pull off a spectacular stunt which caused a sensation in Rangoon. He somehow managed to get a plane and a pilot to fly over Rangoon, dropping leaflets urging a general uprising against Ne Win.

Cowell, Adrian

British television producer of Anglia Television (ATV), London. One of the few Westerners to have really been in the interior of the Shan State, not once but twice following the 1962 coup. Together with his cameraman and co-producer, Chris Menges, he first went in 1965 to film the Shan guerillas of Kengtung which resulted in the documentary, *The Unknown War*. The second time that he entered Shan State (north and south) was in 1972. He lived with SSA troops for one year. This resulted in a colour documentary, *The Opium Warlords* which won worldwide acclaim. From his Shan experience and daily contacts with Shan peasants, Cowell became convinced that active international presence in Shan State and political settlement of the war was the key to the problem of heroin flowing out of Burma. Consequently, he made two more documentaries showing the international aspect of the heroin trade and the attitude of American politicians towards this serious problem. He advocated direct international interaction with Shan peasants, that is, opium growers, and their representatives in solving the opium-heroin problem. Besides being knowledgeable about the Shan, Cowell has also devoted much time to the plight of native Indians of Latin America, particularly Brazil. His documentaries on this subject are regarded as masterpieces in the study of human conditions.

Damrong Rajanubhab

Prince of Thailand. A historian-stateman who served under Rama V, Rama VI, and Rama VII. The Prince was highly esteemed by Shan princes and their families, especially the Kengtung family in the largest Shan principality (12,400 sq miles). After the 1932 coup in Thailand, he left the country and travelled widely, even visiting Burma in 1935 which recorded in a book, *A Visit to Burma*. The Prince's other well-known book concerning Burma is *Thai Wars against Burma* (1971).

Deving

Bo; Shan guerilla leader; of obscure origin, native of Muang Yai; gained local fame in the battle of Tangyan in 1959 — the first major clash of arms between Shan nationalists and the Burma Army. He later led a band and refused to accept the authority of the SSIA founded by university students, but allied himself with like-minded guerilla leaders such as Bo Hsu, Pawlam Ho-mang, Bo Hso-lam, and Bo Gang-yoi. By 1963, when the position of the SSIA had been consolidated, Bo Deving found a powerful ally — Khun Sa, the head of the Loimaw KKY, who had decided to fight the Burmese in 1964. Both contacted U Gondra who commanded the TNA of Kengtung. However, Khun Sa's temporary base on the Thai border was raided by the Thai police for which Khun Sa blamed Bo Deving. Back in the Burmese fold again as leader of Loimaw KKY, Khun Sa waged war on Bo Deving and his allies resulting in Bo Deving fleeing for safety to Thailand around 1966. In the late 1970s, following the failure of his business, Bo Deving attempted unsuccessfully to form a resistance force in the Tachilek area, close to the Thai border. In 1981, he responded to Rangoon's amnesty offer and returned home. At present Bo Deving is operating a small food stall near Loikaw, the capital of Karenni State.

Dorman-Smith, Reginald

Sir; last British Governor of Burma, 1941–46 (interrupted three years by the Japanese Occupation). Sir Reginald was committed to self-government for Burma as outlined in the Government of Burma Act 1921 and Government of India Act 1935. While in exile in Simla, he drew up a plan for post-war Burma called the Simla Plan in which complete self-rule was proposed but in stages following a sufficient degree of economic recovery. However, Aung San and the AFPFL, in control of Rangoon after the war, wanted and agitated for immediate independence. Britain's Labour government then was not interested in keeping Burma (especially since they were leaving India). The rapport between Aung San and Lord Louis Mountbatten, the Allied Far East Commander, who favoured de-colonization, made Sir Reginald, a "lame duck" governor. He therefore had no choice but to resign, made so since he had become the target of Labour MPs in the British Parliament who were sympathetic to the AFPFL.

Driberg, Tom

British Labour MP. A very insistent advocate of immediate independence for Burma, and close friend of Burmese AFPFL leaders. He was vocal in championing Burma's independence in Parliament. In the 1946 session of Parliament, he even led an attack on the British-appointed Governor of Burma, Sir Reginald Dorman-Smith.

E-Bi

Bo; currently heading a CPB composed of Lahu, on the Thai-Shan border. A nephew of Bu-jong Luang who in the mid-1970s went up to the Chinese-Shan border to Pangsang, the CPB headquarters as a result of a personal disagreement with Ja-Erh, the son of Bu-jong Luang. After some time, Bo E-Bi returned to the Thai-Shan border, entered into an uneasy alliance with Ja-Erh, who was attached to the ex-KMT 3rd Army and a Taiwan intelligence unit. In 1982, following the Thai attack on Ban Hintek, Khun Sa's SUA moved into Loi Lang, the Lahu area of operation. In 1983, there were numerous clashes between the SUA and Bo E-Bi, resulting in the latter's expulsion. It was reported in 1985 that Bo E-Bi was fighting with the SUA, making common cause with a Wa group attached to the ex-KMT 3rd Army.

Gang Yoi

Bo; Shan guerilla leader of obscure origin, in appearance very much like Ho Chi Minh. He was the most bitter foe of the student-led SSIA. Though he operated in the far north of Shan State bordering China (Namkham area of Hsenwi), he managed to form an alliance with another bitter foe of the students, namely Saw Yanda, head of the Noom Suk Harn which was based in the extreme south on the Thai border. Bo Gang Yoi teamed up with other leaders who opposed the SSIA such as Bo Deving, Bo Hso-lam, and even U Gondra, head of Kengtung's TNA. He had close contacts with ex-KMT merchant-warlord units in northern Shan State — in Kokang, Muang Si, Kang-muang, Loitao, Loisae, Nakhaa, Muang Sang, and in the Wa State. However, Bo Gang Yoi's band was eventually scattered by the SSA 1st Brigade after some difficult fighting in 1968 (the campaign was commanded by Sai Zam Mai, now one of the vice-presidents of Moherng's TRA formed in 1984). Thereafter he fled into China, but emerged briefly as political organizer for the Burmese communist force in Namkham area in the late 1970s, only to disappear once more; present whereabouts and fate unknown.

Gang Yoom

Bo; Shan guerilla leader, native of Namsan; died in 1982 of old age in Pangsang on the Chinese border in an SSA camp close to the CPB headquarters. Before the Shan resistance Bo Gang Yoom (or Wi-ling), was a village functionary. During the Japanese Occupation, he served under the *khun-muang*, Kham-leng of Muang Yaw, a sub-district of Hsenwi. After the war, he served in the Shan Levies, an irregular force raised by Shan princes to fight the various rebels — leftist PVO, Kachin army mutineers under the famed Naw Seng, and the Pa-O, among others. With the outbreak of the Shan resistance, he gathered together a small band of guerillas in the Namsan-Hsipaw area; but in 1960, he joined the SSIA upon being approached by student leaders, Sai Hla Aung and Sai Myint Aung. He served with distinction in the SSIA and the SSA till his death. He was also one of the vice-presidents of the SSPP.

Gaw Kham

Sai; native of Hsipaw; studied at Rangoon University; joined the first Shan resistance army, the Noom Suk Harn in 1959. Though a student he remained with Saw Yanda when other student leaders (such as Chao Kyaw Toon, Sai Toon Aye, Khun Kya Nu, and Sai Hla Aung) broke away to form the SSIA in 1960. However, a few years later, Sai Gaw Kham was among those (namely, Sang Saw, Sai Nong, Sai Tin Pe, Sai Kyaw Win, Chao Lek, Bo Muangkon and Khun Sing) who deposed Saw Yanda. He was active in the Shan unity efforts initiated by me and Khun Kya Nu which were cut short by the split in the SSA when Bo Moherng, SSA chief-of-staff, broke away and co-operated with the merchant-warlord interests (particularly General Li of the ex-KMT 3rd Army) in 1968. The SNIA (or former Noom Suk Harn) collapsed, and a group led by Sai Nong defected under the Burma Army's KKY programme. Sai Gaw Kham joined Sai Nong, but did not fare well under such conditions. He now lives in obscurity, ill-health, and impoverished circumstances.

Gondra

U, also known as "Chao" Nga Kham; Shan monk; native of Kengtung; president of Kengtung's TNA; assassinated in 1965 by his followers. In the mid-1950s, he was a charismatic nationalist in yellow robes. He gained fame and followers as head of Kengtung's Buddhist Orphanage. He was detained for a time by the MIS during the military caretaker government (1958–60), but continued to agitate for reforms. In 1961, U Gondra went underground (with my help), and met with SSIA leaders near Laikha (Khun Kya Nu and Sai Myint Aung) and he was together with Chao Way (a member of the Kengtung ruling family) appointed the SSIA's representative for Kengtung. However, with the deaths of Chao Way and staunch SSIA leaders in Kengtung, Bo Farang and Chao Kyaw Toon in battle, U Gondra became the undisputed leader. He then proceeded to form the TNA. Ignorant of the outside world and politics, he wasted time and money going after foreign aid (that is, U.S. aid) and fell victim to numerous conmen. He also became increasingly dictatorial, even opposing attempts of the Yawnghwe Mahadevi to create Shan unity in 1964. Due to U Gondra's mismanagement, especially of funds, there soon developed serious friction between him and his commanders and officers, leading to his death.

Goshal, H.M.

Also known as Comrade Ba Tin; Burmese communist leader of Indian extraction; prominent in the communist movement due to his mastery of Marxist dialectics and links with the Communist Party of India. He drew up many of the White Flag communist programmes among which was the decision to seize power by force in 1949. The situation then was favourable as the communists were not only armed but had thoroughly subverted three of the four Burmese regular battalions, the 1st, 2nd and 3rd Burma Rifles, and the paramilitary UMP (Union Military Police). In addition, the PVO (the AFPFL's militia), had been won over by the communists after Aung San's death. The White Flag had also infiltrated the civil service, labour, and students movements. However, when the revolution was launched, the shaky AFPFL under U Nu did not fall, due in the main to British assistance and the staunch support of Shan, Kachin, Chin, and Karenni leaders. Gradually the communists were driven from the towns and cities they had captured into the jungle. Goshal remained influential within the White Flag party until the infusion of cadres who had been exiles in China in the mid-1950s. The Beijing-returned cadres, as they were known, attacked past programmes and plans as being revisionist and anti-revolutionary. And Goshal, being the mastermind, was singled out as a secret enemy agent and liquidated. Along with Goshal, hundreds of leaders and party veterans were killed in a most barbaric manner by a crowd whipped into hysteria. Subordinates were pressured to bring charges against superiors; young people against parents; friends against friends; brothers against brothers or sisters, the accused thrown to the mercy of the almost rabid crowd, to be humiliated and beaten to death.

Gun-hok

Bo; Shan guerilla leader and former village level functionary of Khesi state. He operated in the Muang Kuang-Khesi-Laikha area independently until persuaded by Moherng in 1961 to join up with him. He retired not long after and died of old age.

Gunzate

Bo; also known as Sang Maat; currently vice-president and army chief-of-staff of the TRA (Tai Revolutionary Army, the new name of Bo Moherng's SURA adopted in 1984). He is a native of Laikha, part Tai, Pa-O and Chinese. As a teenager from the late 1940s to the late 1950s, Gunzate participated in the anarchic fighting involving several armies in the Laikha area. After the outbreak of the Shan resistance, he joined Bo Moherng. In 1961, when the SNUF was formed jointly by Bo Moherng and Khun Kya Nu, representing the Noom Suk Harn and the SSIA respectively, Bo Gunzate served as chief-of-operations. When the SSA was formed in 1964 with the Yawnghwe Mahadevi as chairperson, he was chief-of-operations of SSA 3rd Brigade (the commanding officer being Khun Kya Nu). In 1968, when Bo Moherng, then SSA chief-of-staff, broke away to form the SURA, Bo Gunzate was promoted to vice-president with overall command of the troops. Being part Chinese and fluent in Chinese, he enjoyed the special confidence of General Li and the ex-KMT 3rd Army, but Gunzate was loyal to Bo Moherng. Gunzate is of short, squat stature; a brilliant guerilla tactician who though a strict disciplinarian is nonetheless loved by men under his command.

Hearn-kham, Chaonang

(Princess); the Mahadevi of Yawnghwe; Shan; native of Hsenwi; youngest daughter of the legendary Shan hero, Khunsang Ton-huung who in the 1870s cleared Hsenwi of Burmese presence and influence. As was then customary among Shan ruling families and the well-to-do she was sent to study in a Roman Catholic convent in Maymyo till 1937 when she was given in marriage to Chao Shwe Thaike, the Chaofa of Yawnghwe. Being a *Mahadevi* (Chief Queen) and the first First Lady of Union Burma, she was well-known nationally. She gained prominence in her own right in the mid-1950s as an outspoken Shan nationalist. In 1956, the Mahadevi was elected to the Union Parliament (and concurrently to the Shan State Council, the legislature of Shan State). Her criticism of Burmese policy and actions detrimental to the Shan and other non-Burmese ethnic groups made her a formidable figure in Parliament. However, her tenure as MP was cut short by the military caretaker government of Ne Win in 1958. In the general election of 1960, the Mahadevi again contested in the polls, against the wishes of Chao Hom Pha, the Hsenwi prince and her elder brother. The seat was won by another brother, Chao Mun Pha, the *kem-muang* (or heir-apparent) of Hsenwi, the nominee of the prince. Despite this setback, the Mahadevi continued in politics championing the Shan desire for freedom. It was fortunate for the Mahadevi that she was in Britain for medical treatment when the 1962 coup took place. She remained in Britain until November 1962 when her husband, the Yawnghwe prince passed away in the Insein jail. At the end of 1963, she slipped into Thailand and attempted to organize the various Shan armies; but the Mahadevi was able to get only the SNUF and SSA to unite, forming the SSA. She served as chairperson of the SSWC (Shan State War Council) until 1969.

Hla Aung

Sai, also known as Hso-lane; Tai-Palaung, native of Namsan or Tawngpeng; studied for a year or so at Rangoon University, leaving in 1958 to enter politics. He spent some time in the Namsan and Namkham area spreading nationalist ideas clandestinely until the attack and capture of Tangyan in 1959 by Bo Mawng, a former paramilitary police officer. Sai Hla Aung and a group of followers joined Bo Mawng and marched with him to the Noom Suk Harn base on the Thai border. When the SSIA was formed by the students, he joined them, and returned to the north. By 1963, Sai Hla Aung had consolidated the SSIA's position there with the help of Bo Gang Yoom, and a dynamic former high-school student, Zam Muang. In 1964, Sai Hla Aung participated in the formative meeting of the SSA, and was appointed commander of SSA 1st Brigade. In 1968–70, he was moved to the SSA army headquarters on the Thai border. In 1971, Sai Hla Aung took part in the formative conference of the SSPP, and was elected one of its vice-presidents. In

1974, he served as army vice chief-of-staff, and in 1980, he was made president of SSPP/SSA until 1983 when he was deposed. Subsequently he surrendered to the Burma Army together with two followers. Sai Hla Aung's younger brothers, Sai Kyaw Sein, and Sai Loen Mawng, joined the resistance in 1963. Sai Loen Mawng, was a good combat leader and rose to the position of chief-of-operations of a brigade in the late 1970s. When Sai Hla Aung became president and was growing unpopular, there were accusations that he was trying to cultivate Loen Mawng as army chief-of-staff. Caught in a difficult and unhappy (as well as for him, false) position, Loen Mawng surrendered to the Burmese in 1982. The other brother, Sai Kyaw Sein, who had by 1980 become a fairly senior administrative (civilian affairs) officer and a strong and vocal supporter of his brother, Sai Hla Aung was detained by opponents loyal to Sai Lek, acting army chief-of-operations, and Chao Hso-noom, acting army chief-of-staff of the SSA. After Sai Hla Aung's defection, the fate of Sai Kyaw Sein was sealed.

Hla Khin

Saw; a Karen who served with the Shan resistance until he was killed in a clash with the Pa-O organization in 1968. Prior to his involvement with the Shan, he served for several years in the Burma Army. He first joined the Noom Suk Harn in the early 1960s; and when it collapsed, he joined the SSA 3rd Brigade. In 1968, when Bo Moherng formed the SURA, he followed Bo Moherng. He was a combat leader who was gentle and soft-spoken, and very much loved by his men.

Hla Myint

Sai, also known as "Bo Farang", Shan-Pathan, of obscure origin. By profession a long-haul truck driver. When the Shan resistance began, he joined the movement, and not long after, because of his reckless courage in combat, Sai Hla Myint was famous and admired throughout Kengtung and beyond. He is revered even today. He was nicknamed "Bo Farang" because of his "European" (Pathan) features. He accepted the leadership of Chao Kyaw Toon, a student leader and the SSIA man in Kengtung. However, before the SSIA's position could be consolidated in Kengtung both Sai Hla Myint and Chao Kyaw Toon fell in battle (c. 1961).

Hla Pe

Thaton; part Pa-O and part Karen; native of Thaton in Lower Burma; died in 1975, from illness and old age, in Southern Shan State. He was regarded in Shan State as an elder statesman and man of action. Thaton Hla Pe was involved in politics since before World War II in the Burmese nationalist movement. During the Japanese Occupation, he served as Forestry Minister in Dr Ba Maw's puppet government. In the immediate post-war years, Thaton Hla Pe worked closely with the Karen leader, Saw Ba U Gyi, and was one of the founders of the KNDO which spearheaded the armed Karen movement. He also took part in the armed uprising. After the death of Saw Ba U Gyi, Thaton Hla Pe was offered the leadership of the Karen, but he chose to go to the Shan State to organize the Pa-O. As the Shan princes were loyal to the AFPFL government and to U Nu, soon the Pa-O were fighting with the Shan Levies of the princes in Southern Shan State. In 1958, under U Nu's "Arms for Democracy" programme, Thaton Hla Pe and his followers laid down their arms. He was a supporter of the constitutional reform movement set into motion by the Shan government and other constituent states, but escaped detention when all prominent Shan were arrested by the coup-makers in 1962. However, in 1963, during the period of peace negotiations between the military regime and various rebels (about six main groups), Thaton Hla Pe organized peace marches in Rangoon, and was thrown into jail for five years. Upon his release, he joined the Pa-O rebel movement (reactivated by local leaders in 1967), and was recognized as its president. Thaton Hla Pe being a veteran politician was worried by activities of the CPB and recognized the necessity for unity of all resistance groups in Shan State. At this point, the Pa-O movement was riddled with leftists, and this coupled with communist subversion, resulted in a split within the Pa-O rank. The military leader, General Takale, a Karen, broke away to join the communists. Despite this set-back, Thaton Hla Pe worked for Shan State unity, and in 1974 reached a firm understanding with the SSA/SSPP through a series of talks with the SSPP's president, Khun Kya Nu. Unfortunately, before anything concrete could come about Thaton Hla Pe died.

Hom-Pha

Chao; Prince of Hsenwi, and head of Shan State 1958–60, during Ne Win's caretaker government; died of cancer in the mid-1960s. He was the son of the famed Shan hero, Khunsang Ton-huung of Hsenwi who drove out the Burmese in the late 1870s. Chao Hom Pha was educated at Shan Chiefs School, Taunggyi, an institution modelled on English public schools for the benefit of the Shan élite. Before becoming *chaofa* in 1925, he served in the army. After the Japanese war, Chao Hom Pha was in favour of a separate independent Shan State, and was rough with any Burmese politician who dared set foot in Hsenwi. However, as the British refused to consider any alternative but the amalgamation of Shan State and other Frontier Areas with Burma (and under the AFPFL), the Hsenwi prince signed the Panglong Agreement in 1947. In the civil war that followed independence, Kachin mutineers under Captain Naw Seng over-ran Hsenwi, and abducted the Hsenwi Chaofa to get him to join the rebellion. Chao Hom Pha refused and escaped, and at the request of the legal government (the AFPFL) raised Shan levies to fight various insurgents in Shan State. He was appointed Special Commissioner for Northern Shan State by the Shan government at Taunggyi. Chao Hom Pha notwithstanding his earlier anti-Burmese stance, was quick to recognize the real strength and power of the military. He therefore cultivated the goodwill of Burmese army chiefs, particularly Colonel Chit Myaing, and even married off his nieces and adopted daughters to army officers. Consequently, when the military was "invited" by U Nu to form a caretaker government (1958–60), he was appointed Head of Shan State, and it was he who accepted the surrender of power by the princes in 1959. He was not touched by the 1962 coup-makers. Though he seemed to be on good terms with the Burmese, Chao Hom Pha also enjoyed the high esteem of the Shan rebel leader, Bo Mawng, the hero of Tangyan, and Zau Seng, the founder of the KIA.

Hsinphyushin

King; 3rd monarch of the last Burmese dynasty (Alaungpaya dynasty); ruled 1763–76. The second son of the founder, King Alaungpaya, and one of the "unifiers" of Burma. His was a glorious reign as his armies successfully accomplished what Alaungpaya had not — the breaching of Siamese defences and the sacking of Ayuthia. However, due to Thai resistance led by King Taksin and Chao Phraya Chakri (the future Rama I) and more importantly, the Chinese invasion (1766–69), the Burmese had to withdraw.

Hso-gyam

Bo; Shan guerilla leader; formerly a senior village circle functionary of Muangnong state. At the outbreak of the Shan resistance, he became commander of a Noom Suk Harn battalion. Hso-gyam was very close to the Noom Suk Harn founder, Saw Yanda. In the mid-1960s, Hso-gyam was attacked by the Loimaw KKY of Khun Sa, for sheltering the latter's enemy, Bo Deving, and Hso-gyam's forces were scattered. This coincided with the overthrow of Saw Yanda (by Brigadier Sang-saw, and younger, educated officers). Hso-gyam then joined the SSA's 6th Brigade of Sai Pan-mai, and shortly after retired.

Hso-gyam

Bo; Shan guerilla leader who commanded a small band in Hsipaw area at the outbreak of resistance. In 1961, he submitted to student leaders, namely, Sai Myint Aung and Khun Kya Nu, and served with distinction in the SSIA, and later, the SSA. He was killed whilst fighting the Burma Army in the mid-1970s.

Hso-hom

Chao; eldest son of Chao Sam Toon, the Muang Pawn prince, who died with Aung San in 1947. Chao Hso-hom was a brilliant student at Rangoon University, and after graduating in the late 1950s, served as secretary to Chao Khun Khio, the Muang Mit prince and Head of Shan State (and Burma's first Foreign Minister), later joining the Shan Ministry. He became one of the bright stars in Shan government circles. In 1961, Chao Hso-hom was a member of the constitutional reform committee of the Shan government, and was therefore detained by the coup-makers in 1962. However, on Martyrs' Day (29 July), since his presence was required for the ceremony, he was brought out for the occasion and returned at once to prison. He spent five years in jail without being charged or put on trial. He is presently employed at a U.N. agency office in Rangoon.

Hso-lae

Bo; bandit leader who became a key figure in the Hsipaw-Muang Yai area when the resistance began. In 1961, he submitted to SSIA leaders

(Sai Myint Aung and Khun Kya Nu), and served as chief-of-staff of the 1st Battalion, SSIA. When the SSA was formed in 1964, Bo Hso-lae was SSA 4th Brigade chief-of-staff. When I formed the SSA 1st Military Region at a time which coincided roughly with the implementation of the KKY programme by the Burmese, Bo Hso-lae could not resist the temptation and defected with about 500 men (most of whom trickled back). He attempted to get Burmese help to form his own KKY but Khun Sa who was *de facto* chief of all KKY units in Shan State did not approve of Hso-lae's plan. Had he obtained the necessary backing, Hso-lae would have been able to at the very least scatter or even destroy the SSA 1st Military Region in 1970.

Hso-lam

Bo; Shan guerilla leader and former monk in Muang Yaw (Hsenwi state) and a bitter enemy of the "students". He allied himself with Bo Deving who had a similar dislike. But in 1964–65, due to the organizational efforts of the SSA 1st Brigade (of which I was then chief-of-staff), Bo Hso-lam's men defected in large numbers, thus ending the role of one of the anarchic military leaders.

Hso-noom

Chao; born 1947, son of the Muang Loen prince, and educated at Kambawze College (former Shan Chiefs School in pre-war Shan State), he joined the SSIA in 1963 with a force already under him. When the SSA was formed in 1964, Chao Hso-noom was commander of the SSA 2nd Battalion. In 1967, influenced by Sai Kyaw Sein, a renegade student leader (who married Chao Hso-noom's sister), and due to other difficulties, the SSA 2nd Brigade accepted KKY status. In 1970, responding to my call Chao Hso-noom rejoined the SSA 1st Military Region. He was a good officer and rose to command a brigade in 1977. After the disappearance of the SSA acting chief-of-staff, Colonel Zam Muang, and deputy chief-of-operations, Bo Pan Aung in 1979, Chao Hso-noom took charge of all SSA forces. However, ill-health dogged him and he died in 1984.

Hso-wai

Chao; one of my *noms de guerre*.

Hsu

Bo; Shan guerilla leader in Hsenwi area who operated under control of the ex-KMT 5th Army which operated in the Loitao opium producing area. However, in 1965, Bo Hsu submitted to the SSA 1st Brigade, and retired soon afterwards.

Hunter Thahmwe

Saw; president of the Karen movement until 1964. A school inspector before the Karen uprising, he distinguished himself in its early years. After the death of Saw Ba U Gyi, the mantle of leadership fell on Saw Hunter. A strong anti-communist, he spurned all overtures by the Burmese communists. When Mahn Ba-zan, Sgaw Ler-taw, General Mya Maung co-operated with the CPB and formed the KNUP (Karen National Union Party), Saw Hunter presided over the stronger KNU (Karen National Union). During this period, Bo Mya (the present KNU president) was a mere major. In 1963, in the peace talks initiated by Ne Win, Saw Hunter, like all rebels, responded, and in 1964 agreed to go aboveground. (Members of the Karen negotiating team whom I met in Rangoon in 1963 said that their strategy was to achieve their goal through close internal struggle, and urged the Shan to follow suit. I had been in contact with Saw Hunter and Karen leaders while still at university, and even attended the founding conference of the non-communist front, the NLA [Nationalities Liberation Alliance] in 1961). After the agreement with Rangoon, Saw Hunter was rewarded with an appointment as ambassador to Israel. However, the key person at the time, Brigadier Lin Tin of the 5th Kawthoolei Brigade, was killed by the army under mysterious circumstances.

Ja-Erh

Son of Bu-jong Luang, the Lahu holy man; currently at the Shan-Thai border. After Bu-jong Luang fled to Thailand, Ja-Erh commanded the Lahu force but lacking resources, allied himself with the ex-KMT 3rd Army, and also enjoyed the support of a Taiwanese intelligence unit. He also allied himself with the SSA/SSPP, the Shan nationalist force led by students. In 1977, following a re-organization in the Karen sponsored National Democratic Front (NDF), the Lahu force (together with the Pa-O and Wa) was included in the "front". In 1982, following the expulsion of Khun Sa's SUA from Ban Hintek owing to Thai pressure, the SUA moved into the Lahu base at Loi Lang. Ja-Erh for a time co-operated with the SUA who drove out the CPB unit under Bo E-Bi. Not long after, Ja-Erh moved out, establishing himself at Muang-Na, further south of Loi Lang. Lao Su, the notorious heroin refiner and dealer, for whose head the Thai Government had offered a substantial reward, was killed and delivered to the Thai by some Lahu officers under Ja-Erh. Shortly after, Ja-Erh left Thailand and surrendered to Burmese authorities at Muang Ton. In 1984, Ja-Erh re-appeared on the Thai-Shan border. His current activities are not known.

Kawngtai

Chao; Prince of Kengtung; ruled 1787–1804. His rule coincided with the resurgence of Siam's military strength which saw the Burmese defeat and expulsion from Siam. To re-populate the destroyed or deserted cities and towns especially of north Thailand, Siamese-Chiangmai forces took to raiding Kengtung and Sipsongpanna (in Yunnan) and Laos. Kengtung, drained of manpower in the Burmese-Siam war and the Chinese invasion of Burma, both of which occurred in the 1760s and 1970s, was devastated. The Kengtung princely line would have ended then had not one member of the family, Chao Maha-kanan, who "maintained himself gallantly amid many vicissitudes" (*Shan State and Karenni: List of Chiefs and Leading Families* 1946, p. 5), regained power in 1813.

Kawngtai

Chao; Prince of Kengtung; ruled 1881–86; rebelled against the Burmese, expelling them from Kengtung. He also encouraged Shan princes to overthrow the Burmese which many did including Muang Nai, Mawkmai, Lawksawk, and Yawnghwe. Chao Kawngtai was in touch with Chao Khun Seng, Chaofa of Hsipaw, the most enlightened of all Shan. The latter proposed a confederation of Shan free states as in Germany. However, Chao Kawngtai argued that the Shan would not submit to their peers, and an outside suzerain was needed. As such, the Kengtung prince invited a prince of the Alaungpaya dynasty, the Limbin prince, to head the League of Shan Princes. The aim was to overthrow King Thibaw and set up the Limbin prince, the candidate of the Shan, on the throne. However, the

King was instead deposed by the British. At that crucial moment, Chao Kawngtai died, leaving the Shan League leaderless.

Kawngtai

Chao; Prince of Kengtung, became *chaofa* in 1937, but was assassinated in October of the same year. He was educated at Shan Chiefs School, Taunggyi, and at St. Paul, Rangoon. Chao Kawngtai married the eldest daughter of Sir Chao Khe, Prince of Hsipaw. His son, Chao Sai-laung, then aged ten, was recognized as heir. Chao Kawngtai was murdered by a nephew in a conspiracy hatched by some family members. The tragedy stemmed from the fact that Chao Kawngtai was not in direct line to succession. The would-be successor, Chao Phom-lue, was declared ineligible for knowledge of a counterfeiting scheme and his failure to report the matter to the British. He was also implicated in the assassination conspiracy. As such, Chao Phom-lue was banished to Maymyo, and only returned during the Siamese occupation. With Japan's defeat, Chao Pom-lue went into exile. His widow, Chaomae Tippawan, is currently living in Chiangmai.

Kha

Bo; Karen, former member of the famed Wingate's Chindit; enlisted in the armed forces before World War II. Bo Kha served in a Karen battalion of the post-war Burma Army, and joined the Karen uprising of 1949. He went to the Karenni (or Kayah) State with the KNDO, and remained there. Currently vice-president of the KniNPP.

Khammon

Tao-suung; a minister in Hsenwi state in the 1840s. In 1945, the Prince of Hsenwi, Seng Naw-hpa, who enjoyed the support of the Mandalay court executed an influential minister, Tai-suung Toon-kham, his wife, and seven sons. Tao-suung Khammon rebelled and drove the prince out. Mandalay sent the prince back with a Burmese army and after widespread fighting, Tao-suung Khammon was captured and killed. However, the Hsenwi rebellion continued under another minister, Tao Sang-hai, who not only defeated the Burmese but other Shan princes — Muang Mit, Hsipaw, and Yawnghwe, among others, sent to subdue the rebellion. The fight continued until the 1870s when the Hsenwi rebels under the son-in-law of Tao Sanghai, Khunsang Ton-huung (my maternal grandfather), put to flight all armies sent against him, managing to maintain Hsenwi as an independent state until the British arrived in Shan State.

Khe

Chao, Sir; Chaofa of Hsipaw, ruled 1902–28; son of Chao Khun-seng who in 1882 rebelled successfully against King Thibaw. Sir Chao Khe was born in the Mandalay Palace. Until 1902, he held various administrative posts under his father, the Hsipaw prince, becoming the *chaofa* upon his father's death. Like his father, he was bright, intelligent, efficient, and widely travelled. Admired by the British, he was showered with many awards and honours, and was knighted in 1928 (Order of the Companion of the India Empire) — one of the two Shan princes who received a knighthood in the fifty-four years of British presence; the other being Yawnghwe's Sir Chao Mawng (my paternal grand-uncle). One of Sir Chao Khe's daughters was married in 1922 to Kengtung's Chao Kawngtai; and another to Chao Hom Pha (Hsenwi prince) in 1925.

Khin Mawng

Chao; Chaofa of Muang Mit; ruled 1906–36. He along with other princes, namely, Chao Ohng Kya (Hsipaw), Chao Shwe Thaike (Yawnghwe), and Chao Hom Pha (Hsenwi) went to London in 1931 when Burma's self-government was discussed at a Special Round Table Conference. Their objective was to get London to give some consideration to the special status of the Shan, namely, that Shan princes in 1888 and 1889 came under British control not by conquest, but through treaties with individual princes which, in effect, made the Shan states collectively a protectorate, not a colony as was Burma (that is, Burma Proper). It was a fact that at the time of the annexation of Burma, the Shan were no longer under the Burmese throne. Despite this, the British had in 1922, put the Federated Shan States under the Governor of Burma. The Shan were worried lest their homeland be willy-nilly put under the authority of Burmese politicians in the eventuality that the British were to grant Burma greater self-government, and the Shan once more would be subjected to Burmese misrule and oppression. British policy makers ignored the appeals by the Shan because it was in the interest of British bureaucracy in Burma to rule over a larger domain, and such an arrangement (the merger of Shan states and other Frontier Areas with Burma Proper) was less troublesome and cheaper. It could be said that the then British arrangement was an attempt to have their cake and eat it, that is, putting the Frontier Areas and the Shan homeland under the executive power of the British Governor, but outside the scope of the native legislature. Such was the status of the Shan states at the end of World War II and during the period of power play between the Burmese AFPFL and the Labour government in Britain.

Khun Htee

Panglong; Shan trader and politician prominent in the immediate post-war years. He belonged to the younger set who held socialist views and admired the Thakin leaders such as Aung San and U Nu. After independence and the union of Shan State with Burma, Khun Htee was dismayed by Burmese arrogance, and attempts to sow disunity among the different ethnic groups of Shan State, and distressed by extra-legal powers exercised by Burmese army chiefs and treatment of local rural people. In 1961, he joined the movement proposing the re-structuring of the constitution along genuinely federal lines. Following the 1962 coup, Khun Htee was imprisoned without trial. He now lives in Panglong town, the site of the 1947 Panglong Agreement. He was one of the signatories of the agreement.

Khun Hti

Chao; the Khun Muang of Muang Pawn, who in the early 1880s joined in the general Shan rebellion against King Thibaw. A member of the Limbin League which aimed to march to Mandalay to put the Shan candidate, the Limbin prince, on the throne. They would have succeeded if the British had not pre-empted them. Consequently, Chao Khun Hti, like all Shan princes and lords accepted British suzerainty by treaty. Under the British, Muang Pawn state was enlarged with the inclusion of Nawngmon and Namkok. Chao Khun Hti was elevated to rank of *chaofa*. He died in 1922. In ancient days, part of Muang Pawn belonged to Yawnghwe, and the other part to Muang Nai. It was created as a *myoza* state in 1816 in the reign of Bodawpaya as part of the Burmese "divide and rule" policy to weaken the Shan.

Khun Khio

Chao; Prince of Muang Mit, Head of Shan State (before 1956, and 1960–62), the Union's first Foreign Minister, and one time deputy Prime Minister. A Cambridge graduate, he succeeded to the princeship in 1925. Just before the war, he served in one of the two Shan battalions raised for the oncoming conflict. After the war, Chao Khun Khio, though not politically active, was chosen by his peers to succeed Chao Sam Toon (killed together with Aung San) in the central government. As Head of Shan State, he got on well with U Nu and other AFPFL leaders. He played a crucial role in obtaining British aid and sympathy for the AFPFL when communist and Karen rebels held almost all towns and controlled all roads and railways. Though Chao Khun Khio did not support the growing anti-Burmese feelings in Shan State, he was by the late 1950s forced to recognized the existing constitutional imbalance, and the suffering of the population caused by the extra-legal powers exercised by Burma's army chiefs. In 1960, as Head of Shan State (his second tenure), he accepted suggestions by non-princely leaders such as U Kya Bu, Panglong Khun Htee, U Toon Myint Lay and Thaton Hla Pe, for constitutional reform. Chao Khun Khio used his considerable skill and diplomacy to bring together state govern-ments and leaders behind the proposal for constitutional amendments, resulting in the historic Taunggyi conference of 1961. However, U Nu and the AFPFL to whom this move was addressed had, though popularly elected, lost control of the army. In 1962, like many prominent Shan, Chao Khun Khio was jailed for five years without trial. On release, he lived quietly in Rangoon before being allowed to resettle in Britain.

Khun Kya Nu

Shan student leader; founding member of the SSIA (1960), the SSA (1964), and the SSPP (1971); one of the many children of U Kya Bu, a Shan elder statesman. He studied at Rangoon University till 1959, and together with Khun Thawda (a cousin, stepson of Dr Ba Nyan, another elder statesman), he joined the Noom Suk Harn. To their dismay, the students found that Saw Yanda, the founder, had no plans and moreover distrusted them. There was constant friction and the students left to form the SSIA in 1960. Fortunately, Bo Mawng and Chao Kyaw Toon (a former student), the heroes of Tangyan, supported the SSIA. Back once more in the hinterland, Khun Kya Nu together with Sai Myint Aung were able to win over some of the numerous armed groups mushrooming in Shan State, forming them into battalions — the 1st Battalion in Hsipaw-Muang Yai; 2nd Battalion in Muang Loen; 3rd Battalion in Muang Hsu-Khesi; and the 4th Battalion in Hsenwi-Namsan-Muang Mit area. They were able to win over Bo Moherng, leading a Noom Suk Harn group in Laikha-Muang Kung. Khun Kya Nu, as vice-president of the SNUF, and I orchestrated the Shan response to Rangoon's peace call in 1963. This resulted in favourable national publicity for the rebels, and facilitated the meeting of SSIA leaders and further contacts with other Shan armies, thus creating greater Shan cohesion. In 1964, when the Yawnghwe Mahadevi formed the SSA, Khun Kya Nu commanded the 3rd Brigade (former SNUF forces), to the chagrin of Bo Moherng, who though made army chief-of-staff, felt left out. In 1966, he and I reorganized the SSA GHQ which had fallen apart due to squabbles within the SSWC. Plans for Shan unity were implemented. But these were disrupted by the SSA chief-of-staff, Bo Moherng who broke away to form SURA. In 1971, when the SSPP was formed, Khun Kya Nu was elected president and army chief-of-staff; and together with the writer, arranged for Adrian Cowell and Chris Menges of ATV London, to do a documentary on the opium-heroin problem in Shan State. The most brilliant achievement of Khun Kya Nu was the creation of the SSA's southern base on the Thai border in 1973. This was a seemingly impossible feat since the area was under the control of Bo Moherng's SURA and the powerful ex-KMT 3rd Army; besides, he had only thirty men under him. (Thaton Hla Pe, head of the Pa-O army and Shan elder statesman, helped too.) In 1974, Khun Kya Nu as president and chief-of-staff, went into the interior to prevent the CPB from winning over the SSA with offers of arms. He succeeded only in getting the army chief-of-operations, Sai Zam Muang to avoid making any political commitments. In 1976, due to various difficulties, lack of finance, and intrigues by the merchant-warlord interests and the Burmese communists (both fearing a strong SSA presence in the south), Khun Kya Nu was ousted (in a move masterminded by Colonel Sai Pan Aung, a senior SSA officer). Khun Kya Nu then settled down in north Thailand, and is currently self-employed as a trader.

Khun Kyi

Chao; Prince of Muang Nai; ruled from 1875–1914; rebelled against King Thibaw in 1882 because of the oppressive presence of Burmese troops in Muang Nai (it being the Burmese base for Shan State), and the King's attempts to weaken the state. Chao Khun Kyi was one of the leaders of the Shan League which aimed at putting its candidate, the Limbin prince, on the throne. This would have been successful had the British not captured Mandalay. Like all *chaofa*, Chao Khun Kyi signed a treaty with the British in 1888. He was popular with the people and much admired by the British, who showered him with honours and awards.

Khun Kyi

Chao; Khun Muang of Sa-tuung (1925–48) when he died of a stroke. One of the three Shan statesmen who together united the Shan, and prevented Shan State and other non-Burmese homelands from being sold down the river — the other two being, Chao Shwe Thaike of Yawnghwe, and Chao Sam Toon of Muang Pawn. In the years immediately after the war, Britain, having decided to leave India and Burma, was not willing to fulfil any obligations owed to the loyal non-Burmese peoples, and was happy to leave them at the mercy of the Burmese. This put the non-Burmese minorities in a difficult position since Burmese were more politically advanced, having been given better education by the British and had since the 1920s experienced self-government under the British and the Japanese. In contrast, the Karen, Kachin and Shan were insulated and discouraged from even thinking political thoughts. Moreover, they were indoctrinated to think that Britain would always look after them. Further, they were keenly aware of the Burmese inability to govern well (judging from history). It seem that the non-Burmese were about to be disposed of as unwanted baggage. However, the three Shan statesmen, the Kachin and Chin, were able to negotiate as equals with Aung San and AFPFL leaders at Panglong in 1946 and 1947. The ensuing Panglong Agreement in 1947 signified that the Burmese accepted the Kachin, Chin, and Shan as equals, and their homelands as autonomous entities instead of as repossessed former colonies.

Khun Lai and Khun Lu

Legendary figures whom the Shan (that is, the Tai of Shan State, Assam, Upper Burma, north Thailand, Sipsongpanna, and west Yunnan) believe came down from heaven with the Tai/Thai. Khun Lai and Khun Lu and their descendants first founded the kingdom of Muangri-Muangram and later, Chaingsaen-Maoluang from which the later Tai/Thai migrated to found new kingdoms such as Assam, Mao Ava, Chaengsaen, Sukhothai, Chiangmai, among others.

Khun-phung

Sai; brigade commander of the SSA in the late 1970s; killed in a grenade incident; member of the ruling clan of Muang Yane under Hsenwi. He was one of the hundreds of young men who took up arms in 1959 against Burmese rule, and when SSIA leaders and cadres (Sai Hla Aung, Sai Zam Muang, and Sai Nyung, among others) arrived, Khun-phung joined the SSIA 4th Battalion. He proved a good political organizer and a combat leader who rose rapidly in rank, becoming the best officer in the SSA. In the early 1970s, Sai Khun-phung commanded an SSA task force in the Namsan-Muang Mit area which was disputed by the Burma Army, the KIA (and Palaung allies), and the ex-KMT 3rd Army. At one time during this period, Khun-phung fought almost thirty engagements in one month with various foes. In the mid-1970s, he accompanied the SSA chief-of-operations, Sai Zam Muang to the CPB headquarters at Pangsang, and equipped with new weapons, Khun-phung commanded many of the operations against the Burma Army resulting in heavy enemy losses.

Khun Loumpha

Chao; one of my *noms de guerre*.

Khun Sa

Dubbed by international mass media in the late 1970s as "Heroin King of the Golden Triangle". His stepfather was Myoza of Loimaw, a part of Muang Yai state. In the late 1950s, he was head of the Loimaw KKY which helped the Burma Army maintain local peace. After the 1962 coup when Ne Win started his nationalization measures (bringing about the collapse of the economy), Khun Sa decided to fight the Burmese and formed the Anti-Socialist United Army. In 1964, he travelled to the Thai border together with Bo Deving, an independent guerilla leader, who introduced him to U Gondra of the TNA. However, they quarrelled and Khun Sa's camp was raided by the Thai police. He was once again approached by the Burmese and agreed to fight Shan rebels, especially Bo Deving. In 1965, Khun Sa went on a rampage, shattering and scattering Bo Deving's forces, and attacking whoever sheltered him. His success bolstered his confidence, and he attempted to challenge the ex-KMT 3rd and 5th Army which monopolized all cross-border trade. This led in 1967 to pitched battle on the Shan-Lao-Thai border which made international headlines. Not long after, when the Burmese adopted the KKY programme, Khun Sa gained informal status as head of all Shan KKY forces. His authority was challenged by Kokang's Lo Hsin Han who fought CPB units in Kokang, and enjoyed the the trust of the ex-KMT merchant-warlord establishment. Meanwhile, the Burmese were getting uneasy with Khun Sa's independence and increasing nationalism. In 1970, with former Prime Minister U Nu abroad, the Burmese prepared to detain Khun Sa who, in turn, prepared to go underground. He secretly contacted the SSA 1st Military Region (which was under my command), but the Burmese struck first, and Khun Sa was imprisoned. However, his men under Colonel Chang Chu Chuan moved into the jungle teaming up with the SSA 1st Military Region. In 1973, the Loimaw force, now renamed the SUA kidnapped two Russian doctors from Taunggyi. Khun Sa's release was demanded. The Russians were released through the good office of Thailand's General Kriangsak Chommanand, but Rangoon did not respond. In 1976, Khun Sa was released. He did not rejoin the SUA but remained in Burma travelling often between Rangoon and Mandalay on business. In 1982, responding to American pressure, Thai forces attacked Khun Sa's alleged stronghold, Ban Hintek in Thailand, and a large reward for Khun Sa was offered by U.S. officials. There was at one time a rumour that Khun Sa was secretly in league with the Burmese, but this was dispelled following bloody clashes between the SUA and the Burmese in 1984. Khun Sa maintained that he was a patriot and was only taxing opium and heroin refineries; and that he had many times proposed co-operating with the United States and the United Nations in rooting out opium (this was when he met with aides of Congressman Lester Wolfe in the late 1970s). Fortunately or otherwise, the U.S. position was that Khun Sa was a criminal.

Khun Sam

Chao; now deceased; until the 1962 coup served the Shan government in charge of culture. A member of the Khesi ruling family, he was responsible for the renewed interest, especially of the young, in Shan language, literature, folklore, the performing arts, and handicrafts. He encouraged Shan intellectuals, writers, and artistes, which resulted in an intellectual and cultural ferment in the 1950s.

Khun Seng

Also known as Ronald Chang; currently (1985) president of Shan State Patriotic Council set up jointly by Bo Moherng and Khun Sa in 1985; native of Loimaw, Muang Yai state, and younger brother of Khun Sa's mother. He studied at Rangoon University and was known then as Ronald Chang. He joined Khun Sa after graduation when Khun Sa set up the Anti-Socialist United Army in 1964. Khun Seng figured prominently as chief-of-staff to Colonel Chang Chu Chuan in Cowell's documentary, *The Opium Warlords*. In the late 1970's, while fighting the Burma Army, Khun Seng lost an eye in battle.

Khun Thawda

Native of Hsipaw; connected to the ruling family of Hsipaw (his mother was a princess of Hsipaw); adopted son of Dr Ba Nyan, a Shan elder statesman, and an early Shan nationalist; studied at Rangoon University and also accompanied the Hsipaw prince (Chao Kya Seng) to study in the United States in the 1950s. Upon return, Khun Thawda taught for some time at Kambawza College, previously called the Shan Chiefs School under the British. In 1959, together with Khun Kya Nu, he made his way to the Shan-Thai border to join the Noom Suk Harn. After the SSIA was formed, Khun Thawda was invited to join the new organization. In 1963, he headed the joint Shan delegation (SSIA, TNA, Noom Suk Harn) for the final round of peace talks with the Burmese. However, since various rebel groups, especially the White Flag communists were making political capital from the talks, General Ne Win lost interest. Hence the joint Shan team got only as far as Taunggyi and met with a representative of the Revolutionary Council who called upon the Shan to surrender. The Shan team in turn proposed that a genuine federal union be set up so as to bring peace. The talks ended and the Shan team returned to the Shan-Thai border. When the SSA formed under the Yawnghwe Mahadevi in 1964, Khun Thawda was made a member of the SSWC but shortly after, was wounded in a series of assassination attempts by MIS against Shan leaders in the border areas. In 1967, Khun Thawda made an inspection tour of the 3rd, 6th and 4th SSA Brigades covering Laikha, Muang Kung, Hsipaw, Muang Yai, Khesi, and Muang Hsu. In 1968 he retired from active service for personal reasons, and not long after, settled down with his family in Bangkok.

Khun-zom

Sai, or Hso-zom; native of Kengtung and son of the Kengtung police chief, Bogyi Sye-keow (who was imprisoned in 1962 and committed suicide). He was also known as Sai Luung-seng and studied at Rangoon University but transferred to the Police Training School, Mandalay. He was posted to Hsipaw, and after several clashes with Shan rebels, he resigned and joined the resistance in Kengtung. He served as an aide to U Gondra, head of TNA, and represented it in the joint Shan peace talks team (comprising the SSIA, Noom Suk Harn, SNUF and TNA) in 1963. After U Gondra's death, Khun-zom was the general-secretary of the Kengtung forces, now renamed SSA.E (SSA.East); and was active in the SUPC — a body set up to work for Shan unity. In the early 1970s when the Kengtung forces came under CPB control, Khun-zom took part in the communist offensive in Muang Yang area. Not long after, he settled down in Thailand, but surrendered to Burmese authorities in 1979.

Khunsang Ton-huung

Shan rebel leader and hero who in the 1870s repelled all forces (Burmese and Shan) sent against him (this was at the end of King Mindon's reign). Consequently when the British came up to the Shan highlands, they recognized him as Chaofa of Hsenwi. However, to keep peace, a part of the state was designated as south Hsenwi (now known as Muang Yai) and given to the original ruling family of Hsenwi. Khunsang Ton-huung was a native of Ton-huung village on the eastern bank of the Salween in Muang Loen state. Before his marriage to Tao Sanghai's daughter he was known as Sang Yawn. Tao Sanghai was a minister in the Hsenwi court before leading a rebellion against the Burmese. Khunsang

Ton-huung traded in salt by bullock caravan with Mandalay. In the late 1880s, when the British marched into Shan State, Khunsang Ton-huung knew of them through his ally Chao Khunseng of Hsipaw who had travelled widely. Till his death in 1917, Khunsang Ton-huung remained an aloof and dignified figure.

Khunseng

Chao; Prince of Hsipaw; was born during the reign of King Mindon (1853–78), and grew up in the Mandalay Palace as it was usual for Burmese kings to have sons of Shan princes at the court. However, after Chao Khunseng became *chaofa*, the new King Thibaw did not trust him (though King Thibaw was half-Shan, his mother being a princess of Hsipaw, hence the name "Thibaw" which is "Hsipaw" in Burmese). Chao Khunseng therefore fled to British Lower Burma in 1882. There, he killed two men whom he thought were sent to assassinate him which landed him in a British jail. Due to his status and good behaviour he was released and deported. Chao Khunseng lived for some time in Siam (Chantaburi and Bangkok). He then moved on into Karenni state as a guest of Sawphaya Lapaw. When Mandalay fell, he returned to Hsipaw, and entered into an alliance with the famed Khunsang Ton-huung of Hsenwi, and regained control of the state. A much travelled man and a nationalist, he advocated a confederation of independent Shan states. However, since this idea was too advanced at that time, Chao Khunseng opted for British protection and urged them to enter Shan State. Being intelligent, widely travelled, a receptive to new ways, able and efficient, the British admired Chao Khunseng and showered him with honours and awards. He died in 1925, and was succeeded by his son, Chao Khe, who gained even greater honours.

Khunsing

Sai; high school student who served in the Noom Suk Harn (and later in the SNIA). One of the Young Turks who deposed Saw Yanda, the head of Noom Suk Harn. Khunsing even led a force which raided Saw Yanda's house in Chaingdao town in Thailand. The target escaped, but his wife and daughters were captured. Khunsing showed much promise, but eloped with one of his prisoners, a daughter of Saw Yanda, and surrendered in 1967. He now lives in Taunggyi.

Khunsuk

Chao; currently living in retirement in Chiangmai. A senior member of
the Kengtung ruling family. He was educated at Shan Chiefs School, and
underwent administrative training under British officers. He joined the
army and took part in the retreating fight from Burma to India in 1942;
and in the recapture of Burma. Chao Khunsuk who held the rank of major
accompanied British forces into Siam to disarm Japanese forces, and for
a time was appointed British Consul in Chiangmai. In post-independence
years, Chao Khunsuk administered Kengtung on behalf of his nephew,
the then young and inexperienced *chaofa*, Chao Sai-luang. He did not
get on well with Burma Army chiefs and officers who in turn saw him
as an anti-Burmese separatist. In 1958, Chao Khunsuk was summoned
to Rangoon and arrested at the airport, but upon intervention by Shan
leaders, notably Chao Shwe Thaike, he was released. He later fled to
Thailand and was swiftly granted asylum by Field Marshal Sarit (the two
having become friends in Chiangmai immediately after the war).

Ko Latt

Native of Yawnghwe, and long time chief minister of Yawnghwe under
Chao Shwe Thaike. In the early 1950s when Pa-O and KNDO rebels
ran loose, Ko Latt's cool head and efficiency kept the state together. He
was a great help to Chao Seng Hpa, the son and heir of Chao Shwe
Thaike, who was inexperienced having returned from Britain where he
had studied from the age of twelve. Ko Latt was detained for a time by
the military in 1962 although he had retired.

Kolan

Chaofa; also known as Nai Noi. Prince of Mawkmai, 1844–87. A colourful
and adventurous figure who often defied the Burmese at Mandalay. He
distinguished himself in the Karenni war on orders of King Mindon.
Chaofa Kolan jointed the Shan repudiation of Burmese overlordship in
the early 1880s.

Kya Bu

Luung; died in 1983 of old age. A native of Hsipaw, he was educated
at the pre-war Rangoon University, and trained as an agronomist in

British India. He was prominent politically in the immediate post-war years and advocated outright Shan independence. However, since Britain under the Labour Party was deserting those who had been loyal, U Kya Bu signed the Panglong Agreement in 1947, making the best of a bad situation. After independence, he served the Shan government as chief agricultural officer, and was a great innovator. When the resistance began, and one of his sons, Khun Kya Nu joined it, U Kya Bu accepted the task of contacting rebels and persuading them to return home. He went to Thailand, and Khun Maha, the then SSIA president joined him to discuss peace with the Shan government. He was immediately arrested by the MIS. U Kya Bu was, however, undaunted and pushed for constitutional reform. His view was that the rebellion was a by-product of military indiscipline and the extra-legal power of the army in Shan State; the restoration of internal sovereignty as in the spirit of the Panglong Agreement would bring peace. Due to his prominence in the constitutional reform or federal movement in 1961–62, behind which all constituent states rallied, Ne Win imprisoned U Kya Bu, and he spent five years in jail without trial.

Kya Seng

Chao; became Chaofa of Hsipaw after the union of Shan State with Burma. He was educated in the United States, and married a highly intelligent and capable Australian woman, who was the Hsipaw Mahadevi, was much respected by the Shan. Chao Kya Seng was a nationalist and a strong supporter of the Yawnghwe Mahadevi. Though he was hated by the army who regarded him as disloyal, Chao Kya Seng was committed to upholding the Union. Once in 1961, when an SSIA leader, Sai Kyaw Sein was secretly in Rangoon, I asked the Hsipaw prince whether he would like to meet a rebel leader. Chao Kya Seng brought out the Union constitution and read out the oath of loyalty he had sworn as an MP of the Upper House. The Hsipaw prince was last seen under military escort just outside Taunggyi (he was on his way to board a plane for Rangoon) just after the 1962 coup. His wife, the Hsipaw Mahadevi and two daughters managed to leave Burma a few years later. They now live in the United States.

Kyaw Nyein

U; a prominent AFPFL leader who held various cabinet posts (including deputy Prime Minister at various times). During the 1957 split within the ruling AFPFL, U Kyaw Nyein (together with U Ba Swe headed the Stable faction (as opposed to the Clean faction). Though a socialist like all AFPFL leaders, U Kyaw Nyein somehow came across as pro-American, and too clever. During the pre-war years, he worked closely with Aung San, both were student leaders and in the independence movement. He was highly regarded by Aung San.

Kyaw Sein

Sai, also known as Hso-tyen; currently with the SSA faction affiliated to the CPB. Of humble origins, he made it to Rangoon University where he excelled in sports. He was good friend of Chao Kyaw Toon (the hero of Tangyan). In the resistance, he was posted as assistant to Chao Kyaw Toon, the SSIA chief for Kengtung. After the latter's death in combat, Sai Kyaw Sein was forced to flee Kengtung because of his "wild" ways. In 1961 he was at the founding meeting of the NLA at the Karen headquarters. He made the secret trip to Rangoon with me. In 1964, after the SSA was formed, Sai Kyaw Sein served as special aide to the Yawnghwe Mahadevi who was the chairperson. He proved ineffective and ended up in Muang Loen with the SSA 2nd Brigade, and married a daughter of the Prince of Muang Loen. In 1967, he persuaded Chao Hso-noom (son of the Muang Loen prince) and the SSA 2nd Brigade to defect under the Burmese KKY programme, but returned to join the SSA 1st Military Region in 1970 together with Chao Hso-noom. When the SSPP was formed in 1971, Sai Kyaw Sein was a central committee member. In 1977, he was stripped of all army and party posts for misconduct by the acting chief-of-army Staff, Sai Zam Muang, and he defected to the CPB. In late 1984, following the realignment of the SSA with the CPB, Sai Kyaw Sein was moved back to the Shan army.

Kyaw Toon

Chao; also known as Chao Hso-won, the hero of Tangyan. He studied at Rangoon University for several years, excelling in sports, but left to join the resistance army (Noom Suk Harn), on the border. He returned shortly to his native Muang Yai (being a member of the ruling house), and persuaded Bo Mawng an UMP (paramilitary police) to rebel. In 1959, their joint force captured Tangyan town and several army outposts as well. It took the army about ten days of constant fighting with air and artillery support to drive out the rebels. Chao Kyaw Toon and Bo Mawng then marched to the Noom Suk Harn headquarters and threw their weight behind student leaders and the SSIA. He died in battle around 1961 while attempting to bring all Kengtung forces under the SSIA. His hideout in Muang Pyak area was raided by the army and he was wounded. He refused to surrender, and blew himself up with a grenade, taking along several Burmese soldiers. The highest award for valour in the SSA is named after him — the Chao Hso-won Star. His father, Chao Naw Mya — the black-sheep of the Muang Yai family, joined the resistance around 1967, serving under Bo Moherng, then still the SSA chief-of-staff. When the latter formed SURA, Chao Naw Mya was for a time one of the vice-presidents, but soon fell out of favour. Chao Naw Mya left SURA in 1978, and did odd-jobs in Thailand. In 1981, he accepted Rangoon's amnesty offer and returned home.

Kyaw Win

Sai, also known as Hso-nong; a Shan-Intha, native of Yawnghwe. (The Intha live on Inle, or Haiya, Lake of Yawnghwe — a fourteen by seven mile body of water. They speak a Burmese dialect similar to that in the Tenasserim coast, but with a Shan accent. It is surmised that their antecedents were from Tavoy who settled in Yawnghwe during the Pagan dynasty.) In 1963–65, Sai Kyaw Win led the Shan students at Rangoon University. He joined the Noom Suk Harn, and was one of the Young Turks who deposed Saw Yanda. He was sent as an SNIA (formerly Noom Suk Harn) representative to the SSA chief-of-staff, Bo Moherng, who was then a key figure. When Bo Moherg formed a splinter group in 1968, he disarmed the SNIA and detained its leaders. Sai Kyaw Win surrendered shortly after, and resumed his studies.

Kyaw Zam

Sai; currently a senior executive in the TRA (formerly SURA of Bo Moherng). A native of Hsenwi, his father was at one time chief secretary to Chao Hom Pha, the Hsenwi prince. In the late 1950s, he was with

Burma's immigration department, then he joined a small rebel band operating near his town, and later, the SSIA. After the SSA was formed in 1964, Sai Kyaw Zam served in the SSA 1st Brigade as an administrative (civil) officer. From 1966–68, he served as aide to Yawnghwe Mahadevi who was the SSA chairperson. He also served with distinction in the SSA 1st military Region (under me). In 1982, Sai Kyaw Zam together with Sai Zam Mai broke away from the pro-communist SSA faction and joined the TRA.

Kyaw-zaw

Former brigadier, Burma Army; currently with the CPB. He was one of the many young men in pre-war British Burma who was swept by the tide of nationalism. He served in the BIA of Aung San, and in the post-independence Burma Army. Kyaw-zaw was a talented star of the army and gained national fame in action against KMT forces in Kengtung, Shan State. These KMT soldiers had fled China after Mao's victory and with clandestine American support had used the Shan State as a base for a reconquest of China via Yunnan province. Though KMT regulars were evacuated under U.N. supervision in 1954 and 1961, the KMT irregulars remained in Shan State with bases in Kengtung, Wa state, and Kokang which served as depots for the opium-heroin-contraband trade. These ex-KMT bases/depots existed till the early 1970s when all Shan-China border areas were occupied by CPB forces. Despite, or because of Kyaw-zaw's successes against the regular KMT in Shan State, he was dismissed in 1960 from the army for implied connections with the White Flag communists. But in late 1974, Kyaw-zaw made his way from Rangoon by car via Mandalay, Hsipaw, Lashio, Hsenwi, Kutkai, and on to the CPB zone on the Shan-China border. The CPB appointed him their military advisor, and head of the military committee, but in the late 1970s and early 1980s, nothing more was heard of him. There were at one time rumours that Kyaw-zaw was in Laos organizing a pro-Soviet (Vietnam-backed) Burmese force. This rumour proved groundless.

Kyadoe

Brigadier (retired), Burma Army; Karen national, who served in the army under the British, and one of the very few who attended Sandhurst. Kyadoe remained behind when the British retreated from Burma in 1942 before the advancing Japanese. He was active among the loyal Karen of the Irrawaddy delta, and when Burmese nationalists turned against the Japanese in 1944, Kyadoe co-operated with the Burma National Army. After independence in 1948, Kyadoe remained with the newly constituted Burma Army but with the Karen uprising in 1949, he was forced out. He went into a business partnership with Bo Letya, one of the Thirty Comrades, and a defence minister during the early years of independence. In 1965, Brigadier Kyadoe joined Bo Yan-naing and Zali Maw, the son of Dr Ba Maw (the wartime Supreme Leader of Burma under the Japanese), and attempted to raise an armed rebellion against Ne Win. In 1970, when U Nu set up the PDP to overthrow Ne Win, Brigadier Kyadoe joined them, and was instrumental in getting the KNU of Bo Mya to ally with U Nu. With the collapse of the PDP in the early 1970s, Kyadoe retired from active politics to a village in Kanchanaburi province, Thailand. In 1981, Kyadoe responded to General Ne Win's amnesty offer and returned. Shortly afterwards, Kyadoe went back to Thailand but he died soon after under unexplained circumstances.

Lai Oo

Bo; Wa, follower of Bo Mawng; closely connected with the Chinese finance-trade-kinship network, and front-man for both the ex-KMT 3rd and 5th Armies. Due to this connection with elements which enjoyed an economic-military stranglehold in Shan State, Bo Lai Oo became an influential figure. In 1965, he put himself nominally under the SSA 2nd Brigade (of Bo Mawng). In 1967, he accepted KKY status and prospered, becoming a close ally of Lo Hsin Han, head of Kokang KKY, who was much favoured by the Burma Army. In 1974, when the KKY programme was scrapped, Bo Lai Oo sold most of his arms to the SSA, and retired. Not long after, he was killed by a disgruntled underling in Tangyan town.

Lao See

Chinese merchant; leader of one of the KKY units set up by the Burma Army in 1967–73. He co-operated closely with the ex-KMT merchant-warlord armies and was part of the finance-trade-kinship network which dominated sectors of the economy of several Southeast Asian countries that transcended politics and national borders.

Lapaw

Saw, or Sawphaya; Karenni Chief of Eastern Karenni, 1866–89; gained prominence when he helped King Mindon disperse the rebel army (mostly Shan and Karenni) of Prince Myingun who had fled to the Karenni hills after failing to overthrow his father. Consequently, Saw Lapaw was recognized by King Mindon as Myoza of Eastern Karenni in 1866. He was fierce and warlike, much feared by Karenni chiefs and smaller Shan lords such as those in Muang Pai and Samkha. In the early 1880s, when major Shan princes, such as Chao Khun Kyi of Muang Nai, and Chao Khun Seng of Hsipaw, rebelled against King Thibaw, the Karenni chief sheltered them. When the British entered the Shan states in 1887, and the Shan accepted their control, Saw Lapaw refused to do so. In 1888, he attacked Mawkmai town since he bore a grudge against the equally martial Chaofa Kolan, who had died. As Mawkmai was then under the British protection, a unit was sent against Saw Lapaw. In a battle near Loikaw (the present capital of Karenni State) — the British defeated the Karenni with a force comprising mostly Shan. Saw Lapaw subsequently sent his nephew, Sawlawi, to make a submission and he was then recognized as chief by Hildebrand, the British Superintendent of the Shan States in 1889. Saw Lapaw later came out of hiding and settled down as a farmer.

Lek

Sai; currently SSA army chief-of-staff; a native of Hsipaw. He was a mere village boy when he joined the SSIA 1st Battalion in 1962. When the SSA was formed in 1964, Sai Lek was an assistant squad commander. He was a good combat commander, and by 1976 commanded a battalion. With many early SSA/SSPP leaders killed or lost to the enemy, Sai Lek became acting army chief-of-operation in 1981 under Chao Hso-noom. After the latter's death in 1984, Sai Lek assumed overall command of all SSA forces (which today is effectively a junior partner of the CPB).

Limbin

Prince; Burmese; member of the House of Alaungpaya, and one of the sons of the Kanaung prince (crown prince and brother of King Mindon) who was killed in 1866 when Myingun and other princes tried to seize the throne. The Limbin prince was educated in Rangoon, British Burma; and when Mindon died and Thibaw ascended the throne, he fled into British territory to escape the bloody massacre of Burmese princes and royalty by Queen Supayalat and her mother. He was appointed a sub-magistrate by the British, but was pensioned off after attempting to raise a rebellion against King Thibaw. The prince was living in Moulmein when he was approached by agents of Chao Kawngtai of Kengtung, the leader of the Shan League in 1885. He agreed to lend his name to the Shan venture to overthrow Thibaw. While preparations were underway, Mandalay fell to the British at the end of 1885. When the British entered the Shan hills in 1887, the Shan League was undecided on what to do since an altogether unexpected set of circumstances had been created. The British too were in a dilemma. They definitely wished to avoid a protracted Shan war which would invite outside (especially French) meddling. However, this uncertainty ended when the Limbin prince agreed to surrender to the British, thus freeing Shan princes from their loyalty oath (in May 1888). The British consequently had the Shan sign treaties individually accepting British suzerainty in exchange for internal sovereignty. The treaties were with the British as a new paramount power in the area, and not as heirs to the Burmese kingdom which the Shan had, since 1882, repudiated.

Limi

Chinese nationalist (KMT) general and World War II hero. He was in command of the KMT 8th Army in Yunnan when Mao took over China. Consequently, Limi and his 8th Army and other KMT units (26th and 93th Divisions) withdrew into Shan State which borders Yunnan. In accordance with the American cold-war strategy and anti-Mao stance in the 1950s (coinciding with the French Indochina War, the Korean conflict, the shelling by Mao of KMT-held offshore islands, and others), Limi received American support. The plan was for the use of Thailand as a logistics base and the Shan State as a staging point for the KMT invasion of China via Yunnan in preparation for the final sea-borne assault on China from Taiwan. General Limi through various mediators (one of them being Olive Yang, sister of the Kokang Chaofa, and commander of all Kokang forces) tried to get the Shan princes to join the American-Taiwan adventure. However, during the early 1950s, the Burmese communist and leftist forces, and various rebels, were strong, and Shan princes and leaders thought it best for all to support the AFPFL and avoid risky adventures. Hence General Limi was unable to politically consolidate the KMT presence in Shan State. Although the KMT was unsuccessful in setting up redoubts within Yunnan, and regular KMT troops were evacuated in 1954 and 1961, remnants managed to entrench themselves on Shan soil as a finance-trade-military power. They were organized into the 3rd and 5th Armies under Li Wen Huan and General Tuan Shi Wen respectively, and monopolized the opium-heroin-contraband-jade business which enriched the finance-trade-kinship Chinese network in serveral Asian countries.

Lin Tin

Karen; commander (élite 5th Kawthoolei Brigade); now dead. In 1964 following a peace agreement between the Karen president, Saw Hunter Thahmwe, and the government, resulting from the peace talks of 1963, he surrendered. Lin Tin was a flamboyant but inspired combat leader who inflicted numerous defeats on the Burma Army, and in 1961, even raided Maesod town in Thailand. He was one of the few Karen who served under the Japanese during the war. After his emergence from the jungle, Lin Tin made headlines when he married Naw Louisa Benson, a former Miss Burma and film star. He was killed under unexplained circumstances by the Burma Army in the mid-1960s. After his death, his widow, Naw Louisa Benson, led the 5th Brigade back into the jungle, but lost out in a power struggle with General Bo Mya who had not accompanied the Karen president in 1964, but remained behind to build up a new resistance centre. Later, she married an American (a former classmate from the United States where she had studied).

Li Wen Huan

Chinese; a self-made general and multi-millionaire who until the early 1980s was actively in command of the ex-KMT 3rd Army. General Li made international headlines as recently as 1984 when his fortress-like house in Chiangmai, Thailand, was demolished by a powerful bomb placed by unknown people. Of obscure origin and only a minor civilian functionary in pre-Mao Yunnan, Li Wen Huan, who accompanied General Limi into Shan State, proved a shrewd and skilful leader of men. After the evacuation of KMT regular units, Li was, by 1959, in command of an invisible trade-military "fiefdom" covering more than one-third of Shan State. In the chaos, following the outbreak of the Shan resistance, he was in possession of the only organized force in the Shan homeland besides the Burma Army. As such, General Li was able to manipulate Shan forces and rebel leaders to further his trading business — at first in opium-heroin, arms, and ammunition, and later in contraband. General Li's opportunity for more trade and profit was greatly enhanced when Rangoon in the early 1950s embarked on a policy of blanket nationalization causing a scarcity of goods and consumer items. In addition, Rangoon's KKY programme increased General Li's economic power as KKY units needed funds, refining facilities, access to market, and storage areas — all of which he had. Moreover, General Li was able to raise taxes (from the KKYs and outside investors) on protection, storage service, sales (from both buyers and sellers), and even for transport service. Nothing of importance or of commercial value — opium, heroin, gems, cattle, hides, elephant tusks, and all merchandise going into Burma via the Shan border escaped General Li's involvement (directly or through subordinates and agents) or taxation. He was indeed an extraordinary figure who reaped several fortunes from the Shan-Burmese war and Burma's misfortune, and he convinced the world outside that he had no dealings in the opium-heroin business. General Li achieved this by publicly burning twenty-four tons of "opium" in 1971. Thereafter, the ex-KMT armies were re-named CIF (Chinese Irregular Forces) by the United States and portrayed in the mass media as tough anti-communist fighters who grew tea and coffee in Thailand's communist-infested northern frontier. As the 1980s approached however, General Li gradually eased himself out of the business — due in the main to the CPB occupying most opium growing areas and jungle trade routes; and the emergence of Li's old enemy, Khun Sa, as a force to be reckoned with. These factors meant, that he would have to take more risks with less profitable returns, and he was getting old.

Lo Hsin Han

Chinese; native of Kokang, Shan State; currently in charge of a militia under Burmese supervision. He made international news in 1973 when he was "snatched" from inside Shan State by Thai police and spirited to Burma Proper via Bangkok. He was featured prominently in Adrian Cowell's documentary *Opium Warlords* (ATV, London) through which

Lo Hsin Han made an offer along with the SSA to end the heroin trade by helping the United States or any interested governments get hold of all Shan opium crops — thus preventing opium from being processed by criminal elements into heroin. Lo began his career in the Kokang KKY under Olive Yang, sister of the Kokang prince (Edward Yang) who had since the early 1950s been permitted by the Burmese to engage in opium trade in exchange for keeping out KMT regulars (and irregulars) from Kokang which borders China. After the 1962 coup, the army was uneasy about Olive Yang and she was detained. However, one of Olive's older brothers, Jimmy Yang, a businessman (whose businesses and money had been nationalized) and a pre-coup MP, made it to Kokang and raised the banner of rebellion. Lo, who had become one of the key Kokang commanders was persuaded by the Burma Army to submit in exchange for permission to trade. Lo served the Burmese well, and took part in the 40-day battle of Kunlong (in the late 1960s) against the CPB. In the opium-heroin-contraband trade, due to his connections with the ex-KMT 3rd Army and local Chinese financiers and syndicates, Lo prospered. With the detention by the Burmese of Khun Sa of the Loimaw KKY in 1970, he became the unofficial leader of all Shan State KKYs. However, when the heroin problem became a hot international issue, due mainly to American anxiety over drug addiction, and the playing of the opium card by Shan nationalists (that is, the SSA) to attract international attention, the Burmese proceeded to dismantle the KKY programme. The SSA contacted Lo Hsin Han, and he agreed to join them in their effort to bring the world to Shan State and thus gain international sympathy for the Shan cause. However, before any of the SSA's plans could be put into action, Lo Hsin Han was lured onboard a Thai police helicopter, detained, and handed over to Burmese authorities. He was tried in 1974, and sentenced by Rangoon to seven years imprisonment. Upon his release in 1981, he was placed in charge of a Kokang Chinese settlement near Lashio, Shan State, and is believed to be involved in the distillery business and other trading activities.

Maha Kanan

Chao; Shan prince who in 1813 regained control of Kengtung state which had been devastated by the Thai. In one of these raids, Maha Kanan was taken to Chiangmai as prisoner, but he escaped. After years of fighting, often alone, he managed to gain control of Kengtung and

was recognized by the Burmese king at Ava as *chaofa*. He is the founder
of the present ruling family of Kengtung.

Maha Ne-myo

Burmese prince and general who commanded the Shan contingent against
the British in the war of 1824.

Maha Sang

Son of the Wa Chief of Vieng Ngun; currently serving under the ex-
KMT 3rd Army. In the KKY period (1967–73), Maha Sang's Vieng
Ngun group was subordinate to Lo Hsin Han's Kokang KKY, and joined
the SSA after the KKY programme was abolished. In 1977, he set up
the Wa National Army which was accepted by the Karen as a member
of the NDUF (National Democratic United Front), but shortly after he
subordinated himself to SURA (of Bo Moherng). In 1982, Maha Sang
again made a move, joining the ex-KMT 3rd Army.

Mawn-la

Chao; Shan princess of the Muang Mao kingdom who was given in
marriage, or as tribute (Burmese version) to King Anawratha of Pagan
in the eleventh century. She was banished, according to the Burmese
version of the tale, for knowledge of the black arts, while the Shan say
she was a victim of court intrigue. A film depicting this tale, made in
the late 1950s, caused riots in several Shan towns.

Maung Maung

Former brigadier, Burma Army. He was active in pre-war Burmese
nationalist politics, and had served under Aung San in the BDA (Burmese
Defence Army) during the Japanese era. He became one of the key
men in the post-independence Burma Army, and was prominent in the
1958–60 military caretaker government, but was subsequently dismissed
by Ne Win. Maung Maung was given an ambassadorial post and served
in this capacity for a long time.

Maung Maung

Doctor of Law; Burmese; author of Burma's constitution. One of the few Burmese intellectuals who sincerely and deeply admired General Ne Win.

Mawng

Chao; twice the ruling Prince of Yawnghwe (1864–85, 1897–1926) he was granted a British Knighthood in 1916. He was brought up in the Mandalay Palace and adopted by King Mindon as an honorary son. The new king, Thibaw, did not trust Chao Mawng and ordered him to stay at Mandalay. During his absence, a cousin, Chao Chit Su, was made *chaofa* by the rebellious League of Shan Princes. When the British captured the Burmese capital, Mandalay, in 1885, Chao Mawng was there, but he soon returned to Yawnghwe. He was involved in a number of fights with the league and was wounded. He returned to Mandalay for treatment, leaving the state in charge of a half-brother, Chao Ohn, who however proclaimed himself *chaofa*. When the British went into the Shan states in 1887, Chao Ohn was recognized as prince till his death in 1897. Chao Mawng then resumed charge and brought so much progress that he was knighted by the British.

Mawng

Bo; Wa paramilitary officer (Union Military Police) who distinguished himself against the KMT in the early and mid-1950s. In 1959, together with Chao Kyaw Toon, a Rangoon University student, Bo Mawng attacked and captured Tangyan town, holding it for almost ten days. He then made his way to the Noom Suk Harn base on the Thai border believing that American arms and supplies were waiting there. He lost all faith in the Noom Suk Harn president, Saw Yanda, the source of such a tale, and supported the students when they broke away to form the SSIA. Because Mo Mawng was very influential among the Wa in the opium growing area, he was courted by ex-KMT merchant-warlord elements, and he soon fell under their influence, but remained nominally attached to the SSIA and later the SSA of the students. However, by the early 1970s, the CPB began occupying the Wa areas and Kengtung, and all ex-KMT units fled to the Thai border. Bo Mawng refused to have any dealings with the CPB, and surrendered to the Burmese at, ironically enough, Tangyan.

Mawng

Sai, also known Lao-leng; a high school student from Muang Yai who joined the Shan resistance in 1959. He played an important role in the early years of the SSIA, becoming chief-of-operations of the SSIA 1st Battalion; and later of the SSA 4th Brigade. From 1967 to 1972 he was posted to the SSA army headquarters on the Thai border. He was killed in 1973.

Mawrel

Saw; currently president of the KniNPP. Served in one of the Karen Rifles after independence, but joined in the Karen uprising in 1949. Saw Mawrel served under Saw Shwe, a Karenni chief who opposed the joining of the Karenni homeland to the Union of Burma. After Saw Shwe's death, Saw Mawrel became the leader of the Karenni movement. In the early 1970s he co-operated with the SSA and played an important role in founding the National Democratic Liberation Front (NDLF, composed of Karen [KNU], Karenni [KniNPP], Arakan [ALP], Mon [MNSP], Shan [SSA/SSPP], Padaung [KNLP], and the Pa-O, with a Chin group as an ally). Its aim was to contain the CPB's expansion in Shan State, and eventually to constitute a "third force" in Burma's politics.

Mee-Yak

Also known as Ja So Bo; a Lahu leader of the Pangyang KKY which was a small outfit involved mainly in convoy duty for ex-KMT merchant-warlords before and during the KKY period.

Menges, Chris

British who co-produced with Adrian Cowell two documentaries *The Unknown War; Opium Warlords* on Shan rebels. His subsequent fame was in the Oscar-winning films *The Killing Fields* and *The Mission*.

Mindon

King; the tenth monarch (1853–78) of the Alaungpaya dynasty. By the time King Mindon ascended the throne, Burma had lost her lower provinces as a result of the Second Anglo-Burmese War (1852). He was forward-looking and attempted to modernize the kingdom. In 1859, he shifted the capital from Amarapura further down the Irrawaddy River to Mandalay. In 1872, he convened the fifth Buddhist Synod. Though pious and kind, his reign was a troubled one. There was a bloody palace coup attempt in 1866 involving many of his nephews. Mindon's brother and heir, a capable leader, was killed by the plotters as were many senior ministers. King Mindon also faced a major rebellion by the Shan of Hsenwi led by Tao Sanghai and Khunsang Ton-huung which continued after his death. He was forced in 1875 to recognize, jointly with the British, the independence of the Karenni.

Ming-jui

Prince, son-in-law of the Manchu emperor who led the Chinese invasion of Burma 1766–69. In order to get to Ava, the Burmese capital, he had to cross the rugged Shan country (that is, Upper Burma and the present Shan State) which meant that he had to first fight the Shan. This proved very costly and the Chinese were exhausted by the time they reached the Burmese plains. Prince Ming-jui committed suicide to atone for his failure. He was a good commander and much loved by his men.

Moherng

Bo, also known as Kon Zoeng; currently (1985) president of a combined Shan force (TRA and the SUA of Khun Sa). A native of Lai-sak in Yawnghwe, he joined the White Flag communists in the early 1950s in order to counter the rampaging Pa-O rebels. In 1955, a Shan contingent of the White Flag broke away with the aim of setting up a Shan State communist party, but was unsuccessful, and this group (which included Moherng) surrendered. In late 1958, Moherng made his way to the Noom Suk Harn base on the Thai border. In an attack on a Burmese outpost at Bung Pakem, he was wounded and had one arm amputated. In 1960, he made his way back to the Laikha-Lawksawk-Muang Kung area as a Noom Suk Harn organizer, but shortly after combined with the students'

SSIA group under Khun Kya Nu, thus forming SNUF. When the SSA was formed under the Yawnghwe Mahadevi, the widow of the first Union President, Bo Moherng was made army chief-of-staff. However, he did not trust the student leaders, and with the support of General Li of the ex-KMT 3rd Army formed SURA in 1968. In the early 1980s, Bo Moherng distanced himself from General Li, who had gone into semi-retirement, and combining with Sai Zam Mai, the head of the SSA southern faction, formed TRA. At present, Bo Moherng is attempting to set up an informal Shan government-in-exile with the help of Khun Sa. Bo Moherng, as Shan Prime Minister designate, has declared war against narcotics since it is detrimental to the cause of Shan freedom.

Munn Hpa

Chao; died in mid-1960s; younger brother and heir to the Hsenwi prince, Chao Hom Pha. Like most males of Shan ruling families, he was educated at Shan Chiefs School, Taunggyi, and served in the military before World War II. During the war, he was detained by the Japanese for clandestine contacts with the Allies, and was almost executed, Chao Munn Hpa managed the affairs of Hsenwi in the absence of the Prince who served as Special Commissioner of Northern Shan State in the post-independence years. In the election of 1960, Chao Munn Hpa was elected one of the MPs for Hsenwi, unseating his sister, the Yawnghwe Mahadevi.

Mya

Bo; Karen, currently president and commander-in-chief of the Karen movement. Of humble and obscure origin, he took part in the 1949 general Karen uprising. He proved a good combat leader. In 1964, when the then Karen president, Saw Hunter Thahmwe signed a peace accord with the Burmese, Bo Mya remained in the jungle, and by the late 1960s had built up a new Karen army with himself as supreme leader. In the early 1970s, when U Nu, the former Prime Minister of Burma, formed the PDP to overthrow Ne Win by arms, Bo Mya joined the front set up by U Nu. At the same time, Shan SSA/SSPP leaders, together with the Karenni's Saw Mawrel, were attempting to set up a non-Burmese front, and Bo Mya lent his name and energy to this. Thus was the NDLF established, and the Karen withdrew from the PDP front. The NDLF was changed in 1977 to National Democratic United Front (NDUF). Since 1983, Bo Mya and the Karen army have frequently hit international headlines for the successful repulsion of repeated and massive Burma Army assaults against Karen strongholds on the Thai border.

Myingun

Prince; nephew of King Mindon who, in 1866, attempted to seize the throne. Subsequently he fled to the Karenni area and collected a Shan-Karenni force which was, however, defeated by the famed Karenni chief, Saw Lapaw, and other Shan princes. Prince Myingun then sought asylum in British Lower Burma. Disallowed by the British to subvert the Burmese kingdom, he then fled to French Pondicherry in India, and later moved on to Saigon. When the British finally moved to capture Mandalay at the end of 1885, Prince Myingun's presence in French Saigon caused them some anxiety; more so, since the Shan were organized in a Shan League whose original aim was to capture Mandalay, the royal capital. The British did not know what the league would do, but feared that if the Myingun prince was able to win over the league, the French would be able to jeopardize British presence in Burma. This was one of the main reasons why the British went to the Shan homeland in 1887.

Myint Aung

Sai, also known as Hso-khan or Ongbong; Shan, native of Hsipaw; killed in action against the Burma Army in 1979. He studied at Rangoon University for two years before joining the Noom Suk Harn in 1958. When the SSIA was formed by student leaders, Sai Myint Aung played a key role in consolidating it in Northern Shan State. With the formation of the SSA in 1964, Sai Myint Aung was made a member of the SSWC chaired by the Yawnghwe Mahadevi. In 1966, he returned to the front lines and held the SSA together at a time when there was widespread fighting between Khun Sa's Loimaw KKY and other Shan rebel bands, and when the SSA chief-of-staff, Bo Moherng was trying to rally SSA units to his personal banner. In 1968, when I reorganized the SSA into the SSA 1st Military Region, Sai Myint Aung was made senior advisor. When the SSPP was formed in 1971, he was elected one of its vice-presidents. In 1974–75, when the SSA/SSPP was split over whether it should accept weapons from the CPB, Sai Myint Aung headed the majority which favoured a military alliance of convenience with the communists. In 1976, with the removal of Khun Kya Nu from the presidency of the SSA/SSPP, and with the resignation of many staunchly non-communist leaders, Sai Myint Aung became acting president until he was killed.

Myobye Narapathe

King of Ava (1546–52); Shan. He was a nephew of the Prince of Ongbong or Hsipaw, the kingmaker of Ava, and he was also ruler of Muang Pai (which at that time included a large part of Mae Hongson in present day Thailand). His rule coincided, unfortunately, with the resurgence of Burmese power under King Burinnong of Toungoo, and he submitted in 1552.

Naw Hpa

Chaofa; Yawnghwe Chaofa (1858–64), who rebelled against the Burmese, and was forced to flee to Siam. Siam has historically been a place of asylum for Shan rebels. About ten years ago, I was informed of a ninety year old man living in a village not far from Chiangmai who claimed descent from a Yawnghwe ruling prince. He died before I could meet him.

Naw Pha

Chao; one of the numerous offsprings of Chaofa a Khun Pan Sing of Namsan or Tawngpeng state. He was educated at St Paul's High School, Rangoon, and went on to Germany for further studies. In 1968, Chao Naw joined the Shan resistance serving under Bo Moherng in SURA. Currently he is general-secretary of the Tai Revolutionary Council, composed of top leaders of SURA (Bo Moherng) and SUA (Khun Sa), formed in 1985.

Naw Muang

Sai; currently acting president of the northern SSA, in close alliance with the CPB; Shan, native of Bet-kang circle of Kengtung state, a tea growing area. He joined the resistance movement in Kengtung, but unlike other Kengtung military leaders built up the Bet-kang into a fairly disciplined force, and when the Muang Yang Brigade (under Khun Myint) joined the CPB, Naw Muang brought his force into the SSA/SSPP in 1972. In 1983 after Sai Hla Aung's defection to the Burmese, Naw Muang was made acting president and signed a military pact with the CPB.

Naw Seng

Formerly a captain in the Kachin Rifles in the post-1948 Burma Army. He served in World War II under the British. When the Karen took up arms in 1949, Naw Seng joined them and captured Maymyo, an important military base as part of a larger operation which did not succeed. He then fought his way to the Kachin area of Hsenwi via Lashio. Naw Seng also attempted to get Chao Hom Hpa, the Hsenwi prince, to join in the general uprising, but failed. Chased by loyal Kachin and Shan units of the Burma Army, Naw Seng and his band slipped into China. Nothing was heard of him for eighteen years until 1967 when he reappeared in Shan State as military commander of the CPB. Naw Seng proceeded on a dynamic offensive (1967–71), in which the Burma Army lost at least 20,000 soldiers who were killed or wounded, and about 15,000 sq miles of territory. In 1971, the CPB suddenly declared that Naw Seng had died in a hunting accident, but Kachin sources maintain that he was assassinated for being too popular and independent.

Ne Win

Bo, also known as Thakin Shu-maung; Army General; currently chairman of the Burmese Way to Socialism Party (BSPP); in full control of Burma. He was in the pre-World War II days a post office employee, but active in the nationalist movement, and was then known as Thakin Shu-maung. He changed his name to Bo Ne Win when as a member of the Thirty Comrades, he underwent Japanese military training on Hainan island. When the BIA was formed, Ne Win impressed Aung San, the undisputed leader of Burmese nationalists, who made Ne Win the second in charge. During the Japanese years, when Aung San was Defence Minister in the puppet government of Dr Ba Maw, he appointed Ne Win commander of the BDA. After independence, Ne Win commanded the 4th Burma Rifles, the only Burmese unit which was totally loyal. As a result, after the resignation of General Smith Dun, a Karen, Ne Win was made Army

Chief of Staff. In the years that followed, Ne Win kept a low political profile, even giving the impression that he was a playboy. When the ruling AFPFL split followed by a number of government crises, Ne Win persuaded U Nu, the Prime Minister, to hand over power to the military. The caretaker government (1958–60), was very popular with the foreign news media and analysts since it made trains run on time, but was not popular with the people who, returned U Nu to power in the 1960 election by a landslide. General Ne Win was, however, prepared for this, and dismissed all senior army officers who figured prominently in the caretaker years such as Colonel Maung Maung, Tun Shein, among others. In 1962, Ne Win again seized power, giving as pretext the move by the Shan, Kachin, Chin, Karenni, Karen, Mon and Arakan who called for a constitutional reform, and this he and the army interpreted as a threat to national unity. Ne Win embarked on an extreme left path (as opposed to the slightly rightist tone of the previous period), nationalizing all private enterprises and trade. In 1963, Ne Win called all rebels to hold peace talks which he cut short when the public showed more sympathy for the rebels. In 1968, Ne Win formed a 33-member Advisory Committee (U Nu was also a member) to decide on a future constitution, but it was abolished when the majority recommended a federal arrangement. In 1974, he presented the country with a new constitution which made Burma a unitary one-party state, following a closely supervised national referendum. A significant point about General Ne Win is that none of his contemporaries thought very highly of him, and no one thought he could remain for so long in power (from 1962 to the present). A characteristic tough of Ne Win is that prominent subordinates do not survive for long as can be seen from a string of dismissed "No. 2"s such as Brigadier Maung Maung, Aung Gyi, Tin Pe, Tin U, San Yu (elevated to national President, but powerless), and General Tin Oo (former MIS chief, and general-secretary of BSPP).

Nga Mya

Intelligence agent, Burma Army. He infiltrated the CPB. By the mid-1960s, Nga Mya had become a member of Thakin Than Tun's security unit, assassinated the communist leader, and "defected". In the early 1970s, he was captured by the Karen and executed.

Ngaa-muang

Bo, also know as Sara Sang Keng; Shan guerilla leader heading one of the small rebel bands which mushroomed all over Shan State in 1959; formerly a travelling herbal-healer and master tattooist. When the SSIA was formed in 1961, he submitted to student leaders and was made commander of the 1st Battalion. In the SSA, Ngaa-muang was made 4th Brigade commander. He was later placed in charge of the military bureau of the SSA 1st Military Region. In 1973, due to advanced aged, Bo Ngaa-muang went into semi-retirement, and in 1979 he became a monk.

Ni

Bo; MIS officer, Burma Army; currently in prison with General Tin Oo for misuse of funds and power. He served for a long time in Shan State and played an important role in undermining the prestige and influence of traditional Shan leaders. Ni was Home Minister at the time of his dismissal (1983).

Nong

Sai; Shan of Indian descent, currently a village militia (*pyithu-sit*) leader in Muang Nai. Joined the resistance in the early 1960s and had by 1966 become a key figure in the SNIA (formerly the Noom Suk Harn). In 1968, Bo Moherng, then SSA chief-of-staff, collaborating with Saw Yanda (former head of Noom Suk Harn), and with the support of General Li of the ex-KMT 3rd Army, formed SURA, and in the process crushed the SNIA. Sai Nong thereupon defected and formed the Muang Nai KKY, and prospered by smuggling goods.

Nu

U; Burma's Prime Minister from 1948–62; native of Wakema in the Irrawaddy delta region; gained prominence at Rangoon University as student leader and was respected by the younger crop of Burmese nationalists such as Aung San, Kyaw Nyein, and Letya, and though not much older was regarded by them as a senior statesman. After the assassination of Aung San in July 1947, U Nu became Prime Minister. It was due mainly to U Nu's courage, diplomacy, and his close relationship with the Shan, Kachin, Chin, and Karenni leaders that the bid for power by the strong and well-organized communist factions (led by Thakin Than Tun and Thakin Soe) was thwarted. U Nu also did his best to reach an understanding with Saw Ba U Gyi, the supreme Karen leader; but sentiments of hate and distrust were too strong for them to overcome. U Nu strongly supported India's Nehru in the former's effort to chart a non-aligned course for Asian nations, and did all he could to gain the friendship of China. At the same time, U Nu also maintained a good relationship with the West, particularly Britain and the United States, thus gaining for Burma the high regard of both power blocs and many economic and trade benefits. Internally, he handled the insurgency problem wisely so that both the Red Flag (then known as CPB) and the White Flag (BCP of Than Tun) communists became ineffective jungle bands. He also did much to foster Burmese language and literature, and Buddhism — convening a Buddhist synod at the newly erected Kaba-Aye (World Peace Pagoda). U Nu's main weakness was his inability to control the military, and the ruling AFPFL (formed on the eve of Japan's defeat in order to expel the Japanese from Burma). Although he was forced to hand over power constitutionally to the army in 1958, he spent the two following years whipping up democratic and anti-totalitarian sentiments which brought him a landslide victory in the 1960 election. But U Nu failed to curb the military. Though the non-Burmese leaders trusted him, it seemed that U Nu was unable to banish the fear of secession by the Karenni and Shan states in particular. (There was a provision for secession in the constitution.) U Nu's greatest failure was the mishandling of the proposal for constitutional reforms tabled by the constituent states of the Union which gave the military a pretext to stage the 1962 coup. He was put in prison for five years, and upon release Ne Win asked him to head an advisory committee in 1968. To his credit, U Nu very courageously advised that Ne Win hand over power to him (as the legal and popularly elected Prime Minister). Not long after, U Nu was permitted to leave Burma for medical treatment. When abroad, he called upon the people to rise against Ne Win's dictatorship, a call which electrified the country. However, U Nu proved an inept revolutionary. Not only did he fail to win over, and exploit existing Karen, Shan, Karenni, Kachin armies, and dissidents within the Burma Army, he was also ousted from the PDP, the party that he formed. U Nu did not have any realistic plans, and believed that Ne Win would collapse easily, showing the widespread underestimation of Ne Win prevalent among Burmese leaders and politicians. U Nu then went into exile in Bopal (India) in 1973. In 1981, when Ne Win announced an amnesty, U Nu returned to Burma to devote himself to translating Pali-Burmese Buddhist texts into English.

Nyan-win

Sai, also known as Seng Haan; killed in 1983; native of Hsipaw and son of Hsipaw's chief minister and magistrate; graduated from Rangoon University in 1962. In 1963, he accompanied the Yawnghwe Mahadevi and three of her children from Rangoon to the Thai border. Sai Nyan-win served in civil affairs and administration in the SSA 4th Brigade, and later in the SSA 1st Military Region. In 1970, he was moved to SSA army headquarters serving under Khun Kya Nu as staff chief-of-office. In 1977, after the change in the SSA/SSPP leadership, Sai Nyan-win served as head of the external affairs office. In 1981, he was acting general-secretary of the SSA/SSPP, and shortly after, elected general-secretary of the NDUF (composed of Karen [KNU], Karenni [KniNPP], Mon [MNSP], Shan [SSPP], Arakan [ALP], and Pa-O, Wa, and Lahu organizations).

Nyunt

Sai; killed in 1973; Shan; native of Hsipaw, and high school student who joined the resistance in 1959 during the battle of Tangyan. A member of the SSIA since its inception, he served in the 4th Battalion in various capacities. When the SSA was formed, he was assistant head of civil administration in the 1st Brigade, and head of information and intelligence bureau in the SSA 1st Military Region (1968–72). He was moved to SSA army headquarters and while on a mission in Chiangmai, was killed in an assassination attempt on my life.

Ohn

Chao; Prince of Yawnghwe (1885–97); an ambitious member of the Yawnghwe ruling family who was given temporary charge of the state by his half-brother and rightful *chaofa*, Chao Mawng. Chao Ohn thereupon proclaimed himself *chaofa*, an act which in addition to further infuriating the Shan League, also alienated the rightful *chaofa*. As the league was getting stronger, Chao Ohn's position grew increasingly shaky. He appealed repeatedly through Crosthwaithe (the Commissioner) to the British at Mandalay to intervene. The former, worried by possible French intrusion decided to enter the Shan highlands. Fortunately for Chao Ohn, the usurper, it was British policy to recognize the *de facto* ruler so as to avoid any fighting, and he was therefore recognized by treaty as Chaofa of Yawnghwe. Upon Chao Ohn's death in 1897, the position reverted to Chao Mawng, the traditional rightful ruler.

Ohn Kya

Chao; Prince of Hsipaw (1928–38), son of Sir Chao Khe (one of the two Shan who was knighted; the other being Sir Chao Mawng of Yawnghwe). He was educated at Oxford, gaining a Masters degree. On his return, he received training in administration and later served under his father in Hsipaw. He was a modern man and as such saw clearly that the British were disregarding the treaties of 1888 which recognized the Shan principalities of semi-sovereign protectorates. They had in 1922 placed the Federated Shan States under the Lieutenant-Governor of Burma, and the Council of Princes then did not enjoy any legislative or political power. Chao Ohn Kya and some younger *chaofa* feared that when Burma was granted self-government (according to British intentions), the Shan states would be handed over to the Burmese without any political arrangements. The princes as well as the Shan people had no faith in Burmese administration (from past experience), and the Shan had by 1882 repudiated allegiance to the Burmese crown. From the late 1920s onward, Chao Ohn Kya and like-minded princes — Chao Shwe Thaike (Yawnghwe), Chao Kawngtai (Kengtung), Chao Kin Mawng (Muang Mit), and Chao Hom Hpa (Hsenwi), appealed (particularly at the Special Round Table Conference on Burma in 1931) to the British to take into account the special political status of the Shan homeland. However, the British did not respond to numerous pleas made by the Shan, and instead were committed to the amalgamation of the Shan and other non-Burmese areas with Burma. Contrary to Burmese nationalist propaganda that British imperialism divided the country and encouraged separate nationalism, the opposite was actually the case.

Ohn Kya

Khun; chief commissioner of Shan State from the late 1950s to the 1962 coup; native of Hsenwi and at one time the state's chief minister. He was educated at Rangoon University, and married Chaonang Seng-zanda, the sister of the Hsenwi prince. During World War II he was in touch with the Americans (Office of Strategic Services), and in the post-war years served in the Shan State civil service. Khun Ohn Kya and his wife left Burma in 1970 to join their son in Australia. He died in 1979 at the age of seventy-two.

Paan

Bo; one of the many guerilla leaders at the outbreak of Shan resistance; formerly a bandit and adventurer. He also saw service against Pa-O and other insurgents as a member of Shan Levies in the years immediately after independence. He refused to submit to the students, but his band was finally scattered or absorbed by the SSA 1st Brigade when I was its brigade chief-of-staff.

Pan

Sai, also known as Boontai; killed in 1983; native of Kat-tao, Kengtung; studied medicine at Rangoon University but joined the resistance in 1958 before completing his studies. When the SSIA was formed in 1961, he was general-secretary, but did not go up into the interior. In 1963, when Ne Win called for peace talks, Sai Pan went to Rangoon from the Thai border, but had to subordinate himself to the official SSIA-SNUF team which I was head of. When the SSA was formed in 1964, he was made assistant army chief-of-staff, and was a strong supporter of Bo Moherng, the chief-of-staff, but remained with the SSA when Moherng broke away in 1968. Sai Pan spent the next few years with the Kengtung SSA East, and when Khun Myint's Muang Yang Brigade joined the CPB, he fled, arriving at the SSA 1st Military Region. When the SSPP was formed in 1971, Sai Pan became one of its vice-presidents. When the issue on whether or not to accept arms from the CPB arose he supported those in favour, but he made his way to the SSA southern base when the majority opted for an alliance of convenience with the CPB. In 1977, after a change in the SSA/SSPP leadership, and the death of Sai Myint

Aung, he was made acting president. In 1980, Sai Pan was demoted by Sai Hla Aung who became president in 1981.

Pan Aung

Bo; Chinese who joined the Shan resistance in 1959, and served as SSIA deputy chief-of-operations, 4th Battalion; held the same post in the SSA 1st Brigade. In 1966, he was rotated to SSA army headquarters and given charge of arms purchases. In 1972, he escorted the ATV television team (Adrian Cowell, Chris Menges, and a ten-pack mule team) into the Shan State, and enroute, engaged in a running fight with SURA and the ex-KMT 3rd Army. In 1976, Bo Pan Aung staged a mini-coup ousting the SSA/SSPP's president Khun Kya Nu, bringing about a change in leadership. He was made acting army chief-of-operations, but while on a mission in Maesai (Thailand) area with Sai Zam Muang (the acting army chief-of-staff), they and an orderly mysteriously disappeared.

Pan-mai

Sai; commanded at the beginning of the resistance one of the numerous rebel bands, and previously a village circle head (*pu haeng*) in Muang Hsu state. In 1961, he accepted the SSIA and was made commander of SSIA 3rd Battalion. In 1964, he was made commander of SSA 3rd Brigade. In 1968, Sai Pan-mai accepted KKY status offered by the Burmese. Presently he is serving the Burmese as a township-level functionary.

Pao Yung

Bo; Chinese bandit leader and adventurer who commanded one guerilla band in the late 1950s. In 1961, the SSIA organizer for the north Sai Hla Aung managed to win him over. However, Pao Yung was later executed for committing a series of robberies.

Pawlam Ho Mang

Former village circle head in Muang Yai state. At the start of the Shan resistance, he commanded a band and took part in the battle of Tangyan. He refused to submit to the students, and uniting with like-minded others, he resisted SSIA unity efforts. He died of old age in the mid-1960s.

Po Kun

Bo; Burmese politician, leader of the leftist PVO which originally was set up by Aung San, and composed of former BIA, BDA, and BNA (Burma National Army) members who were rejected by the post-war Burma Army. The PVO was to be the vanguard of the armed struggle for independence in the event the British used force. After Aung San's death, the PVO fell under the influence of the communists. Consequently, they joined in the communist uprising in 1949. However, by the late 1950s, the PVO had become a junior partner of the White Flag communists. Bo Po Kun surrendered. When the 1962 coup took place, the regime's leftist and socialist colour appealed to Bo Po Kun who then co-operated with the coup-makers. As a reward, he was appointed ambassador to Thailand in the late 1960s. His present whereabouts and fate are not known.

Pung Ja-sin

Kokang Chinese; currently a senior functionary within the CPB. In 1965, after the Burmese detained Olive Yang and her brother Jimmy Yang who had attempted to make a stand in Kokang and subsequently fled to the Thai border (following the defection of the top Kokang commander, Lo Hsin Han, and others), Pung Ja-sin remained in Kokang. He and his men kept the spirit of resistance in Kokang smouldering, waiting for the return of the main force being reorganized on the Thai border. This force, designated as SSA 5th Brigade (Kokang) came up in 1966, but a large part under its commander, Francis Yang (younger brother of Jimmy Yang), surrendered to the Burmese. Pung Ja-sin then fled to China and was persuaded to join the CPB by the Chinese authorities.

Pungshwe Zau Seng

Kachin leader, killed in 1975. A graduate of Rangoon University, he joined the Shan civil service before eventually joining the KIA. By the late 1960s, Pungshwe Zau Seng had risen to rank of general-secretary of the KIO (the political vanguard of the KIA). In 1973, he accompanied the KIA army chief-of-staff, Zau Tu, to the Thai border. Both were assassinated at the KIA border base camp by an MIS agent (Shengtu, a Kachin national) who had infiltrated the camp.

Saa-tun

Sai, also known as Hso-zeung; killed in 1981; Shan, native of Hsipaw; graduated from Rangoon University, and joined the resistance in 1963. When the SSA was formed in 1964, Sai Saa-tun served as civil administration head of SSA 4th Brigade, and as deputy brigade chief-of-staff. In 1967, he was rotated to army headquarters on the Thai border and played an active role in Shan unity (under me), and going into Laos on liaison missions. In 1968–71, he helped establish the SSA 1st Military Region, and served brilliantly as deputy head of the civil administration bureau and chief political organizer. After the forming of the SSPP, Sai Saa-tun was a member of the political executive committee of the party, and also headed the party security and administrative council with overall command of all irregular units. In 1972 he was rotated to SSA's southern base, serving as head of the trade and revenue department. With the change in the SSA/SSPP leadership in 1976, Sai Saa-tun left the resistance. He was a self-employed trader when he was assassinated by unknown elements.

Sai-luang

Chao; Chaofa of Kengtung (till 1962); was a minor when the Kengtung prince, Chao Kawngtai died. He was educated in Australia and returned to Kengtung only after World War II. As *chaofa*, he was well-loved by the people and did much to foster education in Kengtung, especially providing grants to university students from Kengtung. Chao Sai-luang also lent his support to nationalist activist groups as the Shan State Students Association and Shan Literary Society of the universities in Rangoon and Mandalay. He was highly regarded by all sections of Shan society and would have become a key national figure were it not for the 1962 coup. Chao Sai-luang like many Shan princes and prominent figures was imprisoned for five years without trial. After his release, he was included in the 33-member advisory council set up by Ne Win which advised that a federal structure be adopted. Presently, Chao Sai-luang lives in Rangoon and is highly esteemed by Rangoon's diplomatic community.

Saimong Mangrai

Chao; currently living in Rangoon; senior member of the Kengtung ruling family, and foremost Shan intellectual and educator; educated in Thailand,

Britain and the United States. He served as chief educational officer in Shan State (1948–62), and for a time was the Shan State education minister. Chao Saimong helped to modernize the Shan script, and was attempting to upgrade the teaching of the Shan language throughout Shan State when the army staged its coup in 1962. Shan is now no longer taught in schools, even its teaching outside schools in summer by university students has been banned. Chao Saimong, though apolitical, was like many prominent Shan, imprisoned without trial. His wife Daw Mi Mi Khaing is well-known as the author of *A Burmese Family* (1946), and was one time principal of Kambawza College (formerly Shan Chiefs School) at Taunggyi. She is a Mon-Burmese. Chao Saimong wrote *The Shan State and the British Annexation* (1965), a useful reference book on the Shan State at the point of impact with the British. One of Ne Win's sons by Daw Khin May Than, Pyone Ne Win, married Chao Saimong's daughter.

Samma Duwa Sinwa Naung

Kachin chief who played an important role in the founding of the Union of Burma, and one of the signatories of the historic Panglong Agreement of 1947. After independence, 1948, the *Samma Duwa* (Kachin for "chief") served for a period as Head of Kachin State, and was active in Kachin-Burmese politics, much courted by the ruling AFPFL party. In the 1961 Constitutional Reform Conference at Taunggyi, the *Samma Duwa* urged participants to be more discreet and cautious which, incidentally, was not well received since it was known that he was angling for the Union Presidency. When the 1962 coup took place, the *Samma Duwa* was deprived of the chance of becoming Union President and instead had to content himself with the post of ambassador to Beijing.

Sam Toon

Chao; Prince of Muang Pawn; member of Burma's interim cabinet when he was assassinated with Aung San and other cabinet members in July 1947, six months before independence. He came to the forefront when the political status of Shan State was in jeopardy. During World War II, the Japanese had divided the Shan country into two parts: the smaller (Kengtung and Muang Pan, about 15,000 sq miles) was given to Thailand, and the rest given by treaty to Burma. After the war, the British Labour government had begun the process of decolonization and though it was decided to grant independence to Burma, London had no policy towards the Shan States and "the Karenni country" (which was recognized by Britain as a semi-independent state) or the Frontier Areas (which had been separately administered from the rest of Burma). At the same time, Burmese nationalists demanded the return of these areas, regarding them as part of former Burmese kingdoms, or "lost possessions". There was a real possibility that the Burmese demand would be unconditionally met since the British Labour government was uninterested in undertaking any extra responsibilities. Chao Sam Toon, and two other Shan Statesmen, Chao Shwe Thaike (Yawnghwe prince) and Chao Khun Kyi (Sa-tuung lord) worked together to ensure for the Shan and other hill people (Chin and Kachin) a fair deal in the post-war world. They united the Shan, Kachin, and Chin, thus bringing about the Panglong Treaty of 1947 by which Aung San and the AFPFL recognized the equality and autonomy of the non-Burmese people.

San Thein

Bo; a Pa-O leader who took part in the Pa-O uprising in Shan State, in sympathy with the Karen uprising of 1949, under Thaton Hla Pe. The Pa-O uprising ended in 1958 when Thaton Hla Pe surrendered under the "Arms for Democracy" programme of U Nu. However, in 1966, while Thaton Hla Pe was in prison, Bo San Thein successfully revived the Pa-O army to fight the Burmese. In 1968, at a conference between SURA (of Bo Moherng) and the Pa-O to settle jurisdiction and other problems, there were shots fired. In the ensuring mêlée, Bo San Thein, the Pa-O president, was killed, as was the head of the SURA team and key military commander, Bo Hla Khin (a Karen national).

Sang Sam

Loong; important Shan civil servant; native of Namkham of Hsenwi state. As secretary of the Shan government he played an important role in the constitutional reform movement of 1961. He was imprisoned after 1962 and is believed to have died.

Sang-saw

Bo; native of one of the Chinese Shan States in Yunnan, China. One of the hundreds swept into the resistance movement in 1959, he had by 1963 risen to the rank of battalion commander in Saw Yanda's Noom Suk Harn. When Saw Yanda was deposed in 1966 by the educated Young Turks, Sang-saw assumed the presidency of the SNIA (Shan National Independence Army). In 1968, Saw Yanda with the help of General Li, ex-KMT 3rd Army, captured the SNIA's base camp of Piangluang, and Bo Moherng, the then SSA chief-of-staff, disarmed the SNIA units. Shortly after, Saw Yanda was also pushed out by Bo Moherng, and returned to his farm in Chiangdao, Thailand. One day however, Sang-saw appeared at the farm, and for some time, lived with Saw Yanda. His current whereabouts are not known.

Sanghai

Tao; military leader of Hsenwi who in the 1850s distinguished himself in the Shan repulsion of the Siamese invasions of Kengtung (1850, 1852, and 1854). When he returned, he took command of the smouldering rebellion in Hsenwi against the Burmese-supported prince (Chao Seng Naw Hpa). He was initially successful and defeated various Burmese armies and generals sent against him. However, in accordance with the Burmese policy of pitting Shan against Shan, a combined Shan army (Yawnghwe, Muang Nai, and Muang Mit) was sent to subdue Tao Shanghai who consequently suffered reverses. As it happened, Tao Sanghai had acquired a son-in-law, Khunsang Ton-huung, who proved a better general, and by the mid-1870s, Khunsang Ton-huung had made himself the master of almost the whole of Hsenwi (then covering over 8,000 sq miles).

Saw

U; veteran and prominent Burmese politician executed in 1947 for complicity in the assassination of Aung San and the interim cabinet. He first gained prominence as a fiery nationalist and rabble-rouser in the years when Burmese nationalism was reawakened by the ill-fated Saya San rebellion of 1930. U Saw however chose to work for freedom within the system, and became an important figure in British Burma.

He was made Prime Minister under the British Governor (Dorman-Smith) shortly before World War II. In this capacity, U Saw went to London to obtain Britain's assurance of full independence after the war. In response, Churchill bluntly stated that the Atlantic Charter did not apply to British colonies. Disappointed, U Saw made his way back to Burma via the United States, and while at Hawaii, war in the Pacific broke out. He was unable to return to Burma during the crucial war years, as he spent the period in detention in Uganda for clandestine contact with Japanese agents in Lisbon. When U Saw returned to Burma after the war, the younger nationalists — the AFPFL under Aung San — were in control of the country, forcing the British to negotiate with them, and thus effectively eclipsing him. Added to this bitterness was an attempt on his life in 1946 which he attributed to the AFPFL. This lead U Saw into a rash act the following year which also cost him his life.

Saw Ohn

Colonel (retired), Burma Army; native of Hsenwi and nephew of the Yawnghwe Mahadevi. During World War II, Saw Ohn served in the RAF in the Burma theatre, and after the war received a commission in the Burma Army. In the widespread fighting following independence, he served with the 1st Shan Rifles in Shan State against Kachin mutineers and Pa-O rebels. His eldest daughter was killed in a Pa-O ambush near Panglong. Saw Ohn also served as aide-de-camp to the first Union President, Chao Shwe Thaike, the Yawnghwe prince, for some years before returning to the army. In the late 1950s, while he was posted to Washington as military attache, he came to know General Ne Win who was on a visit. In the mid-1960s, though retired, Saw Ohn was appointed by Ne Win as general manager of the Namtu-Bawdwin Mines (the development of which Herbert Hoover had a part, and he subsequently sold to the British). Saw Ohn was appointed to the Council of State — a senate-like body according to the 1974 constitution, but comprising handpicked and trusted ex-army top brass. Saw Ohn did the SSA a great favour when he refused in the late 1960s to encourage some senior SSA commanders (Bo Hso-lae and Bo Toon-la) who wished to defect under the KKY programme. Had he done so, the SSA 1st Military Region would have collapsed.

Saw-shwe

Karenni chief (or *sawphaya*) of East Karenni who joined the Karen in 1949. He refused to recognize the 1948 Union of Burma since Karenni independence was, since 1875, guaranteed by both the British and the Burmese kingdoms. Unfortunately for the Karenni cause, Saw Shwe did not live long and died of illness in the jungle.

Saw Yanda

Also known as "Chao" Noi; founder of the first Shan resistance body, the Noom Suk Harn (21 May 1958, now celebrated as Shan Resistance Day). A native of one of the Yunnan Shan states who claims to be an illegitimate son of a prince. He first made a name for himself as a nationalist leader among the Shan of Kachin State (who comprise more than 60 per cent of the population) in the mid-1950s, and was at one time jailed for nationalist activities. Being a spellbinding orator and smooth-talker, Saw Yanda managed to convince the Shan in Thailand that he not only enjoyed the confidence of the Shan princes, but the support of the United States and others which enabled him to set up an army on the Thai border. He then styled himself a prince, "Chao" Noi. When patriots from all over Shan State flocked to the border in reaction to Burmese heavy-handedness, Saw Yanda was incapable of capitalizing on the trust he initially enjoyed, resulting in student elements breaking away. In the mid-1960s, Saw Yanda even lost control of the Noom Suk Harn. His house in Chiangdao town (Thailand) was raided by a combined ex-KMT and former Noom Suk Harn force, but fortunately for him he was not at home. In 1968, Saw Yanda attempted a comeback with the help of General Li of the ex-KMT 3rd Army and Bo Moherng, then the SSA chief-of-staff. When SURA was formed, Moherng made Saw Yanda a vice-president, but he was soon pushed out. Saw Yanda now lives the life of a recluse in Chiangdao.

Sein

U; one of the leaders of the KKY units who in 1967–73, were permitted by Burmese authorities to engage in opium-heroin-contraband trade which together with the American presence in Laos and Vietnam contributed to the international heroin business.

Seng Naw Hpa

Chaofa; Prince of Hsenwi who in the 1850s was driven out of Hsenwi by Tao Sanghai, and later Khunsang Ton-huung. Though vigorously supported by King Mindon of Burma, and later by King Thibaw, Chao Seng Naw Hpa was never able to reassert control. When the British went to the Shan State in 1887, the war was still continuing, but with Khunsang Ton-huung winning every engagement. The British managed at the Muang Yai Conference in 1888 to get Khunsang Ton-huung to give some part of Hsenwi to Chao Seng Naw Hpa while retaining the larger share. Thus Hsenwi was divided into North and South Hsenwi, the latter now being known as Muang Yai.

Shao Ser

Chinese trader and a former KKY leader. During the KKY programme (1967–73), he did very well for himself being an ethnic Chinese. He had close connections with the Chinese finance-trade-kinship network, the ex-KMT merchant-warlords, Taiwan intelligence, and with the Burmese authorities. Even after the dissolution of the KKY programme, Shao Ser continued to prosper. But one day, all his consignments (of contraband) were confiscated at Tachilek and Kengtung, and he was thrown into jail for several years. Currently, Shao Ser is on the Thai-Shan border in command of a band under the ex-KMT 3rd Army.

Shwe Thaike

Chaofa; Prince of Yawnghwe; first Union President; Speaker of the Upper House for two terms (1952–60); detained on 2 March 1962, by the coup-makers, died in November 1962 in Insein Jail. According to Shan custom, his body was taken back to Yawnghwe and cremated in full pomp and splendour on a pavilion representing Mount Meru, the abode of the gods. Chao Shwe Thaike was born in 1894, a nephew of the ruling Yawnghwe prince, Sir Chao Mawng. He was educated at Taunggyi's Shan Chiefs School, but not being in the direct line of succession, he enlisted in the army under the British. He served for twenty years, and in World War I was posted to Egypt and Mesopotamia. When Sir Chao Mawng died in 1927, the Council of Ministers of Yawnghwe selected Chao Shwe Thaike as successor. Like other patriotic and enlightened younger princes of the time such as Chao Ohn-kya (Hsipaw), Chao Khin Mawng (Muang Mit), Chao Kawngtai (Kengtung), and Chao Hom Hpa (Hsenwi), the Yawnghwe prince campaigned for British recognition of the Shan homeland as a distinct political entity based on the treaties signed between Britain and the Shan princes in the late 1880s. During the Japanese Occupation, the Shan State was divided by the Japanese: the smaller eastern portion given to Thailand, and the larger part was handed over to Burma by treaty. As a leading Shan *chaofa*, the Yawnghwe prince was much courted by Burmese politicians and pressured to accept the new arrangements. It was a most difficult time for the Shan, more so since there was constant bombings which gave rise to dislocations, and heavy fighting between opposing armies. After the war, the British returned, and with India on the verge of independence, there was no choice for them but to negotiate with Burmese nationalists (AFPFL) under Aung San. In 1946, the British Labour government signed a treaty with Aung San providing for, among others, the amalgamation of the Shan states and other non-Burmese homelands with the independence of Burma — this without any prior consultation with those affected. The Yawnghwe prince together with Chao Sam Toon (Muang Pawn), Chao Khun Kyi (Sa-tuung) — the three Shan statesmen of the period, cabled London saying that Aung San did not represent the non-Burmese, and formed an executive council for Shan State which vested itself with both executive and legislative power. This act, in effect, repudiated British control, and by implication made the Shan State an independent entity. The three Shan statesmen persuaded the Kachin and Chin to unite with them. Thus was the stage set for a major confrontation involving the British, the Burmese, and other national groups (Shan, Kachin, and Chin). However, Aung San proved a great statesman. He recognized and accepted the non-Burmese as partners and negotiated with them resulting in the historic Panglong Agreement of 1947, the founding stone of the Union of Burma. The Yawnghwe prince was made the provisional or first Union President, then served until 1960 as Speaker of the Upper House. Realizing the need to rapidly modernize the Shan State and unite its people, the Yawnghwe prince in 1952 led fellow princes in preparing for the transfer of their power to the Shan government at Taunggyi (which was finalized in 1959 in a ceremony at Taunggyi, attended by General Ne Win who then headed the military caretaker government). In the mid-1950s, he initiated a project to have Burmese Pali Buddhist texts translated into Shan which contributed much to the resurgence of

Shan literature language, and drama, and also national consciousness. When in 1960–61, senior Shan leader such as U Kya Bu, Dr Ba Nyan, and U Toon Myint Lay, initiated a movement for constitutional reforms in order to bring about a genuine federation, the Yawnghwe *chaofa* lent the reformers his immense prestige. At the same time, though a devout Buddhist, he supported the non-Buddhists who protested against making Buddhism the state religion (initiated unwisely by U Nu). Thus he roused the hostility of the Burmese establishment, and newspapers attacked him obliquely, referring to him as "a person as prominent as the sun and the moon fomenting secession". When the coup was staged (2 march 1962), the Yawnghwe prince's residence in Rangoon was surrounded by an army unit who opened fire for half an hour. The prince's favourite son, Chao Mee (aged seventeen) was killed, and the prince was taken away to join other princes, Shan ministers, MPs, civil servants, police officers, prominent businessmen, and leading intellectuals in gaol.

Smith Dun

General; Burma Army (retired 1949); Karen who served in the army under the British, taking part in the evacuation of Burma in 1942, and re-entry in 1945. By then, Smith Dun was in the highest native office, and when the Burma Army was reconstituted after independence, he was made army chief-of-staff. However, when all Karen Rifles mutinied and joined the Karen uprising in 1949, Smith Dun's days were numbered. He was retired and thereafter lived quietly at Kalaw, Shan State until he died of old age. He wrote his autobiography, *Memoirs of the Four-Foot Colonel* (1980).

Soe

Thakin; veteran nationalist and leader of Red Flag communist faction. Unlike other Burmese nationalists, Thakin Soe did not collaborate with the Japanese, but immediately started a resistance movement. In 1944, when Aung San and Thakin Than Tun (a rival communist leader) decided to turn against the Japanese, they had to turn to Thakin Soe and his veteran anti-Japanese fighters who then joined the newly formed AFPFL. Thakin Soe also played an important part in the post-war nationalist agitation for independence. However, the British managed to have Aung San throw out Thakin Soe and his communist faction from the AFPFL, and later,

Thakin Than Tun. Thakin Soe at once formed his own Communist Party of Burma (CPB of the Red Flag), as opposed to Thakin Than Tun's BCP (Burmese Communist Party or the White Flag). The Red Flag creed is a personalized one with a large dose of anarchy, and is closer perhaps to Albanian communism, and moreover, a one-man show. As a result the Red Flag remained a small tight-knit party without much impact except in Arakan, and among students in Rangoon and Mandalay. In 1963, the Red Flag made national headlines when Thakin Soe sent his wife as head of delegation for peace talks with Ne Win. She together with Kyaw Zan Shwee, an Arakanese Red Flag leader, captured the imagination of the Rangoon public with their strong anti-dictatorship platform which, naturally, caused the talks to be quickly terminated. In the mid and late 1960s, when China's radicals ("Gang of Four") opted to support Thakin Than Tun's White Flag, the Ref Flag leader, Thakin Soe, "allowed himself to be captured". He was put on trial and sentenced to death which was later commuted. He now lives on a pension under loose supervision.

Sye-keow

Sai; former officer in the Shan State police who joined the resistance movement in 1968. For a time, in the early 1970s, Sye-keow co-operated with Kokang's Jimmy Yang who had been made commander of Eastern Command (Shan State) by U Nu's PDP. Shortly after, Sye-keow broke away and attempted to rebuild the SSA East which had become defunct when the Muang Yang Brigade (Khun Myint) joined the CPB, and the Bet-kang Brigade (Naw Muang) joined the SSA main force. Sye-keow, however, was unsuccessful, and withdrew in 1978. He is currently self-employed as a trader and broker.

Takale

Bo; currently head of a pro-CPB Pa-O faction. A Karen national from Lower Burma who came up to Shan State in the early 1950s with two elder brothers as part of a KNDO contingent. His eldest brother, Bo Special, made a name for himself in the first Pa-O rebellion as an ambush specialist. In the second Pa-O uprising in the mid-1960s, Bo Takale became the military commander of the movement. However, Takale felt increasingly tempted by the CPB's offer of arms, and in

1974, influenced by communist cadres, attempted to wrest control of the Pa-O movement from the veteran leader Thaton Hla Pe. He lost and with some followers joined the CPB.

Ten Seun-yong

Also known as Bo Gang-hso; currently commanding a Wa unit under the ex-KMT 3rd Army on the Thai-Shan border. A Wa, native of Yunnan (China), who came into Shan State with the general exodus of armed men and refugees following Mao's victory. Served with the KMT in Shan State, and in 1967 became a KKY leader. Like all small KKY leaders, Ten Seun-yong was under the control of ex-KMT merchant-warlord interests. In the mid-1970s, when the CPB moved into the Wa (opium growing) area, Ten Seun-yong fled together with all ex-KMT forces to the Thai border.

Than Tun

Thakin; chairman of the White Flag communists (officially known as the Burmese Communist Party); killed in 1969 by a government agent in command of his security detail. Converted to Marxism in the 1930s, he was very active in the pre-World War II nationalist movement, but often clashed with his brother-in-law, Aung San. By profession he was a school teacher. During the Japanese occupation, Thakin Than Tun served very ably and efficiently as Agriculture Minister in Dr Ba Maw's puppet government, and was thus regarded as a key leader and widely acclaimed. In 1944, with the Allies winning the war, Thakin Than Tun and Aung San formed the AFPFL to fight the Japanese, the former becoming the general-secretary of this front. When the British returned, by encouraging non-communist nationalists under Aung San they managed to get both Thakin Than Tun and Thakin Soe and their communist followers expelled from the AFPFL — thus depriving the communists of any share in power. Unlike Thakin Soe, the former did not plunge into armed rebellion, but prepared together with the AFPFL, notably the PVO (a paramilitary force set up by Aung San), to dispel the British by arms, if necessary. Thakin Than Tun was also convinced that Britain would not grant independence and that the AFPFL would betray the cause. At that time, the relationship between the West and the

Soviet Union was cooling, and Thakin Tun, like all Asian communists, was under pressure by Moscow to seize power. When the Nu-Atlee Agreement was signed which made Burma independent, Thakin Than Tun branded this as "sham independence", and in 1948 staged an armed uprising which reduced the AFPFL government's control to the capital, Rangoon. However, the Chin, Kachin, and Shan leaders — fearing communism — rallied to U Nu. This together with anarchism within the rebel ranks (as they were composed of numerous groups such as the White Flag, the Red Flag, army mutineers, the PVOs, and smaller leftist groups) and the distrust of the left and Burmese on the part of Karen rebels (KNDO), and more importantly, British military aid and support of the West, finally stemmed the "red" tide. Nonetheless Thakin Than Tun managed to keep the armed movement alive despite repeated army offensives, even managing to exert influence in Rangoon notably through student bodies. In 1963, a year after the coup when Ne Win called for peace talks with the rebels, the White Flag sent a team headed by Bo Zeya, one of the famed Thirty Comrades who joined the White Flag rebellion in 1948 at the head of a Burma Rifles battalion. The talk was, however, abruptly broken off by Ne Win when Rangoon's public seemed more sympathetic to the White Flag than the regime. Not long after, due to the anti-Chinese riots in all cities of Burma and the rise of the "Gang of Four" in China, a decision was made in Beijing to support Thakin Than Tun's White Flag. Hundreds of Burmese cadres who had been in exile in China were sent back to lead the party to victory. Thakin Than Tun threw his weight behind these radicals which resulted in a mini-"cultural revolution" in which many hundreds of veteran leaders, military commanders, senior cadres, and even supporters were tried by a kangaroo court, and beaten to death. Consequently, the majority of the horror-stricken and fearful rank and file cadres, and supporters deserted and co-operated with the army which was able to successfully capture all communist bases on the Burmese plains or homeland, and also caused the death of surviving leaders like Thakin Than Tun, Thakin Chit, Thakin Zin, Bo Zeya, and Thakin Tin Tun. Though shorn of all capable leaders, the White Flag with Chinese aid and recruits from the Wa, Lahu, Kokang Chinese, Akha, Kachin, and Shan villages along the border, remains a military force, that is currently operating in the Kachin, Shan, and Karenni states.

Thant

U; the most internationally prominent Burmese having served as the Secretary-General of United Nations in the 1960s; native of Pyimana, and part Shan; died in 1974. He was active in nationalist politics before World War II, and close to U Nu. He was a school teacher by profession. After independence (1948), U Thant served for a long time as secretary to Prime Minister U Nu before being appointed as Burma's U.N. representative. Upon the death of Dag Hammarskjold, U Thant succeeded the U.N. Secretary-General. U Thant, being very prominent, was looked up to by many who opposed military rule in Burma as their champion, but even after retirement, he refused to be involved. Neither did he speak favourably of the army and its rule. Consequently, when he died in 1974, the government did nothing to honour him when his body was brought home. This, however, enraged the students who stole the coffin which was taken to the university campus and laid in state, attracting many thousands of mourners. The government responded by sending in tanks and soldier with fixed bayonets, resulting in violence and deaths.

Thibaw

King; the last king of the Alaungpaya dynasty. He was the son of King Mindon and a Shan princess, the daughter of the Chaofa of Hsipaw — hence the name "Thibaw". He ascended the throne in 1878 engineered by the intrigues of his wife, Queen Supayalat, her mother, and senior ministers such as Kinwun-Mingyi and Daingtha Mingyi, and helped by the frequent and bloody purges of royal princes. During Thibaw's reign, the French were active in Burma, and the court, having lost a large portion of the kingdom within the past fifty years, was hostile to the British. It was mainly to pre-empt a Franco-Burmese alliance that the British decided to move into Burma, which they did at the end of 1885. King Thibaw, Queen Supayalat and the immediate family members were exiled at Ratanagiri, India.

Thihathu

King; youngest of the "Three Shan Brothers" who dominated Pagan after the invasion of Kublai Khan's hordes in 1287. In 1312, Thihathu gained supremacy and moved the capital to Pinya, and his son, Sawyun or Chao Yon, founded Sagaing. Thus began the Shan domination of Burma till the rise of King Burinnong of Toungoo (1551–81).

Thohan-bwa

King (known as Hso Han-hpa by the Shan); son of the Chaofa of Muang Gong (Mogaung) who in 1527 captured Ava and crowned himself king. There was at this time much fighting among Shan princes for the crown which eventually led to their defeat by Burinnong of Toungoo. Thohan-bwa had been made notorious by Burmese historians as a barbarian who killed monks and destroyed pagodas though his deeds were relatively speaking, mild compared to what King Alaungpaya did to the Mon, and their religion, and culture in the 1750s.

Tin-e

U; native of Yawnghwe, and one of the young Shan who, through years at Rangoon University, greatly admired Aung San, U Nu and other Burmese leaders. He was among those in the early post-war years, who agitated for immediate amalgamation of Shan State with Burma. However, like most others who had supported the Burmese, he was soon disillusioned with the AFPFL and the military, and retired from politics. He taught at Rangoon University, and in the early 1960s, supported the federal movement.

Tin Ko Ko

U; probably part-Shan; born in Pyinmana. He was one of the young men who equated Shan nationalism with feudalism, and in the years before the 1962 coup, was a leading opposition leader in the Shan legislature — his main target being the princes. It was widely believed that these men, that is, Tin Ko Ko, Namkham Toon Aye, and Kyaw-zaw, enjoyed the support of the Burma Army in Shan State, particularly the MIS. However, to the surprise of many, Tin Ko Ko and others mentioned tacitly supported the federal movement initiated by the Shan government and other constituent states in the early 1960s. After the 1962 coup, Tin Ko Ko was not given any favour and was even imprisoned for a time by the army. He is currently self-employed.

Tin Pe

Brigadier (retired); Burma Army; from 1962 to 1970 the No. 2 man in Rangoon, and a strong socialist. As a university student he was involved in nationalist politics in the pre-war years. He joined the Burma Defence Army during the Japanese years, and after independence, was one of the senior officers in the Burma Army. Brigadier Tin Pe played an important role in getting U Nu, the Prime Minister to hand over power to the military in 1958 which ushered in the caretaker government. He now runs a sawmill in Rangoon.

Tin Pe

Sai; an Intha, native of Taunggyi. He was educated at Rangoon University and joined the Shan resistance in 1964 (that is, the Noom Suk Harn). Tin Pe was one of the Young Turks who deposed Saw Yanda and set up the SNIA in 1966. After the collapse of the SNIA in 1968 as a result of intrigues and the activities of General Li of the ex-KMT 3rd Army, Saw Yanda, Bo Moherng, and Sai Tin Pe sought refuge with the resurgent Pa-O movement. Sai Tin Pe later went into the service of the Karenni movement as a trade and general liaison officer. In the mid-1970s he settled down in Thailand and is currently self-employed.

Tin Tun

Thakin; communist leader who was killed in action in 1970 while serving as head of the Shan State Party Committee. He was formerly a civil servant in Rangoon. He joined the communists in 1948.

Tin Tut

U; senior and veteran civil servant who gained the trust of Aung San. He became prominent in 1939 when he was chosen as the first elected Chancellor of Rangoon University. In 1942, he accompanied U Saw, the Burmese Prime Minister of British Burma to London in order to obtain greater self-rule for Burma after the war, to which Prime Minister Churchill replied that the Atlantic Charter did not apply to the British empire. After U Saw's arrest by the British in Lisbon for contacts with Japanese agents, U Tin Tut joined the British Governor, Sir Reginald

Dorman-Smith, in exile at Simla, India. He had a hand in drafting the Simla Plan, a blueprint for Burma after the war, which became irrelevant because of the Labour government's decolonization programme. It is a measure of U Tin Tut's capability, integrity, and intellect that he was chosen by Aung San to help him, U Tin Tut, like Aung San believed in treating the Shan, Kachin, and other non-Burmese minorities as equal partners, and he played an important role in getting the non-Burmese to sign the Panglong Treaty in 1947. After Aung San's assassination in July 1947, U Nu, who succeeded him, relied greatly on U Tin Tut who in turn proved a pillar of strength. However, he was not popular with other leaders who resented him because of his close association with the British as a senior civil servant. In 1948, U Tin Tut undertook the task of reforming the Burma Army to make it a real federal armed force, and to weed out undesirable elements, but was killed in a mysterious bomb blast in September 1947.

Toon Aye

Namkham; native of Namsan, a Shan-Palaung. He was one of the young Shan leaders who emerged during World War II, closely linked to young nationalist leaders of Burma. After independence, he led the opposition in the Shan legislature, and constantly attacked the Shan princes, undermining their prestige and dignity. Surprisingly, he tacitly supported the federal movement in the early 1960s. Despite this, he was made Head of Shan State after the 1962 coup, and not long after, he complained about not even having the power to appoint a janitor. U Toon Aye was replaced by Major Toon Yin Law of the Burma Army as Head of Shan State.

Toon Aye

Sai; graduate of Rangoon University who joined the resistance in 1958. He was made one of the vice-presidents of Noom Suk Harn under Saw Yanda. He persuaded a number of Rangoon University students to join the Noom Suk Harn. When the students broke away from Saw Yanda, Sai Toon Aye, being the most senior was elected vice-president of SSIA. He undertook responsibility for organizing the Kengtung force in 1961, but failed dismally due to various reasons. In 1962, dispirited, he surrendered.

Toon Hlaing

Sai, also known as Oum-muang; native of Hsipaw; served as public health assistant under the Shan government before joining the resistance in 1963. When the SSA was formed, he was made the brigade's chief medical officer and also handled civil administration. From 1969–72, he served in the same capacity and also as chief education officer of the SSA 1st Military Region. He did much to improve education, health, and rule of law within the region. After the forming of the SSPP in 1971, Sai Toon Hlaing was made a central committee member and held important posts in various committees dealing with grassroot organizations, education, health, taxation, finance, village governments, and local security. In 1975, after the split within SSA/SSP between those who favoured military alliance with the CPB and those who opposed, Sai Toon Hlaing came down to the southern base together with the president Khun Kya Nu. In 1977, after a change in leadership, Sai Toon Hlaing left the resistance. He is currently living in a border village.

Toon-kham

Taosuung; influential minister of Hsenwi who in the late 1840s was executed together with his wife and seven sons by the Chaofa of Hsenwi, resulting in an uprising. (The Chaofa of Hsenwi fled to Mandalay and with Burmese help defeated the rebels. However, the flame of rebellion smouldered until the 1880s. The Hsenwi rebels under Khunsang Toon-huung controlled all of the state defeating all Burmese and Shan armies sent to subdue them. Peace returned to Hsenwi only when the British arrived in 1887.)

Toon Myint Lay

U; native of Yawnghwe, one of the young Shan leaders with close links to Burmese nationalists who regarded Shan nationalism as feudally inspired and reactionary. Despite his anti-feudalist view, he married a niece of the Yawnghwe prince. After independence, he grew disillusioned with Burmese policies and retired from politics. In the early 1960s, U Toon Myint Lay published a pamphlet, "Whither Shan State", in which he pointed out the monopolization of power by the Burmese-dominated centre to the detriment of the constituent units. In the federal movement which followed, U Toon Myint Lay played a prominent role. Consequently, he was jailed for six years by the 1962 coup-makers. Currently he is self-employed. His eldest son, Tha-gyi, joined the Pa-O movement in 1968, and under the name, Se Leng, gained a reputation as a fearless and accomplished combat leader. He was killed in 1974.

Toon-ohn

U; native of Yawnghwe, related to the Yawnghwe ruling family, and one of the young anti-feudalist Shan leaders who admired Aung San and other AFPFL leaders. He, was later disillusioned by Burmese actions and policies. He died after a long consumptive illness in the early 1960s.

Toon-pe

U; Shan leader who favoured unconditional amalgamation of Shan State with Burma in the immediate post-war years. He became disenchanted with Burmese leaders after independence. He was active in the federal movement in the early 1960s for which he was imprisoned by the 1962 coup-makers.

Toon-shein

Colonel (retired), Burma Army; in the early to mid-1950s he held wide powers in Southern Shan State as the martial law administrator. In the 1958–60 caretaker government, Colonel Toon-shein gained the most publicity as Mayor of Rangoon. After the 1960 general election in which U Nu won a landslide victory on an anti-military platform, General Ne Win was forced to sacrifice many of the top officers who were too prominent during the caretaker period. Accordingly, Colonel Toon-sein was sent off as ambassador to Japan where he died not long after from illness.

Toon Yin law

Major (retired), Burma Army; currently in charge of Shan State. He was a Pa-O and native of Shan State who joined the Burma Army in the mid-1950s. In line with the military-dominated BSPP policy of keeping a tight rein on subsidiary state, and distrust of anyone not from the military, Major Toon Yin Law was made Head of Shan State. It was a wise choice for the BSPP because he was not only a native, but a member of a Shan minority group, the Pa-O.

Tuan Shi Wen

Commander of the ex-KMT 5th Army; a regular officer of the Chinese Army who accompanied units under Limi into Shan State after Mao's victory; died 1980. He took part in the Taiwan-U.S. planned and supported raids into Yunnan in the 1950s which caused U Nu to appeal to the United Nations resulting in the "evacuation" of KMT troops to Taiwan in 1954 and 1961 respectively. Taiwan claimed that communist troops from China were brought into eastern Shan State by the Burmese to fight KMT troops. Though most regular troops and officers returned to Taiwan, a substantial number including locally recruited personnel (mostly Lahu, Wa, and Shan from Yunnan remained behind in bases on the Thai-Shan border and in staging points mainly in Eastern Shan State. The remnants were organized into the 3rd and 5th Armies under General Li and Tuan, respectively. Of the two, General Tuan's was more professional and actively engaged in intelligence-gathering activities for Taiwan and the United States. Though General Tuan engaged in the opium-heroin-contraband trade, he was not obsessed by profits, and believed in the "return to the Mainland".

Wa

Bo; Wa henchman of Bo Mawng, a hero of Tangyan, who before the formation of the SSA in 1964, was the military commander of the SNUF under Bo Moherng. Not long after the SSA was formed, Bo Wa retired and settled down in Thailand. His present whereabouts are not known.

Wareru

King; Shan serving at the Sukhothai court in the late thirteenth century. After the fall of Pagan, Wareru made his way to Burma and established a Shan kingdom in Martaban which was recognized by both Sukothai and Kublai Khan. Wareru also compiled a set of laws known as the *Wareru Dhammathat* which was adopted by the Mon and the Burmese. His descendants inter-married with the Mon and ruled the Mon kingdom

(Hanthawaddy, present day Pegu) which rivalled the Burmese and Shan kingdoms, until laid waste by the Burmese conqueror, King Alaungpaya, in the 1750s.

Way

Chao; member of the Kengtung family who in 1960 was appointed by the students' SSIA, together with U Gondra (a monk), as its representative in Kengtung, and charged with re-organization of all armed groups into a unified command. Not long after however, Chao Way was killed in action together with Sai Hla Myint.

Weng

Chaofa; Prince of Lawksawk; one of the leaders of the Shan confederacy in the early 1880s which not only repudiated allegiance to the Burmese, but also aimed to depose King Thibaw and place its candidate (the Limbin prince) on the throne. Chao Weng was the Shan League's field commander for Southern Shan State and as such, spent most of his energy in fighting Yawnghwe's Chao Ohn whom Chao Weng detested, but who had managed to control the capital. Chao Weng proved a poor match for Chao Ohn of Yawnghwe who got the British to bail him out in 1888 and was moreover recognized as Yawnghwe *chaofa*. The British tried to get Chao Weng to sign a treaty with them, but the Lawksawk prince did not trust them since he had exchanged shots with them. To make things worse, the Limbin prince submitted to the British, and thus freed from previous commitments, other princes (including those of Muang Pawn, Muang Nai, and Mawkmai) signed treaties with the British. There was not much option for the lone dissenter so Chao Weng made his way to the Shan area of Sipsongpanna in Yunnan.

Win Maung

U; Karen national and from 1956–60 Union President. Though a Karen nationalist, he was a pragmatic person who believed in co-operation with the ruling AFPFL party. During World War II, he was parachuted into Japanese-occupied Burma by the Allies and managed to organize a resistance movement among the Karen as well as the Burmese. It was during his tenure as Union President that a split occurred within the

AFPFL, and though U Win Maung did his best to mediate, his efforts proved futile.

Wu Chung Ting

Chinese merchant and KKY leader of Loisae, an important base of the opium-heroin industry in Northern Shan State. Loisae was also used by Taiwan intelligence units as a control point until the early 1970s. With the dissolution of the KKY programme by the Burmese in 1973, and the occupation of all areas on the Shan-Chinese border by the CPB, Loisae was evacuated by the various Chinese trade and intelligence units.

Yan Aung

Bo; communist general, and veteran of Burma's independence struggle; senior officer in the post-war Burma Army, who led army mutineers into the White Flag communist camp. Following the decision by China to aid the White Flag (Burmese Communist Party) in the mid and late 1960s, and the influx of cadres who had been in exile in China, Bo Yan Aung and other top leaders found themselves under attack as traitors, revisionists, among other names. They were hauled before hysterical mobs and humiliated, assaulted, and finally beaten to death. Consequently there was a backlash which resulted in defections and finally the elimination of all communist bases in the Burmese homeland and the deaths of all remaining top leaders, which signified the end of the White Flag as a political force.

Yan-naing

Bo; one of the famed Thirty Comrades; was No. 3 in the BIA and BDA. He married a daughter (Tinza Maw) of the war-time Burmese Head of State, Dr Ba Maw. After independence in 1948, Bo Yan-naing went into business (pearl farming, among others), and also dabbled in politics. In 1965, Bo Yan-naing together with his brother-in-law, Zali Maw, and a Karen leader, former Brigadier Kyadoe, escaped to Thailand and proceeded to raise an army to overthrow Ne Win. Not long after, they were joined by Bo Set-kya another former member of the Thirty Comrades (who died of heart failure in 1969 in Bangkok). In the early 1970s when former Prime Minister U Nu formed the PDP, Bo Yan-naing and his friends joined him. Several of Bo Yan-naing's sons also joined the PDP. U Nu, however, proved inept at leading an armed movement, and was pushed out. The PDP then degenerated into numerous cliques, with all of Bo Yan-naing's sons becoming casualties. In 1981, Bo Yan-naing accepted Ne Win's amnesty offer and returned to Rangoon.

Yang, Jimmy

Also known as Yang Kyin-sen and Chao Ladd; Kokang Chinese, native of Shan State; died 1984. He used to supervise a restaurant run by his wife in Rangoon. He was educated at Rangoon University before World War II and later at Chungking University in war-time China. Served in the Allied China-Burma-India (CBI) theatre as civilian staff. After the formation of the Union of Burma, Jimmy Yang was selected by his brother Edward Yang (Yang Kyin-sai), the ruling Prince of Kokang, as MP for Kokang (till the 1962 coup). Jimmy Yang ran his own business, and managed joint-venture No. 8 allocated to the Shan government. (This was one of the trading corporations set up by the Burmese Government in the 1950s with private participation [48 per cent].) In the early 1960s, he managed the East Burma Bank whose depositors and share-holders were Shan princes and businessmen for Shan State. As MP, Jimmy Yang kept in close touch with Shan students at Rangoon University, inviting them to mahjong games, parties, or to play tennis in the evenings. He also contributed generously to the Shan Literary Society and Shan State Students Association. When the 1962 coup took place none of the Kokang ruling family was touched. But in the mid-1960s, the army detained Olive Yang, the commander of the Kokang KKY, and Edward Yang. Jimmy Yang slipped into Kokang to organize a rebellion, but several important commanders defected, causing him to flee to Thailand escorted by units of the ex-KMT 3rd Army. At the border, several more subordinates mutinied. Despite these troubles Jimmy Yang was accepted by the SSA and made a member of the SSWC. In 1966, a Kokang force, the SSA 5th Kokang Brigade was dispatched to Kokang to join up with Pung Ja-sin, a commander who had remained behind. However, the commander, Francis Yang (a younger brother of Jimmy), faced with command difficulties and defections, surrendered. Stranded in Thailand, Jimmy Yang was however fortunate in landing a job as manager of a hotel in Chiangmai. In the early 1970s when U Nu formed the PDP to overthrow Ne Win, Jimmy Yang joined them, and was made commander of Shan State or Eastern Command. Not long after the PDP splintered and collapsed, and Jimmy Yang went back to hotel managing, but was soon in a Thai jail for illegal entry where he spent about two years. With the help of a French woman journalist, Jimmy Yang was allowed to enter France. In 1981, Jimmy Yang responded to Ne Win's amnesty offer, and returned to Rangoon. When Jimmy Yang was away, his wife, Jean Yang (of Scottish-Chinese ancestry, and a British subject), remained in Rangoon, running a restaurant to support herself. Just before Jimmy's return, she was arrested by the Burmese authorities for running a gambling room on the side, and was imprisoned for a time.

Yang, Olive

Sister of the Kokang prince. She ran the Kokang KKY from the early 1950s to the mid-1960s; a dynamic and forceful character, very much admired for her toughness and ability. While all princes and their families came under attack and pressure from the Burma Army, Burmese politicians, and the media, Olive Yang managed to work with the army top brass in Northern Shan State, and made a fortune in the opium-gold trade, obtaining liquor, meat, and other concessions. Her affairs and marriages to popular songstresses, starlets, and even an established film star, Wa Wa Win Shwe, entertained the reading public.

Yang Shi Li

Chinese adventurer and merchant who amassed a fortune in opium-heroin-contraband trade especially during the KKY period (1967–73). His KKY operated from Kengtung, and he was a "godfather" figure in the town. He was assassinated presumably by a rival in the mid-1970s.

Yape Hpa

Chao; a signatory of the historic Panglong Treaty of 1947. He was the younger brother of the Hsenwi prince, Chao Hom Hpa, and elder brother of the Mahadevi Yawnghwe. He was educated at the Shan Chiefs School, Taunggyi, and served in the military under the British. During World War II he co-operated with the Allies and led a resistance group. After independence (1948), he served in Burma Army, and later transferred to Shan State Police, rising to Deputy Commissioner of Police. He was detained by the 1962 coup-makers. He is now living in Hsipaw and is more than seventy years old.

Yebaw Htay

Veteran White Flag communist leader, and a pre-World War II nationalist. When Beijing decided to support the White Flag communists in the mid-1960s, he fell foul of cadres from China who had been radicalized by the cultural revolution. Like most of the other leaders, he was humiliated by hysterical mobs, beaten, and finally executed.

Yot

Sai; Rangoon University student; native of Kengtung who joined the resistance in 1959. He was one of the founders of the SSIA when the students broke away from the Noom Suk Harn. In 1961, he left the SSIA, married, and settled down in Bangkok.

Zahre-Iyan

Chin leader. He was one of the three delegates at the Taunggyi constitutional reform conference who urged the non-Burmese to be more careful and discreet. He now lives in the United States. He is believed to have left Burma more than ten years ago.

Zam Mai

Sai; currently a vice-president of the TRA set up by Bo Moherng in 1984. Prior to this, he commanded a faction of the SSA/SSPP which opposed an alliance with the CPB. He was a truck driver before joining the resistance. In the SSIA and SSA he rose from private to major (mid-1970s). He has a good combat record, particularly for keeping a cool head in adverse circumstances.

Zam Muang

Sai, also known as Sai Kyaw-khin; high school student, native of Hsipaw, who joined the Shan resistance in 1959 during Bo Mawng's attack and capture of Tangyan. He accompanied Bo Mawng's force to the Noom

Suk Harn base on the Thai-Shan border, and when SSIA was formed in 1960, accompanied other students and leaders to Northern Shan State. He took part in Bo Mawng's war against the Lahu of Muang Loen, and distinguished himself as a combat leader in this campaign. He joined Sai Pan-mai in Muang Hsu and helped in forming the SSIA 3rd Battalion. He then accompanied Sai Hla Aung to the Hsenwi-Namsan-Maung Mit area, and was made chief-of-staff of SSIA 4th Battalion. Sai Zam Muang's rigorous and bold leadership earned the SSIA 4th Battalion a reputation as the best and most aggressive outfit. When SSA was formed in 1964, he was made the chief-of-operations of the SSA 1st Brigade. In 1966, Sai Zam Muang was rotated to army headquarters on the Thai border for further training, and was active in the SUPC (which I was head of) to unite all Shan armies. In 1967, due to internal troubles within the SSA 1st Brigade, and fighting among Shan groups (particularly between Bo Deving and Khun Sa which drew in Bo Mawng, some Noom Suk Harn units, and SSA units), Sai Zam Muang returned to the front. From 1969–72, he served as my deputy in the military bureau of the SSA 1st Military Region and helped in establishing the reputation of the SSA as a disciplined and tough force throughout Shan State. When the SSPP was formed, Sai Zam Muang was elected to the political executive committee of the party and made army chief-of-operations. Not long after, he succumbed to the CPB's offer of weapons and aid. His politicking and CPB intrigues caused a leadership crisis in the SSA from 1972 onwards. At the tension filled the Panghuung conference in 1975, the SSA/SSPP president (Khun Kya Nu) was forced to accept the CPB's military aid, but with the provision that there would be no political entanglement. Sai Zam Muang went up to Pangsang, the communist main base on the Shan-Chinese border, and was able to obtain about 1,000 pieces of small arms (plus some mortars, recoiless rifles, uniforms, and medicine). However, the CPB demanded the SSA's political submission which Sai Myint Aung, one of the vice-presidents accepted. Sai Zam Muang who was with the troops in the Hsipaw-Muang Yai area disapproved and with a task force headed for the southern base. His aim was to accept the plan drawn up by the staunch non-communist leaders who had then retired or were ousted from the leadership in 1976–77 (in particular, myself, and Khun Kya Nu). This was the strengthening of the southern base making the presence of the non-Burmese united front felt in Shan State, uniting Shan armies, and co-operating with the KIA, and other native forces. But before he could take action, Sai Zam Muang, Bo

Pan Aung, and an orderly, mysteriously disappeared in 1979 while on a mission in Maesai town (Thailand).

Zau Dan

Kachin; native of Shan State, graduate of Mandalay University, who together with his elder brothers Zau Seng and Zau Tu, founded the KIA in 1961. He was the most politically astute among his brothers, and militarily capable. He served for a long time as vice chief-of-staff of the KIA and chief-of-operations. When the Chinese began aiding the CPB, the communist military chief being the famed Captain Naw Seng, a Kachin, there sprang up a close relationship between the KIA and the CPB. The Burma Army's offensive against the KIA and the Kachin's need for weapons, plus the good offices of the Chinese, brought about a close alliance between the two forces. However, after Naw Seng's death, relations were not as smooth, and there were clashes between the KIA and the communists. It was in one of these periodic conflicts with the CPB that Zau Dan was killed.

Zau Seng

General; president of the Kachin movement and army commander-in-chief; assassinated in 1975 by an alleged MIS agent (Shengtu) at the KIA base camp on the Thai border. Zau Seng was a native of Hsenwi, and as a teenager, served in the American 101 Force against the Japanese. After the war and independence (1948), he was commissioned as second-lieutenant in the Burma Army, and saw much action against the Burmese communists and leftist rebels. When the Karen joined in the general insurgency, like Captain Naw Seng and other Kachin officers, Zau Seng made common cause with the Karen. He served with the Karen (1949–60), rising to position of brigadier. With the help of his younger brothers, Zau Tu and Zau Dan, and nationalistic Kachin students (from high- and middle-schools), Zau Seng set up the KIA in the Kachin-populated area of Hsenwi, Shan State. He remained in the field until 1965, expanding the control of the KIA into the Kachin State, and building up the Kachin army into a first-class army both in combat and on the parade ground (till today, all drill orders are in English, following the British army). Realizing the need for wider contacts and closer relations with other rebel bodies, General Zau Seng made his way to the Thai border and set up its headquarters. He also set up infrastructure for the export of jade (found in the Shan area of Muang Gong in Kachin State) which boosted the armaments of the KIA. While Zau Seng was at the Thai-Shan border, his brothers, Zau Tu and Zau Dan, were forced by circumstances to contact both the Chinese and the CPB, but cohesion within the KIA remained because of the blood ties. Nevertheless, the CPB, aware of Zau Seng's strong anti-communist feelings, relentlessly strove to undermine his integrity and prestige, accusing him of living in luxurious comfort on the army funds. In the early 1970s, Zau Tu, the army chief-of-staff arrived at the border for consultation on future strategy and various matters. But while in Bangkok on a mission, both were detained by Thai immigration authorities for a year. Not long after his release, while on his way to the KIA headquarters, the commander of the escort party shot and killed the Kachin president, believing that the central committee had ordered such an execution because of Zau Seng's misuse of army funds. The one who arranged the whole plot appeared to be no other than a certain Shengtu who served as personal aide to the army chief-of-staff, Zau Tu. The culprit was caught, "confessed" to being an MIS agent, and was executed. Despite this, doubts still remain as to who was responsible — the Burmese MIS, the Kachin central committee, or the CPB.

Zau Tu

KIA; chief-of-staff and vice-president of the Kachin movement; native of Hsenwi, Shan State. He studied at Rangoon University, and in 1961, staged a spectacular bank robbery at Lashio, Northern Shan State. Zau Tu was caught a few days later, but managed to win over the guards at Hsenwi prison, and emptied the jail. Thus was the money acquired for the founding of the KIA. In the mid-1960s, the Burma Army launched a series of scorched earth sweeps against the KIA in Kachin State, badly battering it. Zau Tu was wounded, and received Chinese permission to seek treatment in China where he was introduced to CPB leaders, in particular, the famous Captain Naw Seng. A military alliance was agreed upon which enabled Naw Seng to gain a foothold in Hsenwi, Shan State, which was expanded to Kokang, the Wa areas, Muang Loen, and northeastern Kengtung. After Naw Seng's death in the early 1970s, the KIA's relation with the CPB worsened, but a complete split was prevented by the Chinese. In order to plan a future strategy with his brother Zau Seng, who was president of the KIA and had been on the Thai border since 1965, Zau Tu and the KIO (the political arm of the KIA) general-secretary, Pungshwe Zau Seng, made their way to the Thai border. However, both Zau Seng and Zau Tu were arrested by Thai immigration officials and detained for some time. In 1975, not long after their release, while on the way to the headquarters, Zau Tu and Pungshwe Zau Seng were ambushed and killed by the headquarters' security force on orders believed by the soldiers involved to be from the central committee. The next day, a note was dispatched to General Zau Seng who was in Chiangmai asking him to go to the headquarters, and he was shot near the base. Later, the KIO central committee denied any involvement, saying that all the cabled orders were forged by Shengtu, a trusted aide of Zau Tu, who was reportedly an MIS agent.

Zeya

Bo; communist general; one of the famed Thirty Comrades who "liberated" Burma. He served in all the pre-independence Burmese armies (BIA, BDA, BNA, PBF, among others), and after independence, was among the top echelon of the Burma Army. He had by that time become a communist, and when Thakin Than Tun launched an armed rising, Bo Zeya joined the armed movement at the head of a Burma Rifles battalion. He reappeared again in public eyes in 1963 as head of the White Flag team for preliminary peace talks with the strongman, General Ne Win. It was at the time rumoured that Bo Zeya was flown in from Kunming by the Chinese, and that he had been in China for some time. After the talks broke down, or rather were abruptly terminated by Ne Win, fighting resumed. Bo Zeya was killed in action in the late 1960s.

Zin

Thakin; Burmese communist leader. One of the few leaders of the BCP (White Flag communists) who was not killed by radicals in the bloody purges of the party in the mid-1960s. These extreme leftists who initiated a Chinese-style "cultural revolution" were mostly those party cadres who went to China in the 1950s. Most had married Chinese cadres, and like all in China at the time, became very radicalized or had to be. These Burmese cadres-in-exile were especially enthusiastic since it was Lin Biao, Jiang Qing, and to a lesser extent, Zhou Enlai who decreed that the Chinese people and party should aid the Burmese communists in a war of national liberation. These China-based Burmese cadres infiltrated into Burma with Chinese help in the mid-1960s, and the brutal slaying of veteran topline leaders was in reality, the bid of the "new blood" to take over power in the party. Though the China-returnees were more than successful in doing away with established leaders, commanders, cadres, and all those who stood in their way, their extreme actions resulted in mass defections of not only the activists, but villagers who had long supported the party. Aided by embittered and angry former communists, the Burma Army was able to easily destroy all White Flag strongholds and bases, hunting down remaining top leaders such as Thakin Chit (who succeeded Thakin Than Tun), and Thakin Zin, as well as the China-returnees. It thus eliminated the White Flat communists as a political force in Burma, though it remains a formidable military force in Kachin, Shan, and Karenni states.

Zingda

Bo; one of the leaders of the numerous rebel bands that sprang up all over Shan State in 1959. Bo Zingda was formerly one of the drivers of Chao Hom Hpa, Special Commissioner of Northern Shan State and Hsenwi prince. He commanded one band of rebels which operated in the areas around Hsenwi town, refusing to submit to the SSIA (under Sai Hla Aung). However, after the SSA was formed (1964), while I was chief-of-staff of the 1st Brigade, Bo Zingda submitted, and his men were inducted into the 4th Battalion. Soon after, Bo Zingda requested leave which was granted. Nothing was heard of him afterwards, presumably he resettled somewhere, living quietly.

APPENDICES

Appendix I

HISTORIC DECISIONS AND AGREEMENTS PRIOR TO INDEPENDENCE

A. Decision Arrived at by the Shan-Kachin Committee at Panglong on 6 February 1947 at 2.30 p.m.

The Committee is of the opinion that the freedom for the Shans and the Kachins would be achieved sooner through the co-operation with the Burmese. As such the two races would send in their respective representatives to take part in the Executive Council of the Burmese Government during the transition period, with the following conditions:

(1) Same status, rights, and privileges as enjoyed by the Burmese on democratic lines.

(2) The Shan and Kachin members in the Executive Council would be responsible for all their respective internal affairs and would jointly be responsible for common subjects, for example, Defence, Foreign Affairs, Railways, Custom, and so forth.

(3) This Committee supports the demand of the Kachins for their desire to have a distinct separate Kachin State.

(4) The terms of agreement arrived at between the Burmese delegates and His Majesty's Government is not to be binding on the Shans and Kachins.

(5) The right to secede after attainment of freedom from Confederation with Burma if and when we choose.

Shan Committee [Signatories]

Khun Pan Sing   Chao Shwe Thaike
Chaofa Luang of Tawngpeng   Chaofa Luang of Yawnghwe

Chao Hom Hpa   Chao Num
Chaofa Luang of North Hsenwi   Chaofa Luang of Laikha

Chao Sam Htun   Chao Htun E
Chaofa Luang of Muang Pawn   Chaofa Luang of
                                           Has-Muang Kham

Khun Paung   Tin E
Htun Myint   Kya Bu
Khun Saw   Chao Yape Hpa
Khun Htee

Kachin Committee [Signatories]

Sinwa Naw (Myitkyina)   Zau Rip (Myitkyina)
Dinra Tang (Myitkyina)   Zau La (Bhamo)
Zau Lawn (Bhamo)   Labang Grong (Bhamo)

B. Decision Arrived at by the Combined Chin-Kachin-Shan Committee at Panglong on 7 February at 9.00 p.m.

The Chin Delegation having arrived on the night of the 6 February 1947 was welcomed to the meeting. It consisted of:

(1) U Hlur Mung, ATM, IDSM, BEM, (Falam, Chin Hills)
(2) U Thawng Za Khup, ATM (Tiddim, Chin Hills)
(3) U Kio Mang, ATM (Haka, Chin Hills)

The terms of the decision arrived at yesterday by the Shan Representatives and the Kachin Delegation at their Meeting at 2.30 p.m. was duly read out and explained to the Chin Delegates who approved of the decisions and subscribed to the same with the following additions which was unanimously approved by all:

(a) All rights and privileges as regards Central Revenue enjoyed by the Shans shall also be extended to the Chin and Kachins on population basis.
(b) Any deficiency in local finance to be made good from Burma Revenues.

(c) There shall be formed a Supreme Executive Council of the United Hills Peoples (SCOUHP) composed of representatives of Shans, Kachins and Chins which shall have full power of decision on all matters of policy between the Hill Peoples and the Government of Burma.

Shan Committee [Signatories]
Khun Pan Sing, Tawngpeng Chaofa Luang
S.S. Thaike, Yawnghwe Chaofa Luang
Chao Hom Hpa, Hsenwi Chaofa Luang
Chao Num, Laikha Chaofa Luang
Chao Sam Htun, Muang Pawn Chaofa Luang
Chao Htun E, Has-Muang Kham Chaofa Luang
Maung Pyu, Representative of Hsa-htung Chaofa Luang
Khun Pung
Tin E
Tun Myint
Kya Bu
Khun Saw
Chao Yape Hpa
Khun Htee

Kachin Committee [Signatories]

Sinwa Naw (Myitkyina)	Zau Rip (Myitkyina)
Dinra Tang (Myitkyina)	Zau La (Bhamo)
Zau Lawn (Bhamo)	Labang Grong (Bhamo)

Chin Committee [Signatories]

Hlur Mung (Falam)	Thawng Za Khup (Tiddim)
Kio Mong (Haka)	

C. The Panglong Agreement 1947
Dated: Panglong, 12 February 1947

A Conference having been held at Panglong, attended by certain members of the Executive Council of the Governor of Burma, all Chaofa and representatives of the Shan State, the Kachin Hills, and the Chin Hills.

The members of the Conference, believing that freedom will be more speedily achieved by the Shans, the Kachins, and the

Chins by their immediate co-operation with the Interim Burmese Government.

The members of the Conference have accordingly, and without dissidents, agreed as follows:

(1) A representative of the Hill Peoples, selected by the Governor on the recommendation of representatives of the Supreme Council of the United Hill Peoples (SCOUHP), shall be appointed a Counsellor to the Governor to deal with the Frontier Areas.

(2) The said Counsellor shall also be appointed a member of the Governor's Executive Council without portfolio, and the subject of Frontier Areas brought within the purview of the Executive Council by Constitutional Convention as in the case of Defence and External Affairs. The Counsellor for Frontier Areas shall be given executive authority by similar means.

(3) The said Counsellor shall be assisted by two Deputy Counsellors representing races of which he is not member. While the two Deputy Counsellors should deal in the first instance with the affairs of their respective areas and the Counsellor with all the remaining parts of the Frontier Areas, they should on Constitutional Convention act on the principle of joint responsibility.

(4) While the Counsellor, in this capacity as Member of the Executive Council, will be the only representative of the Frontier Areas on the Council, the Deputy Counsellors shall be entitled to attend the meetings of the Council when subjects pertaining to the Frontier Areas are discussed.

(5) Though the Governor's Executive Council will be augmented as agreed above, it will not operate in respect of the Frontier Areas in any manner which would deprive any portion of these areas of the autonomy which it now enjoys in internal administration. Full autonomy in internal administration for the Frontier Areas is accepted in principle.

(6) Though the question of demarcating and establishing a separate Kachin State within a Unified Burma is one which must be regulated for decision by the Constituent Assembly, it is agreed that such a State is desirable. As a first step towards this end, the Counsellors for Frontier Areas and the Deputy Counsellors shall be consulted in the administration of such areas in the Myitkyina and the Bhamo Districts as are Part II Scheduled Areas under the Government of Burma Act of 1935.

(7) Citizens of the Frontier Areas shall enjoy rights and privileges which are regarded as fundamental in democratic countries.

(8) The arrangements accepted in this Agreement are without prejudice to the financial autonomy now vested in the Federated Shan States.

(9) The arrangement accepted in this Agreement are without prejudice to the financial assistance which the Kachin Hills and the Chin Hills are entitled to receive from the revenues of Burma, and the Executive Council will examine with the Frontier Areas Counsellor and Deputy Counsellors the feasibility of adopting for the Kachin Hills and the Chin Hills financial arrangements similar to those between Burma and the Federated Shan States.

Shan Committee [Signatories]
Khun Pan Sing, Tawngpeng Chaofa Luang
Chao Shwe Thaike, Yawnghwe Chaofa Luang
Chao Hom Hpa, Hsenwi Chaofa Luang
Chao Hom, Laikha Chaofa Luang
Chao Sam Htun, Muang Pawn Luang
Chao Htun E, Hsa-Muang Kham Chaofa Luang
Khun Pung, Representative of Panglawng Chaofa Luang
People's Representatives: U Tin E
                            U Htun Myint
                            U Kya Bu
                            Khun Saw
                            Khun Htee
                            Chao Yape Hpa

Kachin Committee [Signatories]
Sinwa Naw (Myitkyina)   Zau Rip (Myitkyina)
Dinra Tang (Myitkyina)   Zau La (Bhamo)
Zau Lawn (Bhamo)   Labang Grong (Bhamo)

Chin Committee [Signatories]
U Hlur Hmang (Falam)   U Thawng Za Khup (Tiddim)
U Kio Mang (Haka)

Burmese Government [Signatory]
Aung San

D. Representation Made by the Shan State to the Frontier Areas Commission of Enquiry (FACE), 1947

(1) The Shan States shall participate in the forthcoming Constituent Assembly, members to be nominated by the Shan States Council on population basis.

(2) In the Constituent Assembly no decision shall be effected in matters regarding the Shan States or any change, amendment, modification effecting the Shan States in the future Constitution of the Federation, without a clear majority of two-thirds of the votes of the members from the Shan States.

(3) Association with Burma shall be on Federal basis with —
   (a) equal rights and status;
   (b) full internal autonomy for the Shan States;
   (c) right of secession from the Federation at any time after attainment of freedom.

(4) Federation on subjects which cannot be dealt with by the Shan States alone, such as:
   (a) Defence
   (b) Foreign and External Affairs
   (c) Railways, Post and Telegraph
   (d) Coinage and Currency
   (e) Customs, etc.
   Which would be defined as common subjects by the Constituent Assembly.

(5) The selection and appointment of the judges of the Supreme Court to interpret the Constitution should by Convention be approved by the majority of the Frontier members of the Federal Government.

E. Representation Made by the Frontier Areas Regarding the Constituent Assembly and the Federal Constitution, 1947

(1) Representative members to the Constituent Assembly to be nominated by the Provincial Councils proportionately on intellectual basis, irrespective of race, creed, and religion as far as the Hill Areas are concerned.*

(2) To take part in the Burmese Constituent Assembly on population basis, but no decision to be effected in matters regarding

particular areas without two-thirds majority of votes of the representatives of the areas concerned.

(a) Equal rights for all

(b) Full internal autonomy for all representatives of Hill Areas

(c) Right of secession at any time after attaining freedom.

(3) It is resolved that due provision shall be made in the future Burmese Constitution that no diplomatic engagements shall be undertaken or appointments made without prior reference to the Hill States.

(4) In matters of common subjects, for example, Defence, and so forth, no decision shall be made without the prior consent of the majority of the representatives of the Hill States irrespective of the Burmese votes.

(5) The provision shall be made in the Constitution of the Federated Burma that any change, amendment, or modification affecting the Hill States, either directly or indirectly, shall not be made without a clear majority of two-thirds of the Representatives of the Hill States.

(6) When opinion differs as to the interpretation of the terms in the Constitution, the matter shall be referred for decision of the High Court of Judicature** at Rangoon comprising of the Chief Justice and two other Justices.

(7) The total number of the Burmese members in the Federal Cabinet shall not exceed the total number of the members of the Frontier States in the said Cabinet.

Note: * Special consideration for the Chin in view of divergence in language, custom, and difficult means of communication.

** Or the Supreme Court, the appointment or selection of which should by convention be approved by the majority of Frontier members of the Federal Government.

Source: Resolutions of the Steering Committee (Shan State) for Reform of the Constitution, Taunggyi (1961) Annex 6, 7, 9, 11, 12.

Appendix II

SHAN PROPOSALS TO TERMINATE THE OPIUM TRADE IN THE SHAN STATE

A. The 1973 Proposals by the Shan State Army (SSA) with Lo Hsin Han

(1) The Shan State Army and its allies will invite observers from the United States Narcotics Bureau, or any similar body to visit the opium areas of Shan State and to transmit information about opium convoys on their wireless transmitters.

(2) The SSA and its allies will ensure that all opium controlled by their armies is burnt under international supervision. The opium will be sold at a price to be negotiated later, but the basis for negotiation should be the Thai border price.

(3) The SSA and its allies will attack all opium convoys which will not subject to an agreement based on these proposals.

(4) In return for these temporary measures, the SSA and its allies will expect help in finding a more permanent solution to the problems of the Shan State.

    (a) Because the opium trade can only flourish in a state of anarchy, and since this anarchy will never cease until the people of Shan State are allowed to have democratic elections and political self-determination, foreign organizations interested in an end to the opium trade will be expected to use their influence to persuade the Government of Burma to return to the legal Constitution of Burma.

    (b) Once the Shan State has a democratically elected govern-
        ment, those countries which will gain from an end
        of the opium trade will be expected to provide financial
        help for an economic and agricultural campaign to assist
        the people of Shan State to replace opium with other
        crops.

(5) If the assistance is received, the political parties signatory
    to these proposals will ensure that the elected government of
    the Shan State will — after an agreed transition period — allow
    helicopters under international supervision to search out and
    destroy any opium field that still remain.

[Signatories]

Lo Hsin Han	Boon Tai
President	Vice-President
Shan State Unit Action Committee	Shan State Progress Party
Shan State	Shan State

B. The 1975 Proposals by the Shan State Army Jointly with the Shan United Army (SUA) and Shan State Army (East)

(1) As representatives of the Shan people, the signatories to these
    proposals are concerned by the misery caused by narcotic
    addiction throughout the world and increasingly inside Shan
    State. However, as the opium trade thrives on anarchy, and
    as many Shan people depend on opium for their livelihood,
    its cultivation will never cease until Shan State has a demo-
    cratic and representative government, supported by a majority
    of the Shan people, capable of carrying out long-term agro-
    economic programmes to replace opium with equally viable
    crops.

    The signatories to these proposals guarantee that as soon as
    a democratic Shan government is elected, a treaty will be
    negotiated whereby opium is abolished after an agreed transition
    period in return for international aid and expertise.

During the intervening period of civil disorder, the signatories propose the following temporary measures:

(a) The signatories will sell the annual Shan opium crop at the Thai border price to any recognized international or governmental body.

(b) The signatories will co-operate with the purchaser to prevent opium grown in Shan State being marketed by parties not subject to the terms of this agreement.

(c) The signatories will permit inspection inside Shan State.

(d) The signatories will assist and participate in any economic, agricultural or sociological research aimed at replacing opium with alternative crops.

(2) To initiate negotiations for the sale of the 1975 opium crop, the following immediate steps are proposed:

(a) Before 1 May 1975, the sale of 1 ton of opium at the current border price of 3,100 baht per viss.

(b) On the satisfactory conclusion of this sale, a price will be determined, on the basis of the prevailing border rate, for a further purchase of 5 tons of opium from each separate resistance organization that attends a Shan opium conference to be held on the Thai border in July 1975 where a fixed price for future opium sales and a long-term agreement will be negotiated.

Khun Loum-fa   Sao Fah Lang
Secretary-General   Chief-of-Staff
Shan State Progress Party   Shan United Army
(Shan State Army)

Hsai Keow
Vice-President
Shan State Army (East)

Source: Shan State Army (SSA) Archives.

Appendix III

NOTES ON THE FILM, *OPIUM WARLORDS*

1. Introduction

For people seriously interested in Thailand, particularly northern Thailand, the subject of opium and the politics of Burma cannot be avoided although in reality not much opium (less than 100 tons, according to official figures) is produced in Thailand, and the politics of Burma and Shan State does not directly concern this country.

Nevertheless, it is impossible to talk about opium and the politics of Burma without mentioning Thailand, and vice versa. There are several reasons. Firstly, Thailand shares a long border (over 1,000 miles) with Burma. Secondly, a variety of ethnic groups (Mon, Karen, Karenni, Lahu, Lisu, Akha, Shan or Thai-yai — the latter named being ethnically Thai) straddle this border and their respective homelands form, since time immemorial, a buffer between the Thai and their ancient foe, the Burmese. Thirdly, these groups while maintaining a close and peaceful relationship with the Thai, have been at war with the Burmese Government for at least twenty years. Fourthly, Thailand serves as a transit and refining area for the 400–700 tons of opium (according to accepted figures though I find this high) from Shan State, and the cities of Thailand (Bangkok, Mae Hongson, Pang, Maesai, Chiangrai, and Chiangmai) are centres from where heroin trafficking is financed and controlled.

This state of affairs poses for Thailand a number of difficult and awkward problems. For instance, regarding opium and drug trafficking, Thai officials and even the government have often been accused by some foreign governments and bureaucrats, and sundry journalists as well, of involvement in the trade, or of not being really serious about stopping the flow of drugs.

Furthermore, because the non-Burmese ethnic groups of Burma enjoyed cordial relations with the Thai, the Burmese Government or Rangoon have for long been extremely suspicious of Thailand. Rangoon would very much like to see Thailand involved in a mini-war with the rebels of Burma.

Recently, there has been attempts to link the rebellions in Burma with opium and heroin. Some credence have been given by certain governments to the allegation made by Rangoon that the rebels of Burma equals opium and drug trafficking. This implies that the eradication of opium and drug trafficking will be brought about with the elimination of these anti-Rangoon rebels.

As one who knows something about Burma, I think that the tying of the solution to the opium problem with the military victory of Rangoon is disturbing. Disturbing because some governments are accepting as a fact what in reality is politically motivated slander made by one warring party to discredit its enemies.

I will not say that anti-Rangoon rebels are not involved in opium and drug business but this is not the crux of the matter. The crucial point is: nothing much is known about Burma since no one (not even diplomats or U.N. officials) is allowed by Rangoon to travel about freely, or permitted to carry out independent studies of conditions within Burma. For example, no one really knows how much opium is produced in Shan State since there has been no field survey — the figure bandied about, 400–700 tons, is pure guesswork.

The film *Opium Warlords*, is an attempt by some Shan nationalists to tear apart the dark veil of secrecy imposed on their homeland by Rangoon. It is my hope that the film, while answering some of the question in your minds, will at the same time, raise many more questions which I will be honoured and happy to answer.

2. The Making of the Film

The film was first conceived of in 1971 by the SSA — Shan State Army — a nationalist organization led by former Rangoon University students.

The SSA was at that time faced with a serious new problem — that is, the Chinese Communist Party (influenced by the "Gang of Four" and the Red Guards) had decided to support the CPB. Since

Shan State adjoined Yunnan province, China, it was the strategy of both the parties to use Shan State as a battleground whereby the Burma Army would be drawn out and smashed — a killing ground, as it were. This strategy would bring considerable loss to Shan State especially in human lives as local people who already hated the Burma Army would be recruited as cannon fodder.

While such a development was unfolding within, there appeared in the outside world a growing concern for and interest in the outflow of opium from Shan State. This was a good opportunity to focus world attention on the situation in the Shan State. The SSA believed, perhaps too naively, that the threat of communism and the world-wide concern over opium would stimulate governments of the Free World to some positive action which would end anarchy and war prevailing in Shan State since 1959.

At that juncture, there appeared an Englishman, Adrian Cowell, who was interested in Shan affairs. He had in 1964 entered Kengtung, the eastern Shan State, and lived there for some months with a band of Shan guerillas, and had produced a film, *The Unknown War*, on the activities of this band.

Adrian Cowell and his cameraman, Chris Menges, spent more than a year (April 1972–July 1973) with SSA units in Shan State, and the film, *Opium Warlords* was the result.

3. Aftermath

The film was shown on TV, more widely in Europe than elsewhere, and it won many top prizes in 1976 at various film festivals in New York, Hong Kong and elsewhere.

However, though the film was a success, it did not have the impact the SSA hoped for on governments and international agencies. Instead of coming to see the opium problem as a real problem linked firmly to the social, economic and political problems of Shan State and Burma, politicians and bureaucrats especially persisted in seeing the opium question through eyes of Hollywood scriptwriters complete with heroic cops and powerful godfathers, or "opium kings", played first by Lo Hsin Han, then by Khun Sa and his SUA and more recently by the CPB. The search for a solution to the opium problem became a search for scapegoats.

Worse, the hunt for a scapegoat is on its way to becoming, at present, a search for a military victory in Rangoon's favour since it is now believed by some governments that the eradication of opium hinges on Rangoon gained effective control of the country — meaning the defeat of various armed rebels.

Therefore, one must ask: Is a military victory by Rangoon feasible or possible? Rangoon has been fighting various rebels for a long time (Burmese communists and other leftists, Mon, and Karen since 1948; the Shan since 1959; the Kachin since 1961, and the Karenni since 1965). The only tangible result has been, to date, the increase in the numbers and types of rebels. At present there are some 25,000–35,000 armed rebels at the very least. As opposed to this, the Burma Army has 40,000–50,000 men in 100 battalions.

It is therefore not too difficult to conclude that military victory by either Rangoon or the rebels is not even conceivable for a very long time to come.

4. Conclusion

I would very much like to believe that serious and wholehearted efforts are being made to eradicate opium. Unfortunately, as things stand, I cannot but feel that very few people are genuinely interested in seeking a solution especially when governments and international agencies have shown very little willingness to tackle the problem at its source, that is, in Shan State. The usual excuse is that nothing can be done since Rangoon does not welcome international presence in Burma, and dislike foreign interference. This attitude is most incredible since the opium problem can never be solved so long as the area which produces the bulk of Southeast Asia's opium is ignored.

More incredible than this is the frenzied efforts by governments and international agencies to eradicate opium in Burma through Thailand — which is like trying to pull out a tooth in order to cure a stomach ache.

I sometimes wonder whether the opium problem has not become a goose that lays golden eggs — enriching, on one hand, the drug syndicates and traffickers and on the other providing multi-national and international bureaucracies with more jobs, funds and good living.

Chao Tzang Yawnghwe
(Eugene Thaike)
Chiangmai
February 1983

Abbreviations

AFPFL	– Anti Fascist People's Freedom League
ALO	– Arakan Liberation Organization
ALP	– Arakan Liberation Party
ASEAN	– Association of Southeast Asian Nations
BCP	– Burmese Communist Party
BDA	– Burma Defence Army
BIA	– Burma Independence Army
BNA	– Burma National Army
BSPP	– Burmese Socialist Programme Party
CPB	– Communist Party of Burma
FACE	– Frontier Areas Commission of Enquiry
KIA	– Kachin Independence Army
KIO	– Kachin Independence Organization
KKY	– Local defence force, or homeguard
KMT	– Kuomintang (Chinese nationalists)
KNDO	– Karen National Defence Organization
KniNPP	– Karenni National Progress Party
KNLP (Padaung)	– Kayan New Land Party
KNU	– Karen National Union
KNUP	– Karen National Union Party
MIS	– Military Intelligence Service
MNSP	– Mon New State Party
NDF	– National Democratic Front
NDLF	– National Democratic Liberation Front
NDUF	– National Democratic United Front
NLA	– Nationalities Liberation Alliance
NLUF	– Nationalities Liberation United Front
OSS	– Office of Strategic Services (U.S.)

PBF	– Patriotic Burmese Forces
PDP	– Parliamentary Democracy Party
PVO	– People's Volunteer Organization
SCOUHP	– Supreme Council of the United Hill Peoples
SEATO	– Southeast Asian Treaty Organization
SNIA	– Shan National Independence Army
SNUF	– Shan National United Front
SSA	– Shan State Army
SSA.E	– Shan State Army East
SSIA	– Shan State Independence Army
SSCC	– Shan State Command Council
SSPP	– Shan State Progress Party
SSWC	– Shan State War Council
SUA	– Shan United Army
SUPC	– Shan Unity Preparatory Committee
SURA	– Shan United Revolutionary Army
TNA	– Tailand National Army
TRA	– Thailand Revolutionary Army
TRC	– Tai Revolutionary Council
UNDF	– United Nationalities Democratic Front
UMP	– Union Military Police (paramilitary police)

Glossary

Baht	– Thai currency
Bo (Burmese)	– military leader
Chao	– Shan royal rank
Chao Haw Khan	– Shan royal rank
Chao Haw Seng or Chao Wong (Shan)	– emperor
Chaofa (Shan)	– "Lord of the Sky" (prince); *Sawbwa* in Burmese
Chaofa Luang	– senior Chaofa
Farang (Thai)	– white-skinned (foreigner/westener)
Haw (Shan)	– palace
Hso (Shan)	– a tiger; in ancient times, names of kings of princes as, for example, Chao Hso-khan Hpa, but nowadays adopted by military leaders
Ka-kwe-ye (Burmese)	– local defence forces
Kawthoolei	– Karen nationalist movement
Kem Muang	– heir apparent to the Chaofa
Keng (Shan)	– a fortified town as in Kengtung; in Thai, "Chiang", as in Chiangmai
Kham	– Shan royal rank
Khun	– Shan royal rank
Khun Haw Kham	– non-Tai kings
Khunmuang	– lord; *myoza* in Burmese
Kyat	– Burmese currency
Mahadevi	– Shan title for Chief Consort or Queen
Muang (Shan)	– Town or urban centre; sometimes spelled "Mong"

Noom Suk Harn (Shan)   – "Brave Young Warriors" (the first resistance
                           group)
Poy (Shan)   – a fiesta or celebration; *pwe* in Burmese
Pyithusit (Burmese)   – village militia organized by the Burmese
                           army
Sai (Shan)   – a boy or young man; also for addressing a
                           young male
Sala (Shan) or zayat   – pavilion on monastery grounds
(Burmese)
Sanad   – grants bestowed upon the Burmese by the
                           British
Saw   – Karen form of address for an adult male
Thakin (Burmese)   – master
U (Burmese)   – form of address to an adult male
Zat-pwe (Burmese)   – opera

Bibliography

Books

Barua, Rai Sahib Golap Chandra, ed. *Ahom Buranji*. Calcutta: The Baptist Mission Press, 1930.

Cady, John F. *A History of Modern Burma*. Ithaca, New York: Cornell University Press, 1958.

Chao Saimong Mangrai, *see* Sao Saimong Mangrai.

Christian, John Leroy. *Burma and the Japanese Invader*. Bombay: Thacker, 1945.

Cochrane, Wilbur Willis. *The Shans*. Rangoon: Government Printer, 1915.

Colquhoun, Archibald Ross. *Amongst the Shan*. London: Field and Tuer, 1885.

Crosthwaithe, Charles. *The Pacification of Burma*. London: Frank Cass and Co. Ltd., 1912.

Damrong Rajanubhab. *Thai Wars against Burma* [in Thai]. Bangkok: Silpa Banakharn, 1971.

Hall, D.G.E. *A History of Southeast Asia*. New York: Macmillan Press Ltd., 1955.

Harvey, G.E. *History of Burma*. London: Frank Cass and Co. Ltd., 1925.

Htin Aung. *A History of Burma*. New York: Columbia University Press, 1967.

Kraisri Nimmanahaeminda. "Put Vegetables into Baskets, People into Towns". In *Ethnographic Notes on Northern Thailand*, edited by L.M. Hanks et al. Cornell Data Paper No. 58. Ithaca: Southeast Asia Program, Cornell University, 1965.

Lehman, F.K., ed. *Military Rule in Burma since 1962*. Singapore: Maruzen Asia, 1981.

Lintner, Bertil. "The Shans and the Shan State of Burma". *Contemporary Southeast Asia* 5, no. 4 (1984): 403–50.

Maung Maung Pye. *Burma in a Crucible*. Rangoon: Khittaya Publishing House, 1951.

Mi Mi Khaing. *Burmese Family*. London: Longmans, Green and Co. Ltd., 1946.

Milne, Leslie. *Shans at Home*. London: J. Murray, 1910.

Ratanaporn Setakul. "Political Relations between Chiangmai and Kengtung". Paper presented at Payab College seminar, Chiangmai, 1983.

Sao Saimong Mangrai. *The Shan States and the British Annexation*. Cornell Data Paper No. 57. Ithaca: Southeast Asia Program, Cornell University, 1965.

Scott, James George and Hardiman, J.P. *Gazetteer of Upper Burma and the Shan States*. Rangoon: Superintendent of Government Printing, 1900.

Silverstein, Josef. *Burma: Military Rule and the Politics of Stagnation*. Ithaca, New York: Cornell University Press, 1977.

Smith Dun. *Memoirs of the Four-Foot Colonel*. Cornell Data Paper No. 113. Ithaca: Southeast Asia Program, Cornell University, 1980.

Steinberg, David. *Burma: A Socialist Nation in Southeast Asia*. Boulder, Colorado: Westview Press, 1982.

Taylor, R.H. "British Policy and the Shan States, 1886–1942". Paper presented at Payab College seminar, Chiangmai, 1983.

Tinker, Hugh. *The Union of Burma*. London: Oxford University Press, 1967.

Trager, Frank N. *Burma: From Kingdom to Republic*. London: Pall Mall Press Ltd., 1966.

Yebaw Mya et al. *Last Days of Thakin Than Tun*. Vols. I and II [in Burmese]. Rangoon: Mya-ya-bin Press, 1970.

Records and Chronicles

Burma and the Insurrections. Rangoon: Government Printing Press, 1949.

Burma Frontier Areas Commission of Enquiry. Rangoon: Superintendent Government Printing Office, 1947.

Constitution of the Union of Burma. Rangoon: Government Printing and Stationery Office, 1948.

Hmannan Maha Yazawintawkyi [The Glass Palace Chronicle]. Rangoon: Rangoon University Press, 1960.

Kuomintang Aggression against Burma. Rangoon: Government of Union Burma, 1953.

Records of the Constitutional Reform Conference 1961 at Taunggyi. Rangoon: Shan State Government, 1961.

Records of the Shan State Council 1957–58 Session. Rangoon: Shan State Government, 1958.

Resolutions of the Steering Committee (Shan State) for Constitutional Reform. Rangoon: Shan State Government, 1961.

Shan State and Karenni: List of Chiefs and Leading Families. Simla: Government of British Burma in Exile, 1946.

U Kala Yazawungyi [U Kala's History], edited by Pe Maung Tin. Rangoon: Hanthawaddy Pitagat Press, 1960.

U.S. Congressional Hearings on the Narcotics Situation in Southeast Asia: The Asian Connection. Committee on International Relations, House of Representatives, 3 April 1975. Washington D.C.: U.S. Government Printing Office, 1975.

U.S. Congressional Hearings Before Select Committee on Drug Abuse, July 1977. Washington, D.C.: U.S. Government Printing Office, 1977.

World Almanac 1980. New York: Newspaper Enterprise Association, Inc., 1980.

Index

Index to photographs in the book is indicated by italicized numerals.

THE AUTHOR

The late **Chao Tzang Yawnghwe** was educated at various Roman Catholic mission schools in Shan State. He was a son of the first President of the Union of Burma. He graduated from Rangoon University in 1969 and was a tutor in English at the university until 1963 when he joined the Shan resistance movement. He left the movement in 1976 and settled down in Chiangmai, Thailand, where he worked in several finance companies and kept in close touch with Shan political and cultural activities. He has contributed articles to the *Bangkok Post* and Chiangmai University. He left Chiangmai in 1985 and lived in Canada. He passed away on 24 July 2004.